IMAGES
*of America*

# ROCKRIDGE

**ON THE COVER:** Legend has it that Rock Ridge (at one time two separate words) was named after Cactus Rock, seen here *c.* 1912, in the 1870s by mining tycoon Horatio P. Livermore's wife, Helen, who liked to picnic nearby. Horatio Livermore made his fortune in the Natoma Water and Mining Company in El Dorado, California, then settled with Helen on a large estate in the Rockridge hills. Later much of the Livermore estate became part of Rock Ridge Properties, which sold lots for middle-class housing. The Laymance Real Estate Company marketed the development by promoting the legend of the rock, known as Cactus Rock. In an alternative explanation, the name Rockridge came from a quarry that was for many years the largest employer in Rockridge. In the 1860s, the Oakland Paving Company opened this quarry at Broadway and Pleasant Valley Road to provide crushed rock for paving Oakland's dirt roads. The quarry, which can still be seen at the Rockridge Shopping Center, sits at the end of a long stony ridge that forms the Rockridge hills. (Courtesy Oakland History Room.)

IMAGES
*of America*

# ROCKRIDGE

Robin and Tom Wolf

ARCADIA
PUBLISHING

ISBN 978-0-7385-4799-2

Published by Arcadia Publishing
Charleston, South Carolina

Printed in the United States of America

Library of Congress Catalog Card Number: 2007925805

For all general information contact Arcadia Publishing at:
Telephone 843-853-2070
Fax 843-853-0044
E-mail sales@arcadiapublishing.com
For customer service and orders:
Toll-Free 1-888-313-2665

Visit us on the Internet at www.arcadiapublishing.com

*This book is dedicated to the many people who were interested in seeing the history of Rockridge preserved in photographs. They made their photographs available to us, brought artifacts to photograph, opened doors by introducing us to people with photographs, and gave us references to articles they had written about Rockridge.*

# Contents

# ACKNOWLEDGMENTS

This book is the result of a community effort. Newspaper articles asking for photographs and stories about Rockridge were written by Annalee Allen, Erika Mailman, and Ortrun Niesar in the *Oakland Tribune*, *Montclarion*, and *Rockridge News*. As a result, the community opened its door to us. Special thanks goes to Raymond Raineri, Jennifer Dowling, Bill Larkins, Annalee Allen, John Harder, the Louis Siegriest estate, Fr. Christopher Renz and Brother Raymond and the Western Dominican Province, Patricia Browne Arthur, Edmund Clausen, Don Kinkead of the *Rockridge News*, the Claremont Country Club, John Bosko and Lynn Bosko, Evelyn Avidano Clevenger, Barbara Maltvy Follini, Kevin Flynn and Marilyn Citron, Neville Desouza, Bill Morrison, Ed Archer and Diane McIntyre of Dreyer's Grand Ice Cream, John and Jo Coffin, John Gelinas, Janice Woo of California College of the Arts, Shelly Lewis and David Yoas of the East Bay Regional Park District, J. Kent, David Kruse, Roger Heller, Susan Montauk, the Oakland History Room, Betty Marvin, Marian Combs, David and Christine Wright, Pastor Bill Beaty, Bill Chung, Alan Simpson, and countless others who supplied photographs, artifacts, articles, stories, and encouragement in this project.

# Introduction

Two decades after gold rush San Francisco established itself as the metropolis of the Bay Area, the cross-bay town of Oakland was put on the map when it became the western terminus of the transcontinental railroad in 1869. Only recently, it had been a Mexican rancho and, before that, a site of an Ohlone Indian village. Oakland now was an industrial city, producing timber, processing crops, making farm machinery, running train yards, and fabricating boilers for locomotives and ferryboats.

As Oakland expanded northward toward the college town of Berkeley, Rockridge (then Rock Ridge) was part of the hinterland in its path. Rockridge lay just east of the stagecoach line on the Telegraph Road. The Broadway of downtown Oakland could be projected straight through Rockridge, though at that distance, Broadway was a rough dirt trail that ran over hilly terrain to meet up with the stagecoach line to Contra Costa County. Oakland's expansion to the north would follow this trail.

As the town of Oakland boomed and private wells were exhausted or contaminated, the city franchised its first commercial gravity-driven water system, a reservoir and pipeline to be developed by Anthony Chabot in the Rockridge hills. Also at Rockridge, a massive rock formation became a quarry where Italian immigrant workers ran machinery to crush stone that would pave Oakland's streets for years to come. Oakland's cemeteries were being forced out by urban congestion and relocated to the Rockridge slopes, now served by horsecars running on schedule.

The Rockridge hills above Broadway and College Avenue became a favored spot for the estates of tycoons in mining, dredging, and other earth-pushing fields. Meanwhile, on the flatter terrain below Broadway, vegetable farming grew up along the creek sides. But Rockridge was never simply distant farmland. There was always an urban tinge to Rockridge. Farmers could truck their produce to Oakland and Berkeley. Magnates could easily reach their headquarters in Oakland by horsecar and in San Francisco by horsecar and ferry. In the 1870s, a horsecar line ran on Telegraph Road to Berkeley. Another horsecar line ran on Piedmont Avenue to the Mountain View Cemetery in Rockridge. A College Avenue horsecar provided rail transport through the center of Rockridge with direct connections to downtown Oakland and Berkeley.

Victorian houses began to appear near horsecar lines in the 1880s and 1890s, along with a dozen buildings on College Avenue and more in western Rockridge near Telegraph Road. In 1904, an electric streetcar replaced the College Avenue horsecar and spurred further development. Around 1912, a destination resort hotel, the Claremont, was erected in the hill just beyond Rockridge, and the Key System fast electric interurban train ran from there to the pier of the San Francisco–bound ferry, stopping at College Avenue en route.

After the 1906 earthquake, refugees from San Francisco poured into Oakland, and their tents covered Rockridge farmland. Happy with the excellent housing, transportation, and sunny climate, many settled permanently there. Following the quake, residential estates were subdivided into home building sites, and they found a ready market. The largest development of home site lots was Rock Ridge Properties east of Broadway, which opened in 1909. It became a trendsetter for middle-class housing development in the Bay Area.

In the midst of the Rockridge building boom, another electric interurban train system—the Oakland, Antioch, and Eastern Railway, which later became the Sacramento Northern Railway—extended its line through Rockridge in 1912–1913 with stops at Broadway and College Avenue. This line connected Contra Costa County (and the state capital) with Rockridge. Passengers could continue on to catch the ferry to San Francisco. By 1913, Rockridge had numerous local rail options.

The College Avenue commercial district developed apace with Rockridge housing during the second decade of the 20th century. By the 1920s, College Avenue boasted the Chimes movie theater, confectionery shops, pharmacies, and groceries, along with new car repair shops. In spite of the demand for home sites and the construction frenzy between 1910 and 1930, several Rockridge estates remained intact and were transformed into other uses. These new uses included the Claremont Country Club, St. Albert's Priory, and California College of the Arts.

Rockridge has long been attractive to artists because its sunny climate provided an extended season for outdoor painting, and artists were attracted by the natural light. The Society of Six, an influential group of painters, met weekly in the Rockridge hills at the Chabot Road cabin of Selden Gile to paint and have dinner, sometimes with Jack London and Ambrose Bierce. One of the most famous of these painters was Louis Siegriest, a Rockridge resident whose papers are now collected by the Smithsonian Institution.

# *One*

# Hinterland

The area that became known as Rockridge had been open land lying just east of an Ohlone Indian settlement on Temescal Creek. On Vicente Peralta's rancho, cattle grazed along creek paths that in the future would correspond with Broadway Terrace and Highway 24. Starting with the gold rush, squatters founded Oakland, Peralta's rancho was squeezed into a small area, the railroad boosted Oakland, and the outlying acres of Rockridge became the site of a gravel quarry, cemeteries, the estates of mining tycoons, and a scattering of farms.

In addition to open land, Rockridge's resources included free-flowing creeks with abundant water. Demand for a dependable gravity-driven water supply for the town of Oakland led hydraulic mining figure Anthony Chabot to form the Contra Costa Water Company and look to Rockridge. His horses stomped down an earthen dam on Temescal Creek on the eastern edge of Rockridge to form a reservoir, today's Lake Temescal.

As Oakland prospered, development pressures led to the relocation of downtown cemeteries to land in Rockridge. The nonprofit Mountain View Cemetery Association purchased 200 acres in the Rockridge countryside in 1863, and the buried were reinterred there. The all-day trip from downtown to the cemetery was streamlined when the Piedmont Avenue horsecar railroad opened in 1876.

Some say the name Rock Ridge (then two words) was inspired by the rock quarry operated by the Oakland Paving Company, which was located at the end of a rocky ridge that ran through the hills. Others say it was named by Helen Livermore, wife of mining tycoon Horatio Livermore, after a gigantic rock (shown in chapter three) on their estate.

The boundaries of Rockridge are unofficial, and in the public imagination, they have shifted over time and will be subject to debate. Roughly speaking, Rockridge lies between Telegraph Avenue on the west and Lake Temescal on the east, Berkeley on the north and Fifty-first Street on the south, though it dips farther south to pick up Rockridge's neighborhood high school, Oakland Technical, and some businesses that served Rockridge's Bilger Quarry in the early 1900s, such as the Rockridge Saloon and the Broadway Market.

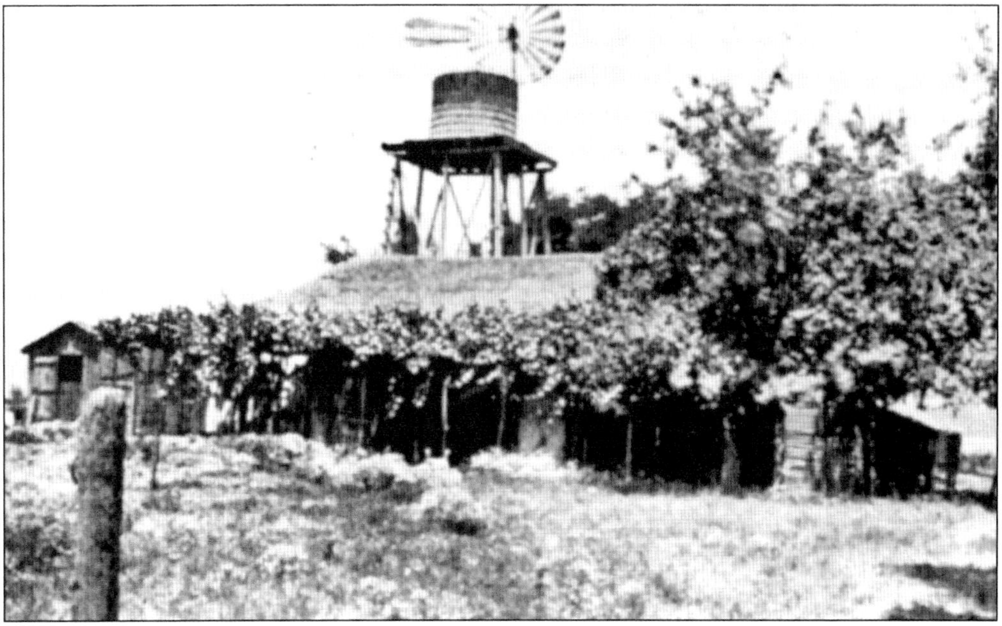

**VICENTE PERALTA ADOBE.** Luis Peralta went on an expedition with Juan Bautista De Anza that brought him to the foothills of Rockridge in 1776. He then received a large land grant from the Spanish king that included present-day Oakland and Berkeley. Peralta later gave his son, Jose Vicente Peralta, land that included the present-day Rockridge. Vicente built his adobe on Temescal Creek on what is now Vicente Street just west of Rockridge where he raised cattle and cut timber. (Courtesy Oakland History Room.)

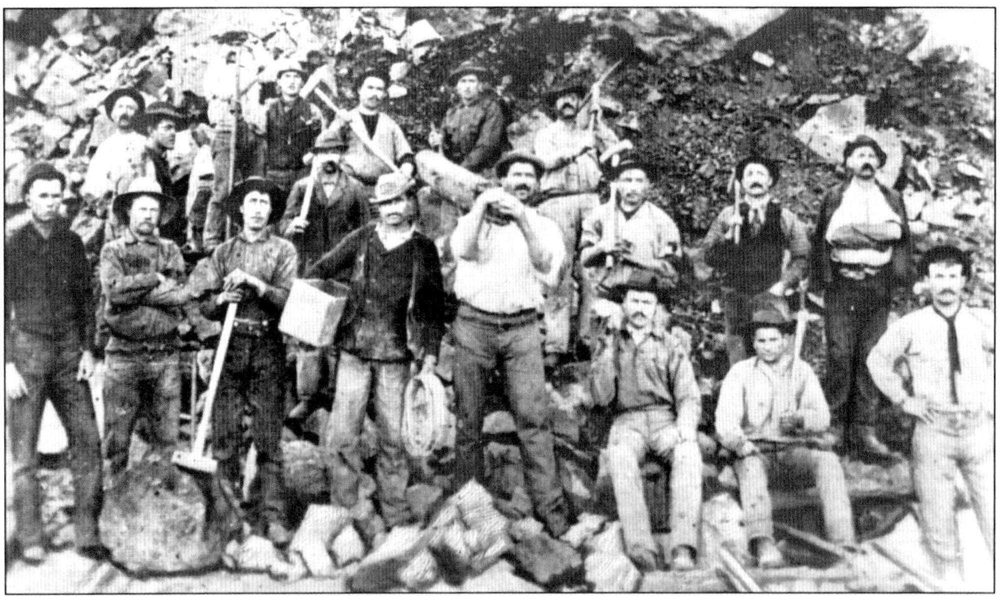

**QUARRY WORKERS, 1898.** Early Rockridge was hinterland, or open countryside, that lay between Oakland and Berkeley. Rockridge included both flatlands and the rocky hills that formed a ridge ending at the rock quarry opened by the Oakland Paving Company in the 1860s. It is possible that the name Rock Ridge came from the rock quarry, later known as the Bilger Quarry. (Courtesy Oakland History Room.)

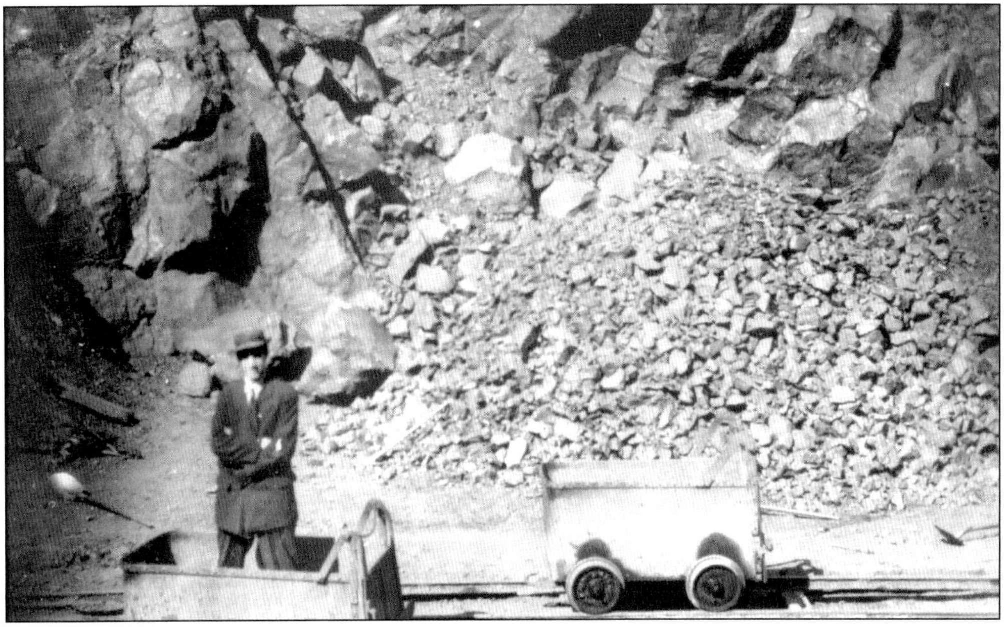

**BILGER QUARRY, EARLY 1900S.** A company official stands in one of the rail carts that carried rock from the pit at the Bilger Quarry to the surface, where it was crushed into gravel. The Bilger Quarry opened in the 1860s and was a major employer in Rockridge in the second half of the 19th century. At its height, the quarry employed over 200 workers. An on-site dormitory operated by the quarry housed 125 workers, most of whom were recent immigrants from Italy. The dormitory organized bocce ball teams that represented the villages in Italy from which the workers came. (Courtesy Ray Raineri, R. J. Hill photograph, Vernon Sappers collection.)

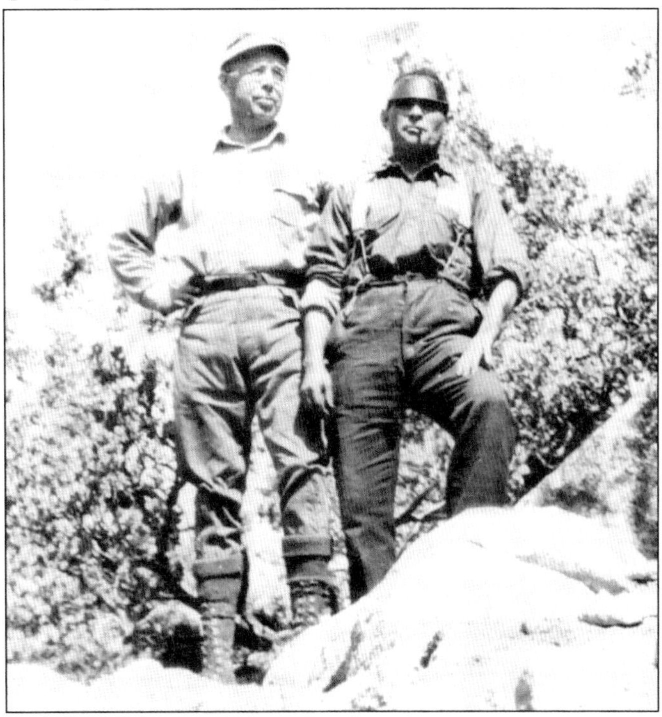

**QUARRY WORKERS, C. 1915.** Guiseppe Ollino, right, is standing at the Bilger Quarry with a fellow worker. Ollino worked his way up from blasting rock to operating the rock-crushing machine. He was able to purchase land on Broadway across from the quarry and build the Broadway Market with living quarters upstairs. Ollino then brought his wife, Eliza, and two daughters, Jemira and Camilla, over from Italy to operate the market. (Courtesy Evelyn Avidano Clevenger.)

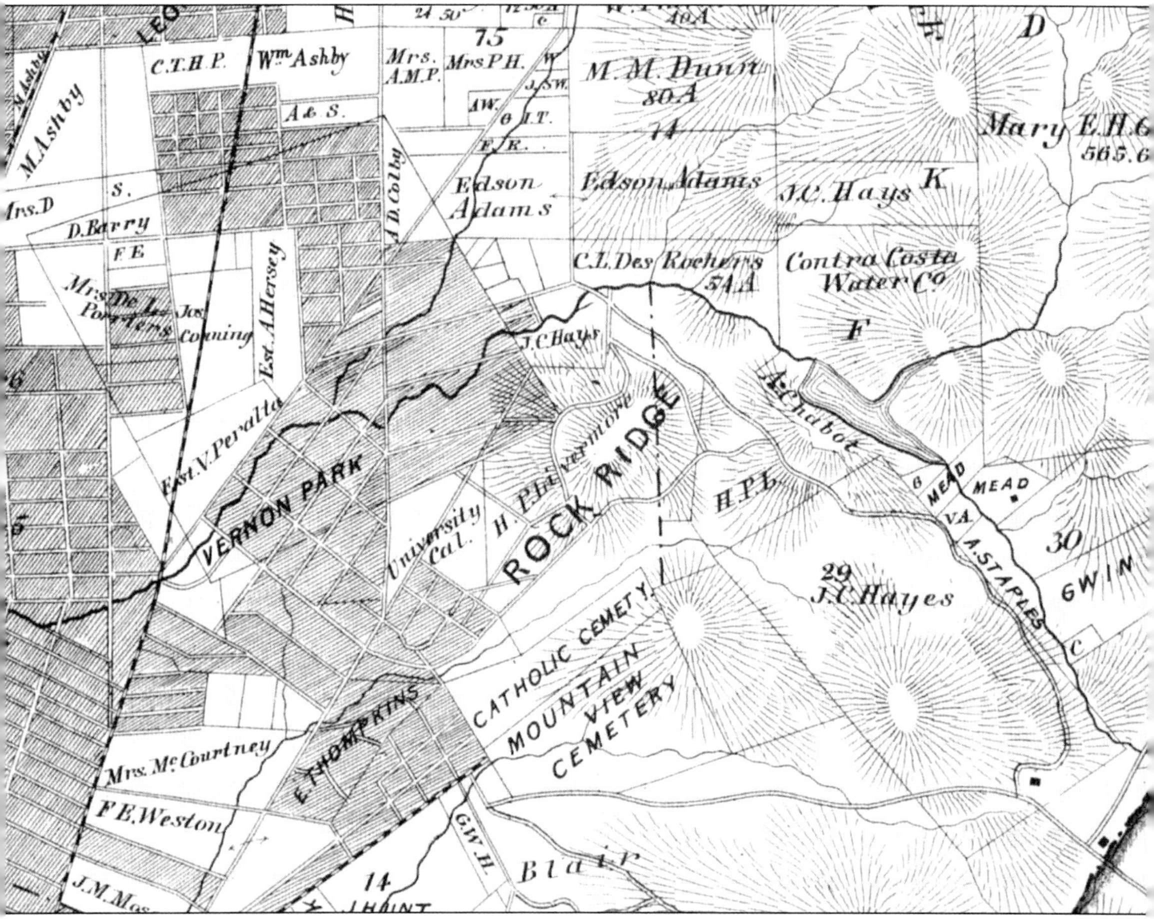


**Map of Early Rockridge.** In this Thompson and West Atlas map from 1878, Rock Ridge is two words. The two dark, broken lines are horsecar railroads. One runs vertically on the left along Telegraph Avenue, and the other runs diagonally along Piedmont Avenue ending at Mountain View Cemetery. The triangle just above the words "A. Chabot" is the Contra Costa Water Company reservoir, now Lake Temescal. The words, "University Cal." are written over the street of Broadway and denote vacant land owned by the university that later became Thomas Avenue and Carlton Street. Beside the "U" in the word "University," College Avenue branches off of Broadway. The Vernon Park development to the left contains tracts of land that were farms between College and Claremont Avenues. (Courtesy Oakland History Room.)

**ADVERTISEMENT FOR THE BILGER QUARRY.** The quarry was operated by the Oakland Paving Company and was important to the development of both Rockridge and Oakland at large. It provided crushed "blue" (actually gray-blue) stone for paving Oakland's dirt roads. (Courtesy Oakland History Room.)

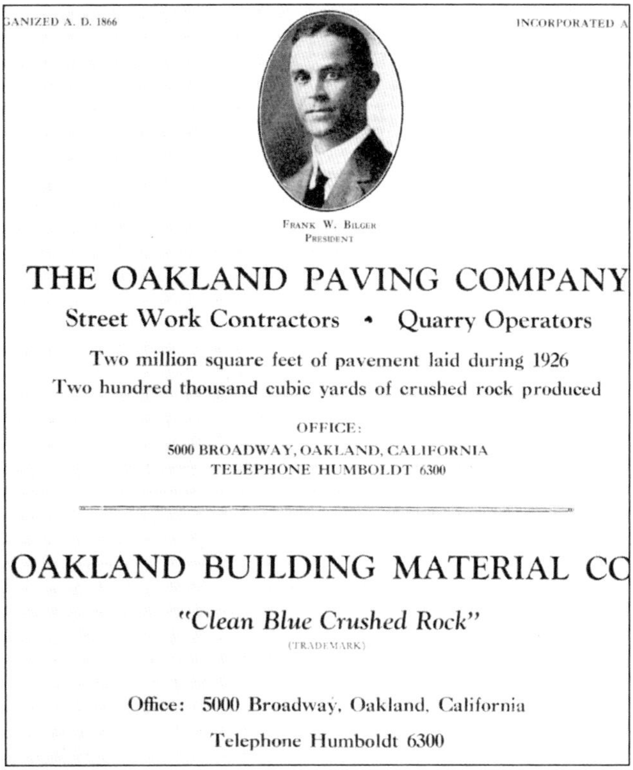


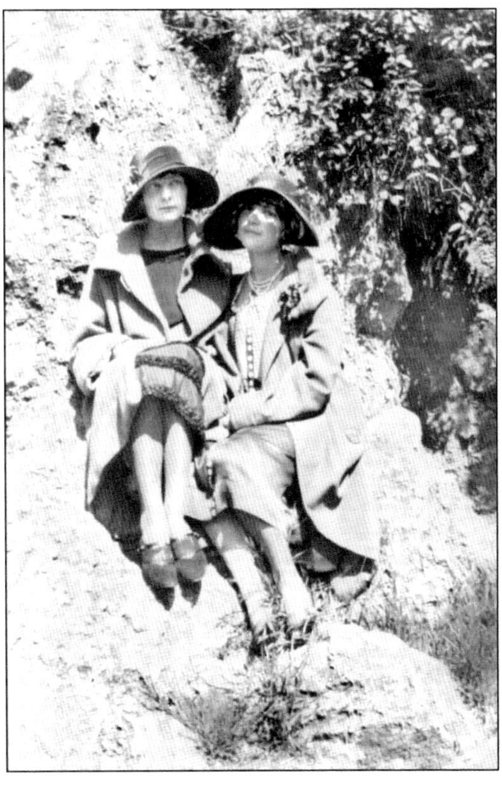

**PICNIC AT THE QUARRY, 1920S.** Jemira Ollino, on the right, is the daughter of a quarry worker. She and her friend Angelina Falcone are sitting on quarry rocks at a picnic. Weekend picnicking at the quarry was a popular pastime of quarry worker families. Jemira lived above the Broadway Market across from the Bilger Quarry. (Courtesy Evelyn Avidano Clevenger.)

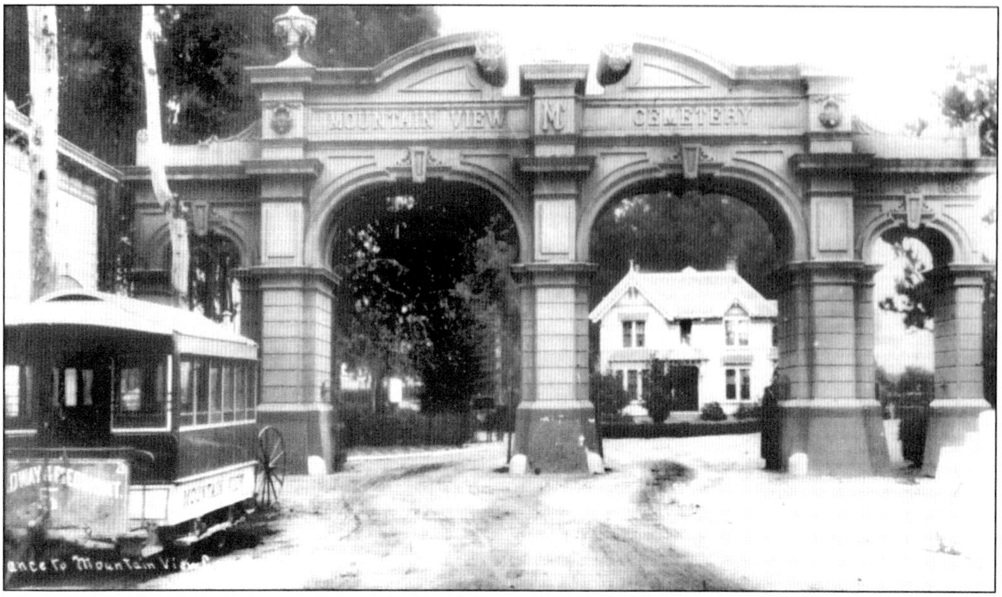


**MOUNTAIN VIEW CEMETERY, 1880S.** In the 1860s, a nonprofit association of Oakland businessmen moved Oakland's downtown cemetery to the Rockridge countryside. Before this, bodies in Oakland's cemetery had already been dug up once and moved once to make way for city expansion. On the left of the cemetery gates is a Mountain View horse-pulled streetcar. The superintendent's house is seen through the gates. (Ted Wurm collection, courtesy Ray Raineri.)

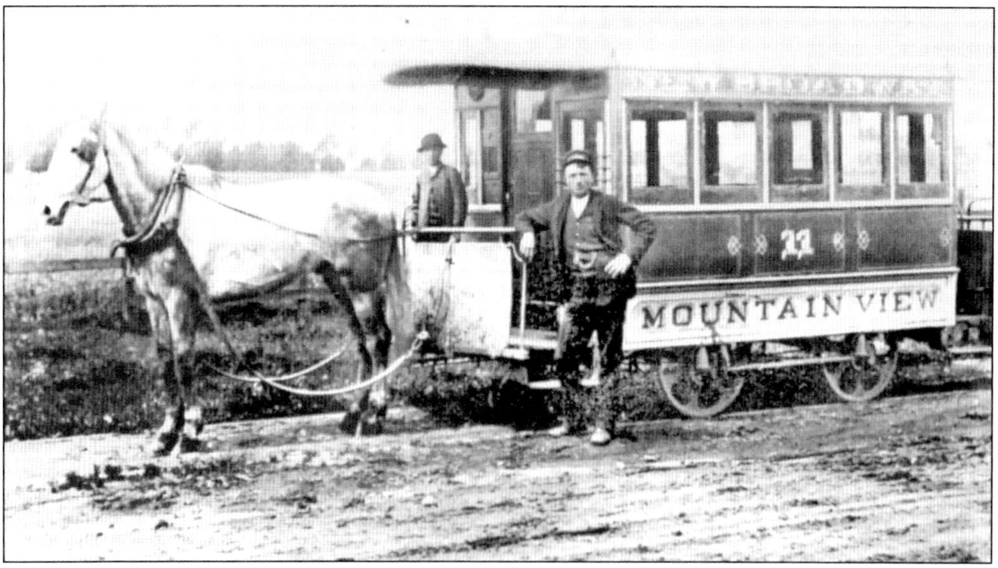


**PIEDMONT HORSE RAILROAD.** In 1876, a horsecar began running from Seventh Street in Oakland to Mountain View Cemetery in Rockridge. Before that time, a round-trip to the cemetery from Oakland had taken a full day by horse carriage. Laying streetcar rails on the dirt streets made transportation more reliable because travelers did not have to worry about getting a wagon wheel stuck in the mud. (Courtesy Ray Raineri.)

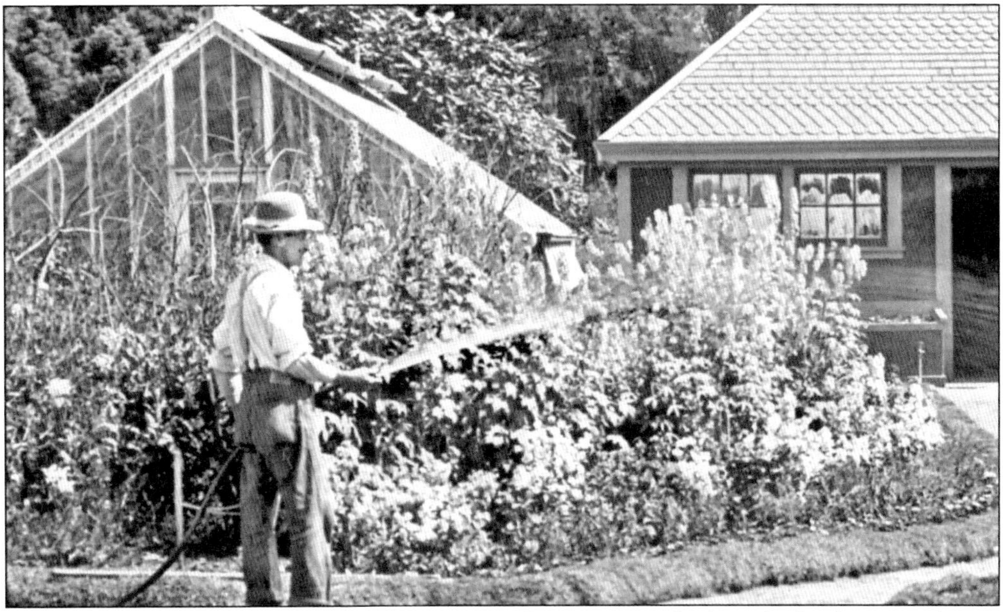

**CEMETERY WORKER, C. 1900.** Mountain View Cemetery was laid out by landscape architect Frederick Law Olmsted, who designed Central Park in New York. Oakland city fathers chose Rockridge for a cemetery site because they wanted the deceased to be surrounded by the beauty of nature. In addition, moving the downtown cemetery to Rockridge made way for the growth of downtown. (Courtesy Oakland History Room.)

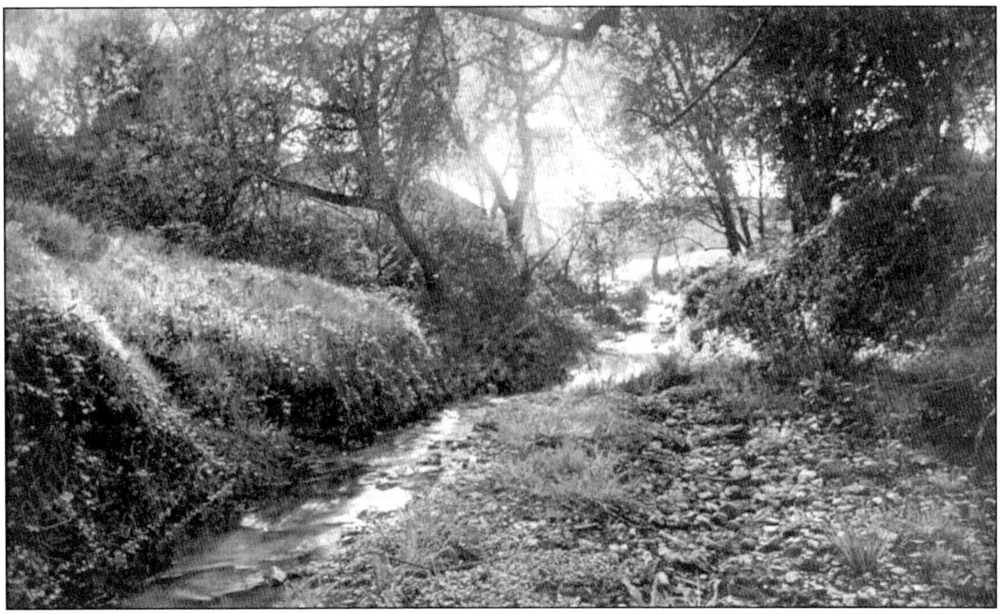

**TEMESCAL CREEK, C. 1911.** Here a branch of Temescal Creek runs through the Rock Ridge Park, a Laymance Company subdivision in the vicinity of Acacia Avenue. Rockridge was still wilderness in 1911. Creeks, particularly Temescal Creek, were an important part of the early history of Rockridge, providing water for farming. Anthony Chabot, who made his fortune in hydraulic mining, dammed Temescal Creek and formed Lake Temescal to supply Oakland with water. (Courtesy Edmund Clausen.)

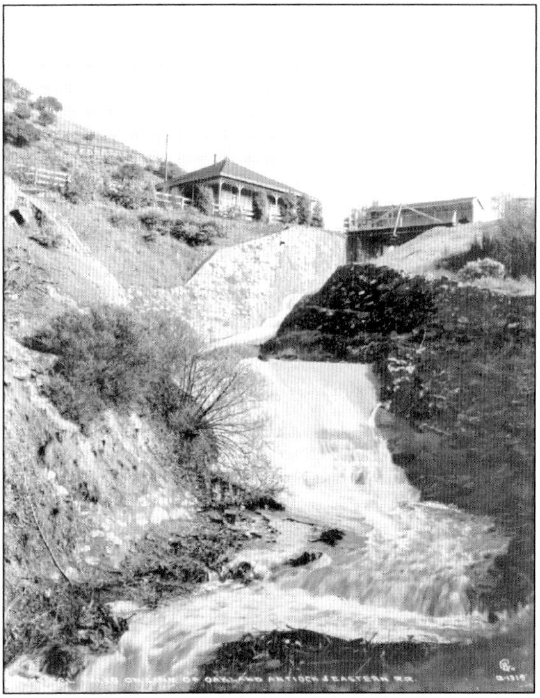

**Dam Keeper's Cottage.** Here a dam keeper lives by the dam at Lake Temescal, monitoring the flow of water into Temescal Creek. Anthony Chabot created a dam across Temescal Creek to form Lake Temescal. He ran mustang horses back and forth over the earthen dam to compact the dirt. Chabot had developed the technology of hydraulic mining in the Sierra, and he brought his talents to Rockridge in building Lake Temescal. (Courtesy Ray Raineri.)

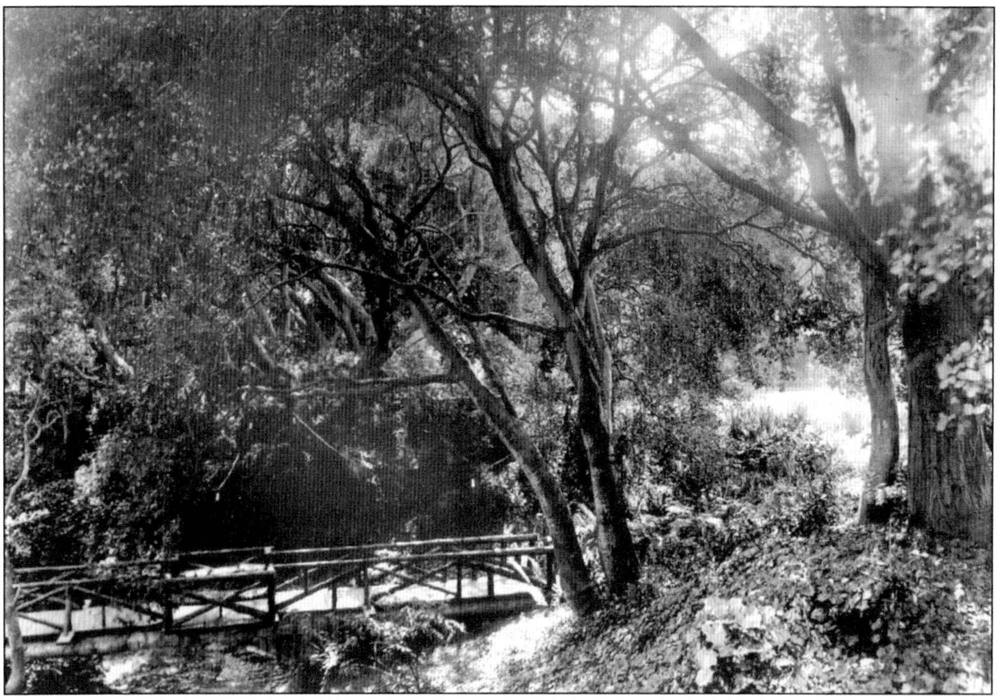

**Temescal Creek, 1915.** This bridge spans one of several branches of Temescal Creek as it ran through the Perry Estate on Chabot Road. Temescal Creek ran free before it was put underground in 1917. Temescal Creek joined Harwood Creek west of College Avenue behind the current Market Hall at Forrest Street, where its width sometimes reached 100 feet from bank to bank. (Courtesy of Patricia Browne Arthur.)

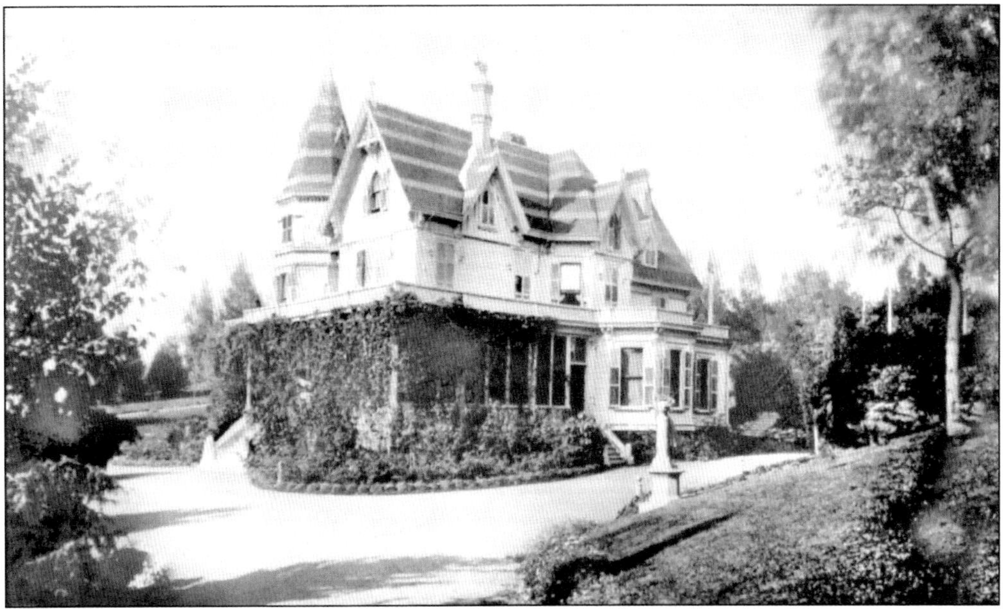

**LIVERMORE MANSION, C. 1870.** Horatio P. Livermore, who gained his wealth through the Natoma Water and Mining Company, bought over 600 acres of Rockridge land from land speculator Jack Hays in 1869. Livermore and his wife, Helen, built their home on McAdam Street, now roughly Broadway Terrace. Legend has it that Rockridge was named by Livermore's wife, Helen, who was fascinated by the large rock on their property that attracted picnic outings. (Courtesy Oakland History Room.)

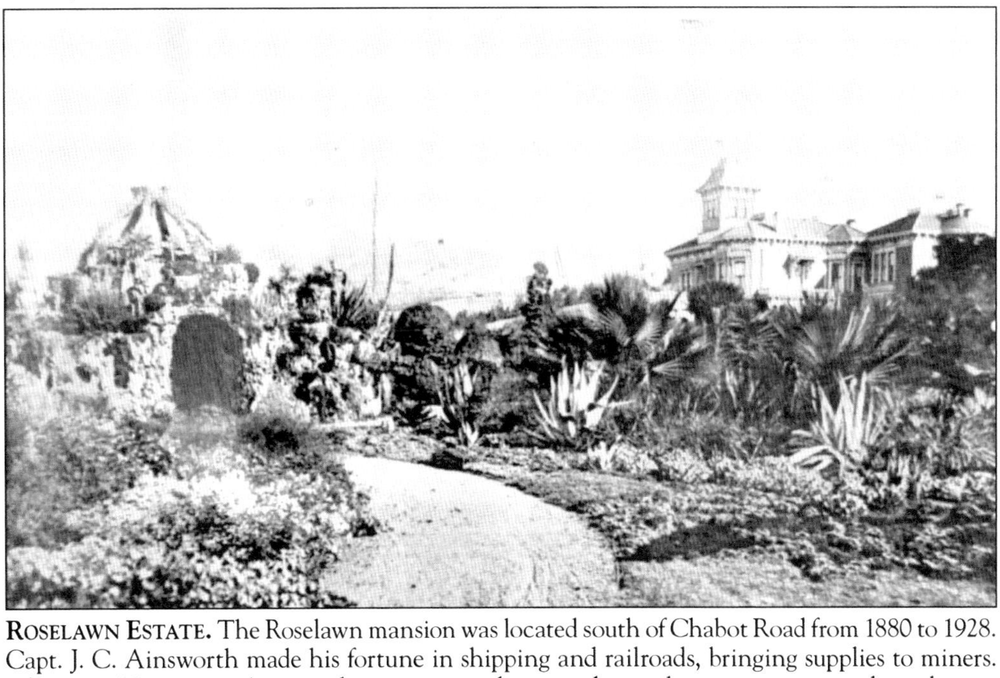

**ROSELAWN ESTATE.** The Roselawn mansion was located south of Chabot Road from 1880 to 1928. Capt. J. C. Ainsworth made his fortune in shipping and railroads, bringing supplies to miners. Like many Victorians, Ainsworth grew exotic plants, such as palm trees, cactus, and eucalyptus. On the right is the mansion, and the structure on the left is probably an exotic gazebo. (Courtesy Oakland History Room.)

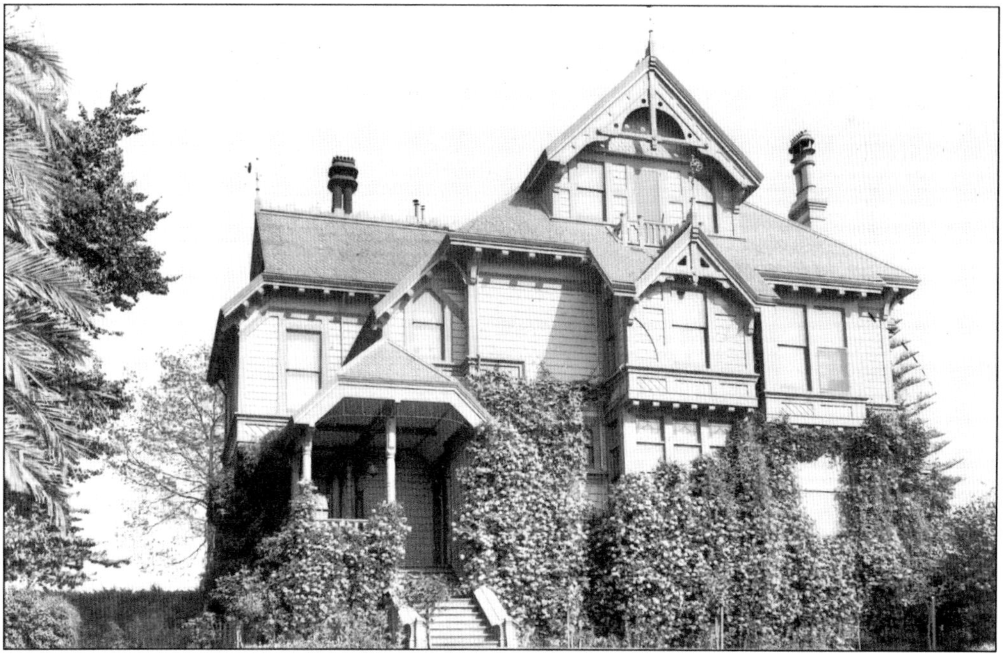

**TREADWELL MANSION.** Built around 1879 by a former miner, William Hale, the mansion was bought in 1899 by James and Louisa Treadwell who housed displaced friends after the 1906 earthquake. In the early 1920s, the mansion was sold to California College of Arts and Crafts (now California College of the Arts or CCA) and became Macky Hall. (Courtesy the archives of California College of the Arts, Meyer Library; © California College of the Arts.)

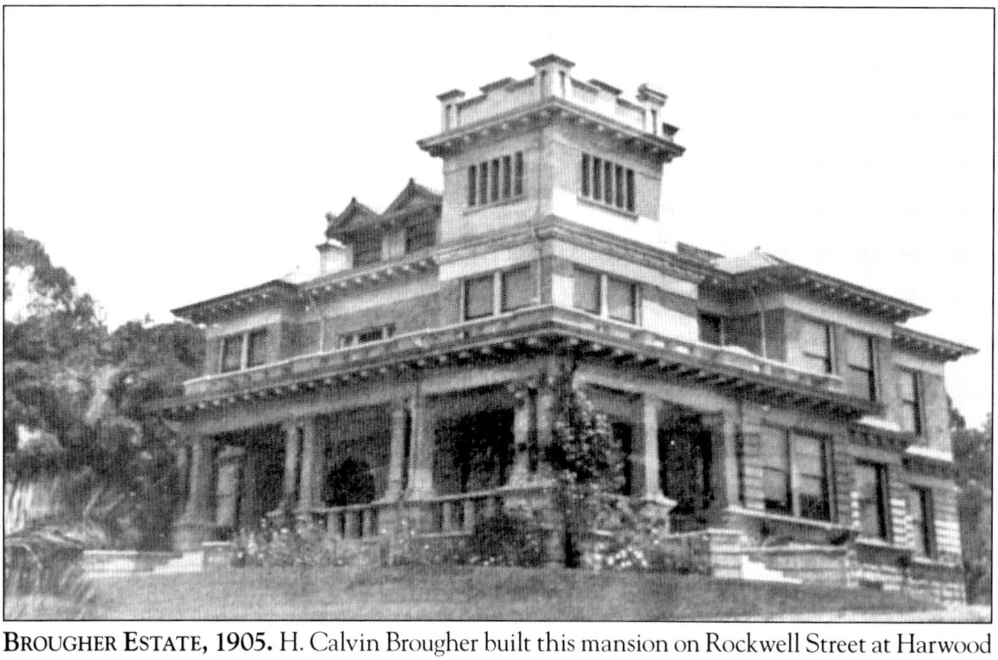

**BROUGHER ESTATE, 1905.** H. Calvin Brougher built this mansion on Rockwell Street at Harwood Avenue in 1905 after becoming wealthy from Nevada mining. He named a street on the property Elsie Street (now Ivanhoe Road) after his wife, Elsie Belle, who was 33 years younger than her husband. (Courtesy Jennifer Dowling.)

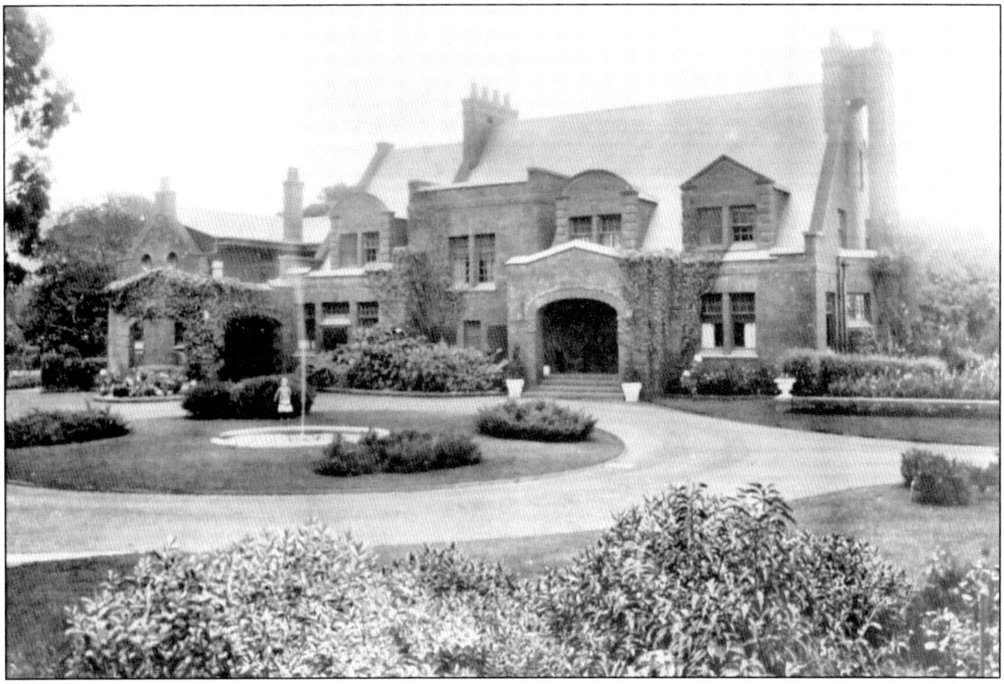

**PERRY ESTATE, 1910.** One of the last country estates to be built in Rockridge was the Perry mansion, constructed in 1910. Raymond Perry had a company that dredged many ports in the United States and abroad, including the Oakland ferry slip for the Key System ferry to San Francisco. (Courtesy of Patricia Browne Arthur.)

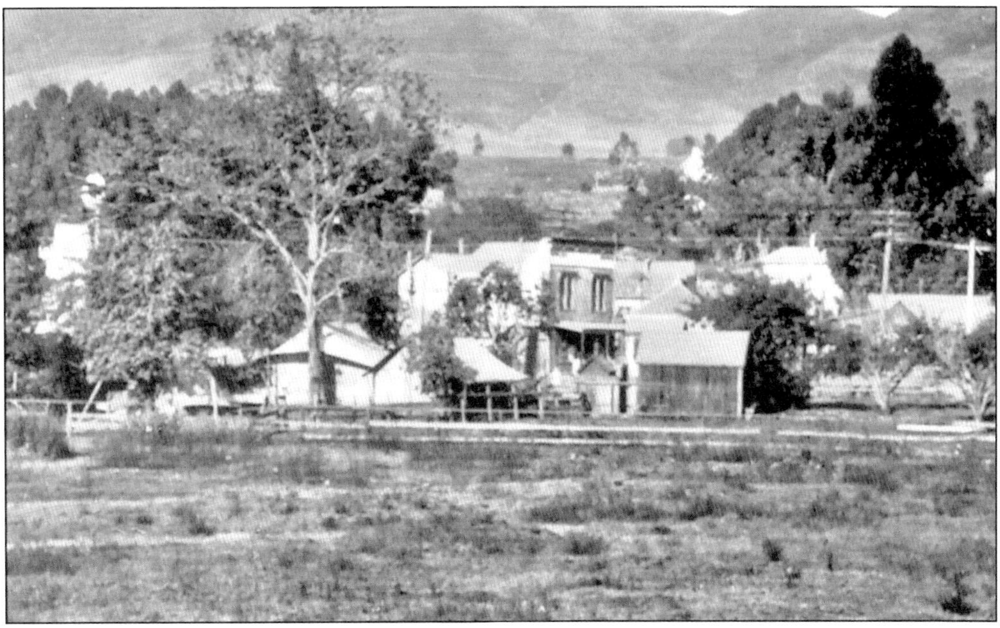

**FARMS SOUTH OF COLLEGE AVENUE, 1906.** This view of the back side of College Avenue looks north toward College Avenue and Claremont Avenue from the surrounding farmland. Newly installed poles carrying electricity can be seen lining College Avenue. On the left is a windmill that pumps water for a nearby farmhouse. (Courtesy Kevin Flynn and Marilyn Citron.)

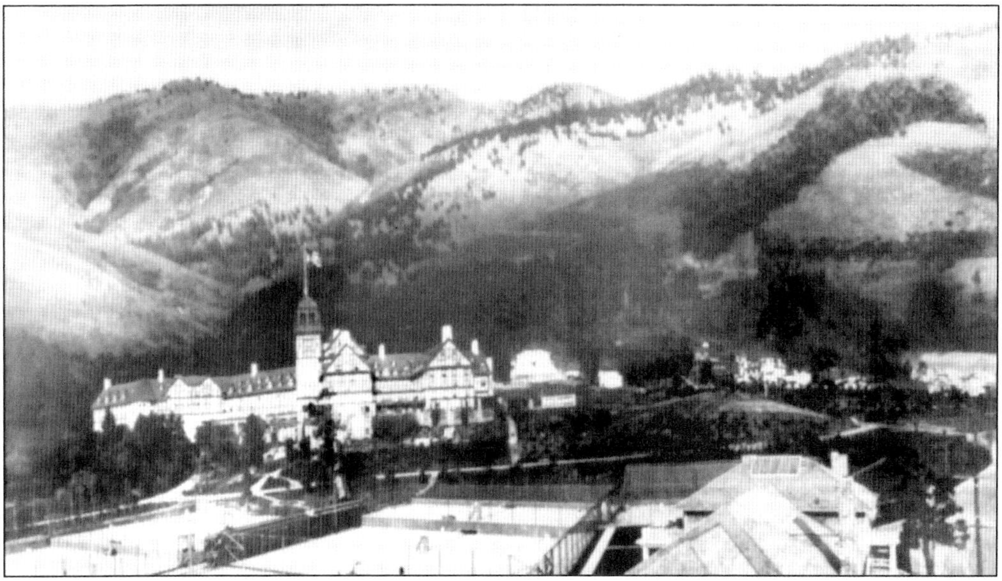

**The Claremont Hotel.** The Claremont Hotel was built between 1906 and 1915 by land speculators as an attraction that would bring wealthy people to the edge of Rockridge in hopes that they would then purchase a home site. A streetcar can be seen between the tennis courts. Originally the rails were planned to end in the hotel lobby, but the hotel foundation would not support the weight. (Courtesy Oakland History Room.)

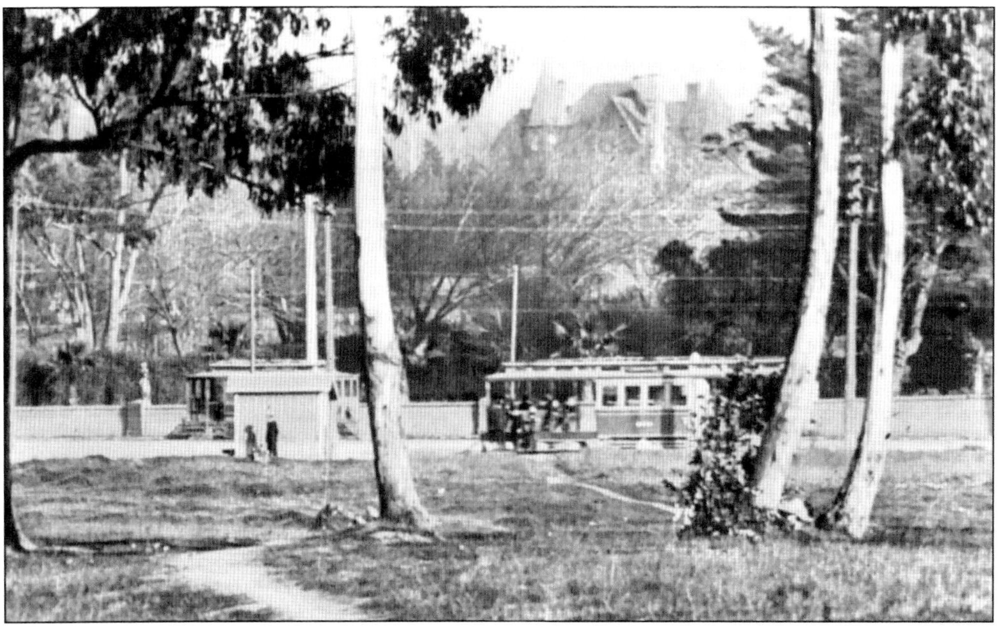

**Broadway Trolley.** In the early 20th century, a streetcar ran up Broadway to Clifton Street where Broadway intersects College Avenue. From here, passengers could transfer to the College Avenue streetcar. In the background, the Livermore mansion can be seen through the trees. (Courtesy Oakland History Room.)

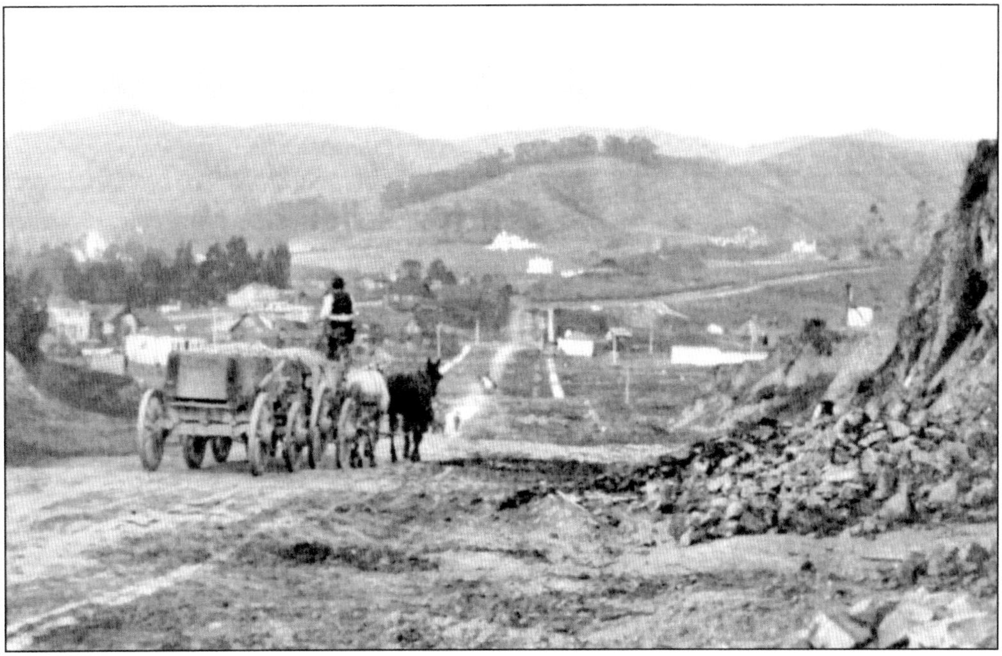

**ROAD REPAIR WAGON, 1908.** Here a road worker uses a horse-drawn wagon to work on Broadway. This view is from the crest of the Broadway hill, and Jennifer Dowling has identified the street to the left of the driver's elbow as Lawton Avenue. The Claremont Hotel can be seen in the distance. (Courtesy Ray Raineri and OHR.)

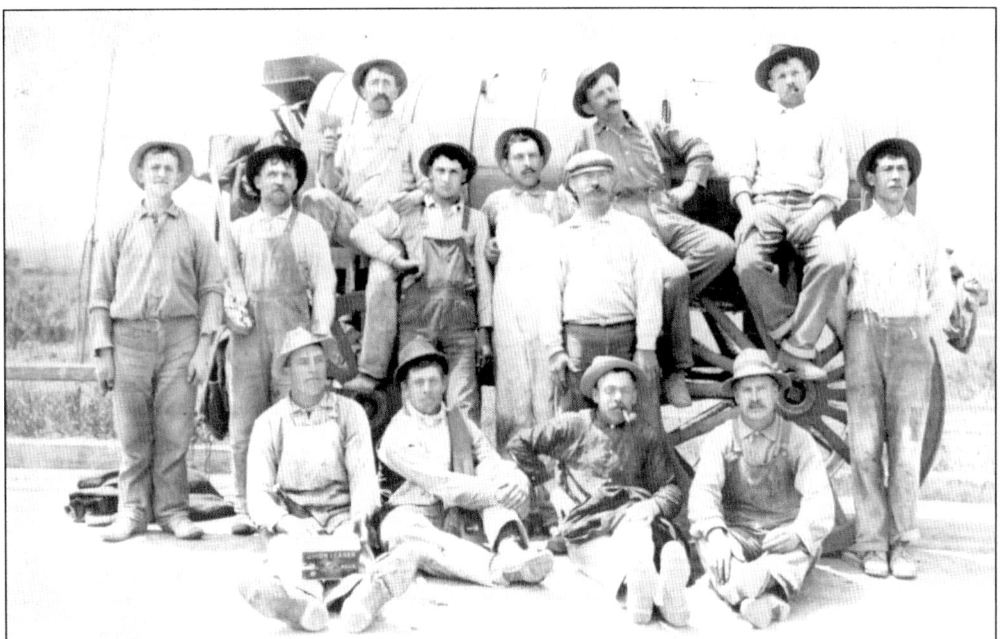

**CITY ROAD CREW, 1906.** This crew of workers has the job of paving some of Oakland's dirt roads. Crushed rock from the Bilger Quarry was used to tame the mud of Rockridge's winter roads. In the middle row, second to the left is Italian immigrant Alessandro Scuero. The portion of Broadway in Rockridge was paved in 1909. (Courtesy Oakland History Room.)

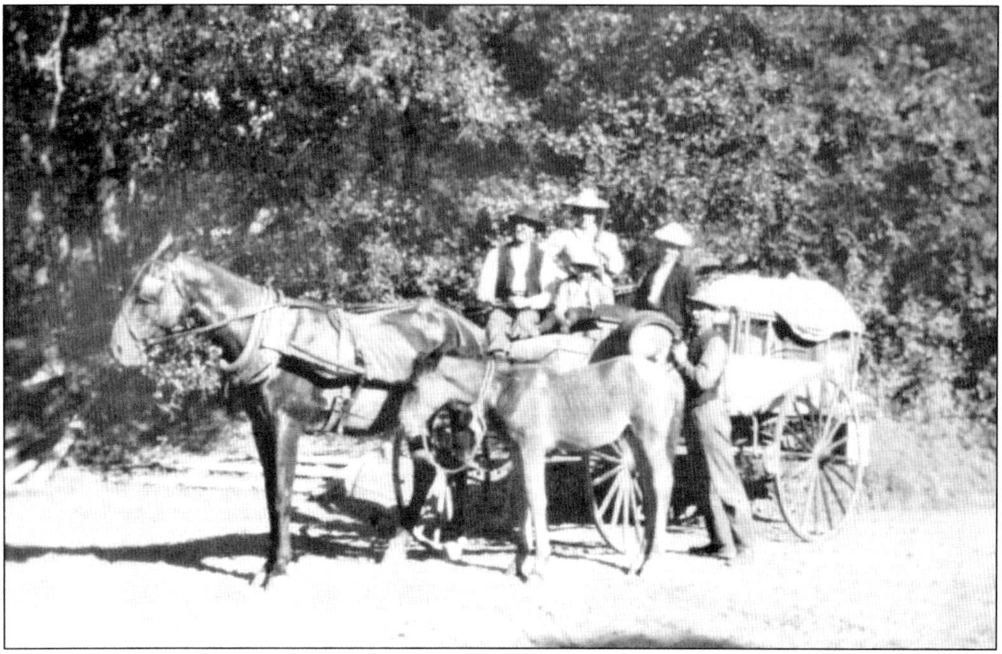

**CAMPING TRIP, C. 1902.** The Louis Napoleon Siegriest family takes their annual vacation. Siegriest loaded up gear, family, and some neighbors and drove this wagon from his Miles Avenue home, through Rockridge, over the hills behind the Claremont Hotel, and into Orinda for a summer vacation, camping on a relative's farm. (Courtesy Louis Siegriest estate.)

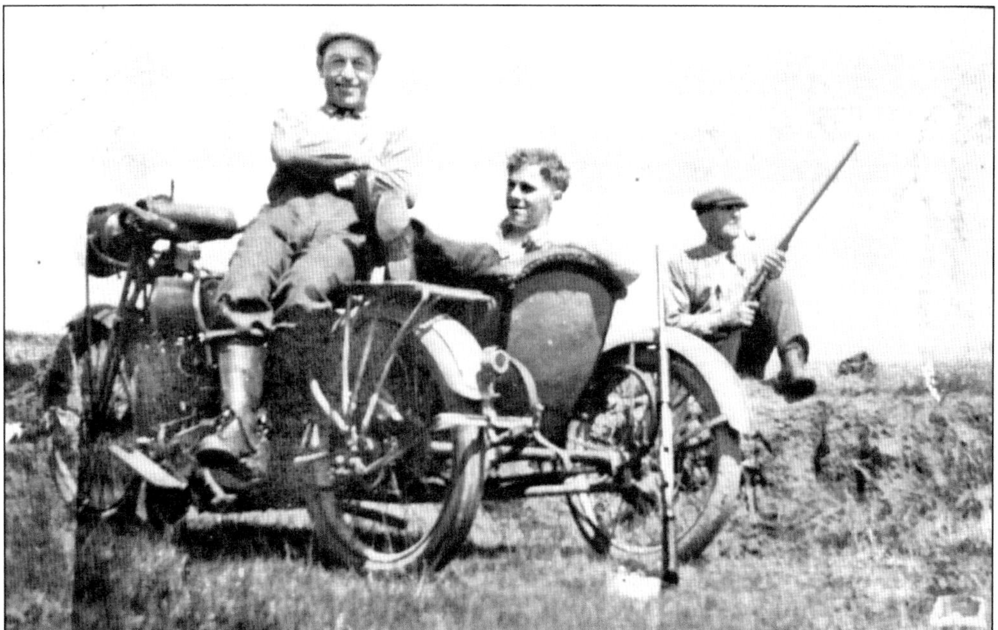

**HUNTING IN ROCKRIDGE, C. 1915.** Much of the hill country of Rockridge was still wilderness in 1915. Here the family of Thelma Milliff uses their motorcycle for a hunting outing in Rockridge. (Courtesy John and Jo Coffin.)

*Two*

# Streetcar Suburb

In the late 19th century, the lack of street paving was partly overcome by laying steel rails on dirt streets to carry streetcars into the countryside in all weather, to spread development and still keep commute times tolerable.

At that time, Rockridge was home to orchards and truck farms. Several creeks ran through Rockridge, including Temescal Creek, which coursed down Miles Avenue and across Telegraph Avenue at Fifty-first Street. The creeks of Rockridge helped irrigate the truck farms. In the foothills around Chabot Road, orchards provided fruit for the Lusk Cannery in the town of Temescal near Telegraph Road.

Horse-drawn streetcars began running along Telegraph Road on the western edge of Rockridge soon after the transcontinental railroad came to Oakland in 1869. Running through farmland and open fields, the streetcars linked downtown Oakland with the newly established University of California in Berkeley. This line encouraged the building of sparsely scattered Victorian homes in the 1880s and 1890s, with construction activity edging eastward toward College Avenue.

The College Avenue car line, at first horse-drawn then electric, connected Rockridge with Berkeley and played a major role in the commercial development of that street. A reliable streetcar system was in place when the 1906 earthquake sent thousands of refugees to Oakland, many of whom settled in Rockridge. For commuters bound for San Francisco, the Key System interurban train ran down Claremont Avenue from the Claremont Hotel, stopped at College Avenue, and proceeded to the ferry terminal. The Sacramento Northern Railroad, also electric, was extended through Rockridge in 1912–1913 with stops at Broadway and College and connecting with the Key System trains at the depot at Fortieth Street and Shafter Avenue.

By the 1920s, streetcars were fighting to share streets with a growing number of automobiles. Reflecting the trend to cars, the Bilger Quarry churned out crushed stone to meet the needs of road-paving projects in Rockridge and elsewhere. Paved streets and automobiles brought Rockridge into the car-commuting orbit of San Francisco, and the demand for cars reshaped the residential landscape of Rockridge and the character of College Avenue.

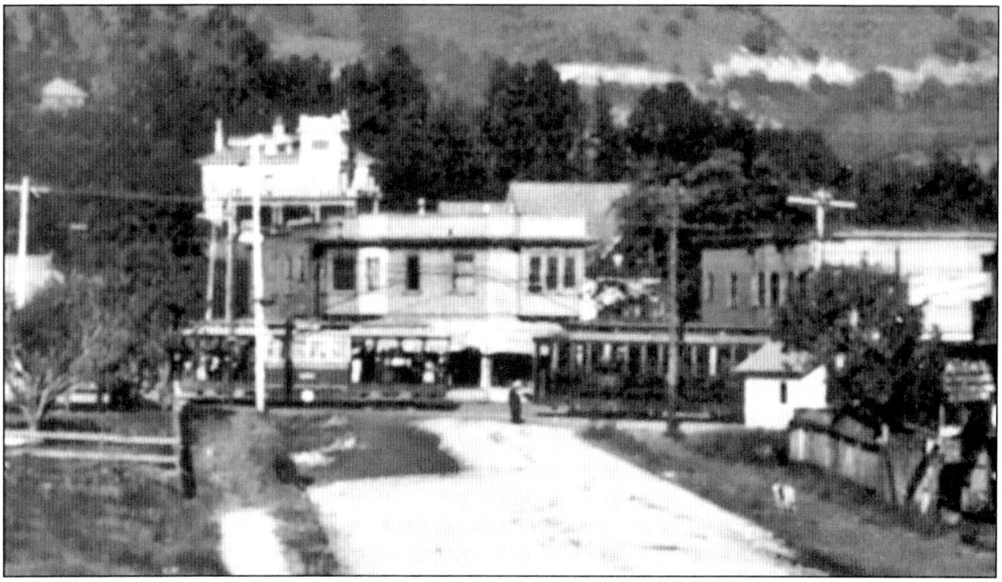

**College Avenue Streetcar, c. 1907.** This view looks east on Sixty-second Street to see two electric streetcars passing on College Avenue (then University Avenue). The No. 6 College Avenue line began in Rockridge at the intersection of College Avenue and Broadway and ended at the University of California in Berkeley. Prior to building the electric streetcar line in 1904, horses pulled a trolley on rails along College Avenue to Berkeley. (Courtesy Kevin Flynn and Marilyn Citron.)

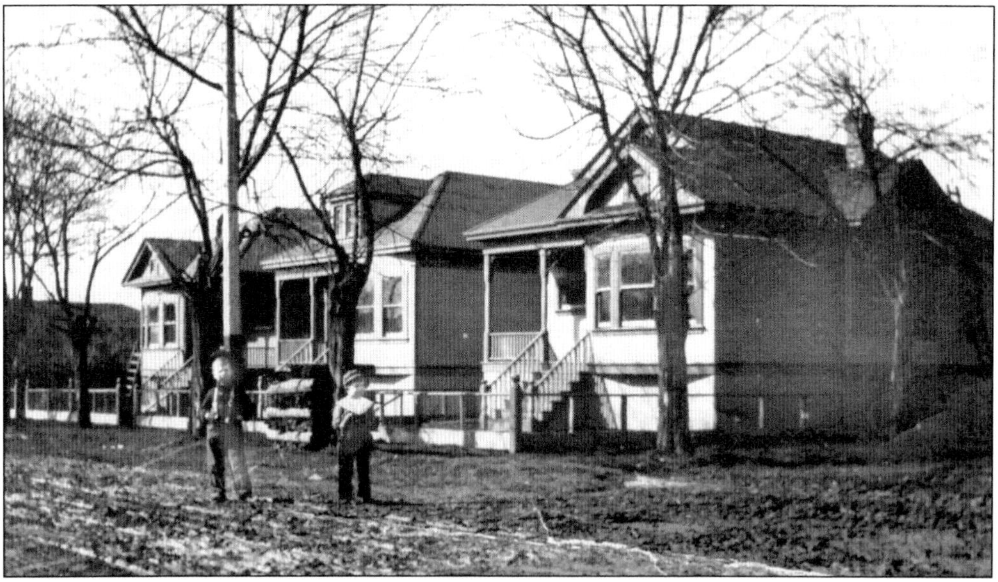

**Victorians on Shafter Avenue, c. 1906.** Louis Siegriest (right) and friend Dewey Westaway play on Shafter, then a dirt road, near the corner of Cavour Street before the Sacramento Northern Railway tracks were laid. Siegriest's father, Louis Napoleon Siegriest, worked as a horse trainer at the horse-drawn streetcar barn at the nearby corner of Fifty-first Street and Telegraph Road. Victorian houses sprang up around the Telegraph Avenue streetcar line in the 1880s and 1890s, bringing commuter homes to the area of Rockridge east of Telegraph Avenue. (Courtesy Louis Siegriest estate.)

**MILES AVENUE HOME, 1901.** One-year-old Louis Siegriest is pictured with his mother, Amelia, on Miles Avenue across the street from their home. This was one of a number of Victorian homes built in Rockridge in the 1890s to serve commuters to Oakland and San Francisco. In 1869, when the transcontinental railroad arrived in downtown Oakland, a horsecar railroad was also built along Telegraph Road. It was extended from downtown Oakland to Fifty-first Street in the 1870s to the point where Temescal Creek crossed Telegraph Road at Fifty-first Street. (Courtesy Louis Siegriest estate.)

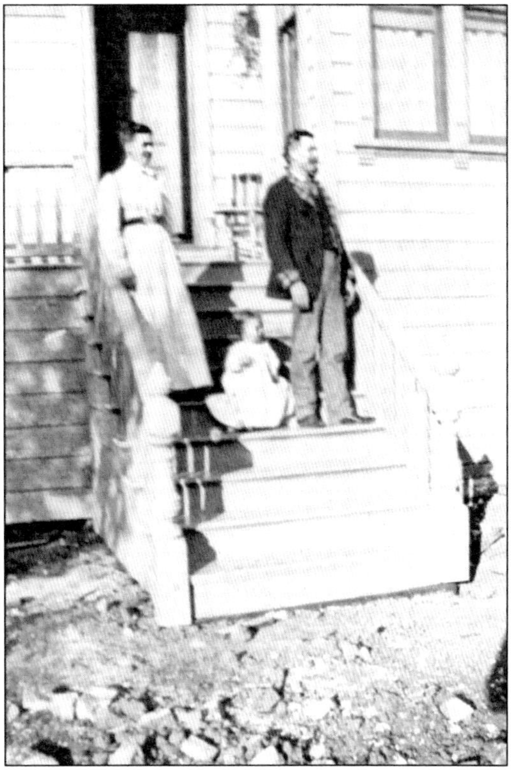

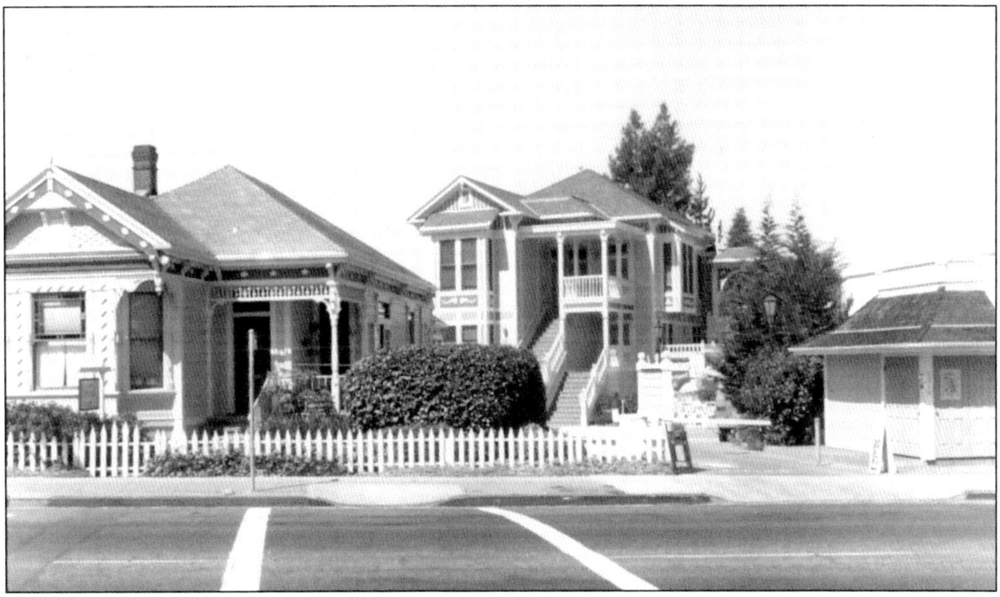

**COLLEGE AVENUE VICTORIANS.** These two houses were built in the 1880s on College Avenue at Bryant for commuters to San Francisco. The house on the right was first owned by John Avan, a San Francisco police officer. The house on the left belonged to Charles Shields, who worked as a scene artist in San Francisco theaters. The Avan house was moved across the street and raised to put an additional story underneath the original house. (Courtesy Don Kinkead, Don Kinkead photograph.)

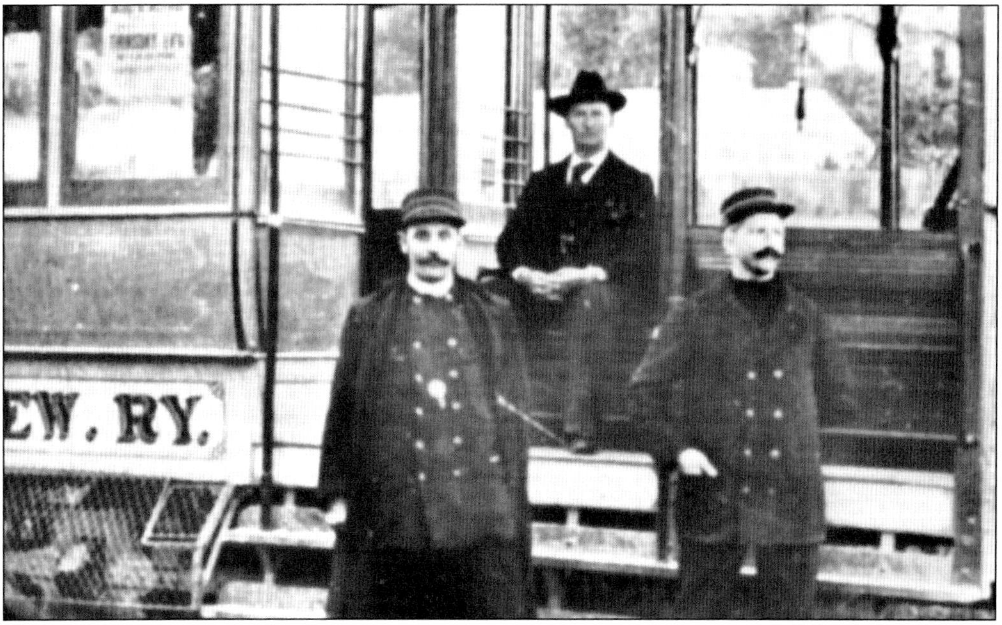


**STREETCAR WORKERS, C. 1900.** These are workers on the Piedmont and Mountain View Railway, which later became part of the Oakland Traction Company. In turn, the Oakland Traction Company became a division of the Key System called East Bay Street Railways. The electric streetcar replaced the horsecar on Piedmont Avenue in 1904 and was then replaced by buses in 1938. (Courtesy Oakland History Room.)

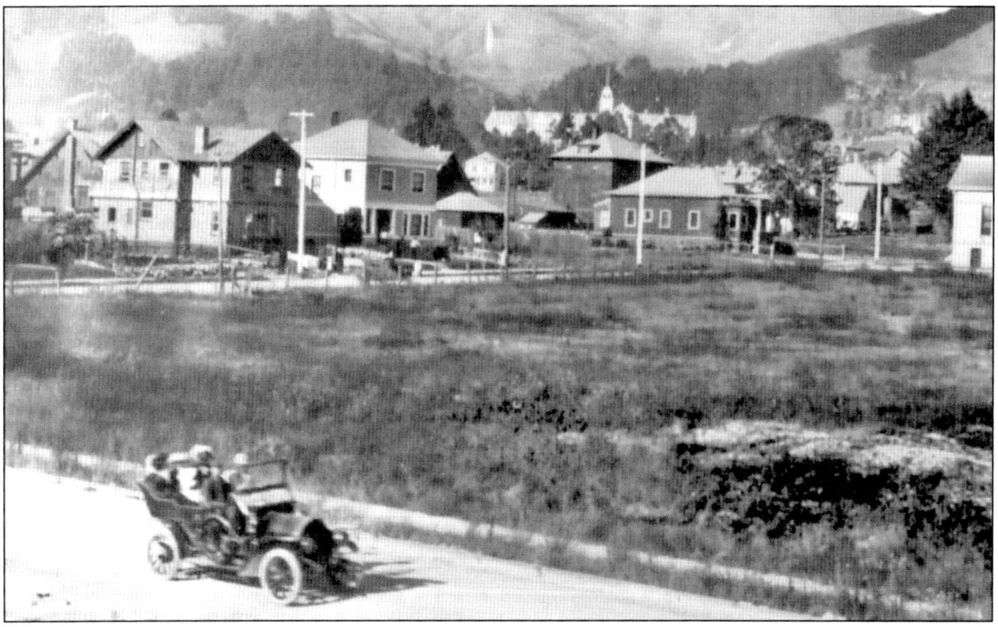

**COUNTRYSIDE BEGINS TO DEVELOP, C. 1906.** This photograph looks northeast toward the intersection of Claremont Avenue and College Avenue. The farmland is turning into housing a block below the College Avenue streetcar line. The Claremont Hotel is in the background in the center. Most streets in Rockridge were still dirt roads in 1906. (Courtesy Kevin Flynn and Marilyn Citron.)

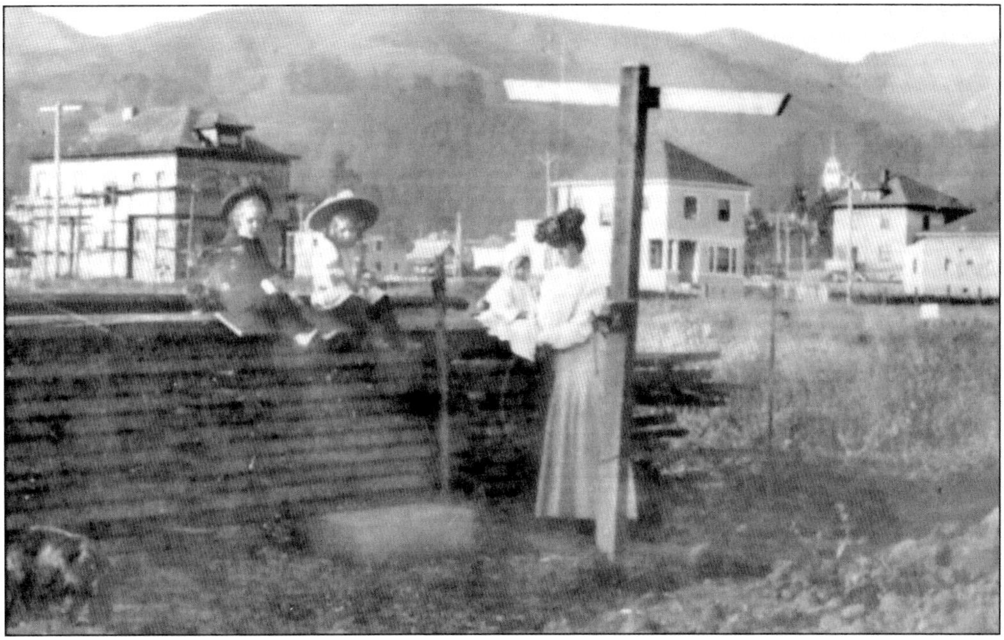

**OPEN FIELDS WEST OF COLLEGE AVENUE, C. 1906.** A woman stands holding an infant near a stack of lumber for building a new house in farmland west of College Avenue. The view looks northeast toward Sixty-third Street and College Avenue. (Courtesy Kevin Flynn and Marilyn Citron.)

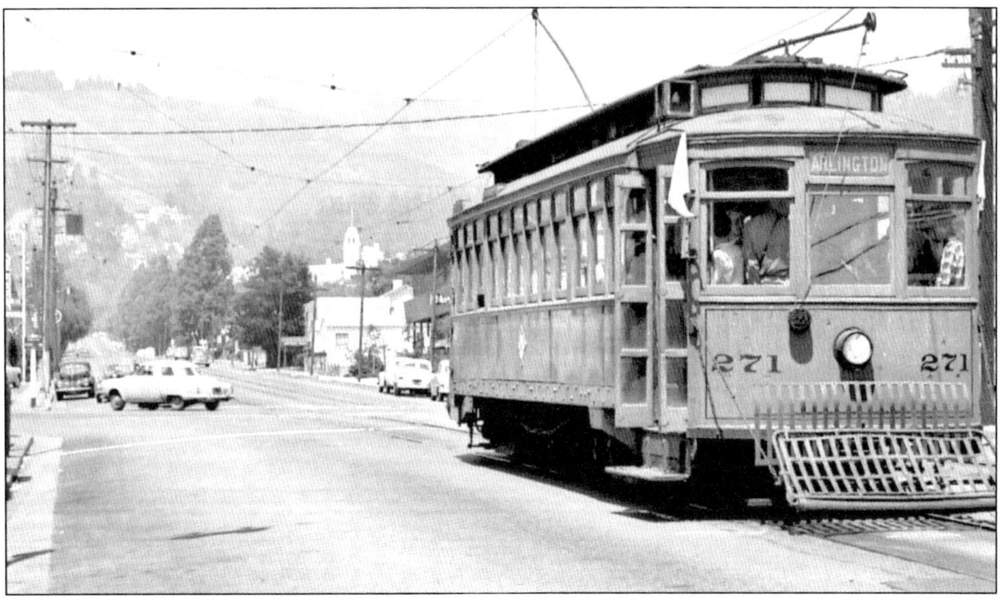


**REMEMBERING STREETCARS.** This streetcar at the intersection of College Avenue and Claremont Avenue was brought back for a commemorative run on May 22, 1955. The Claremont Hotel is in the background. The streetcar is using the E line right-of-way on a Bay Area Electric Railway Association excursion. (Courtesy Ray Raineri.)

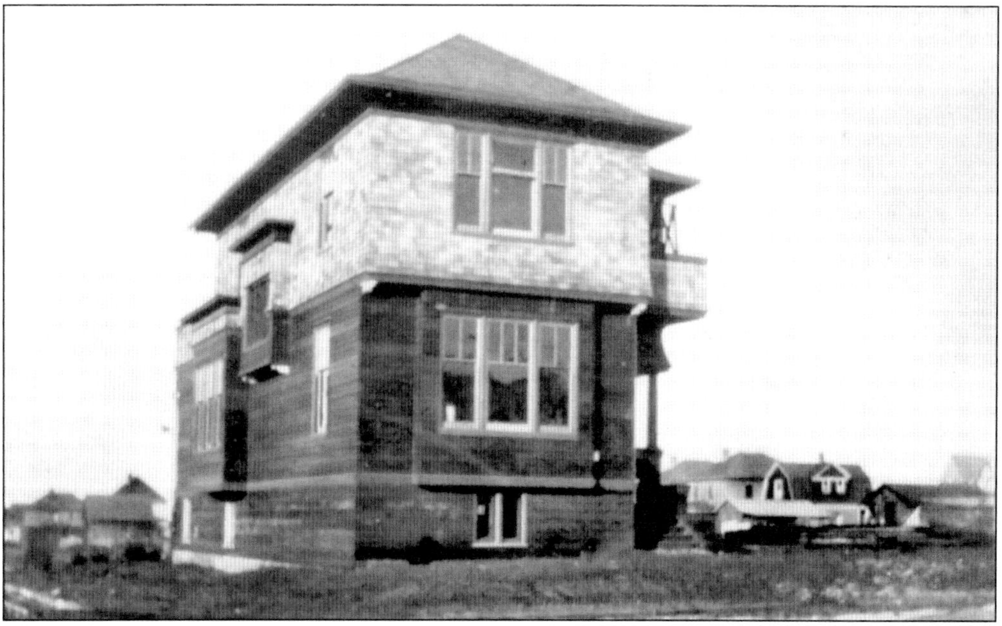

**RUSSELL HOUSE, 1907.** Good streetcar transportation attracted commuters to Rockridge in the early 1900s. This house was owned by Thomas Russell, a pattern maker at Phoenix Iron Works in downtown Oakland. Phoenix Iron Works was important in the development of Oakland's street system because the company made non-rattle manhole covers and street lamps. Russell bought a piece of farmland at the corner of Hillegass Avenue and Sixty-second Street near College Avenue and had this house built in 1906–1907. (Courtesy Kevin Flynn and Marilyn Citron.)

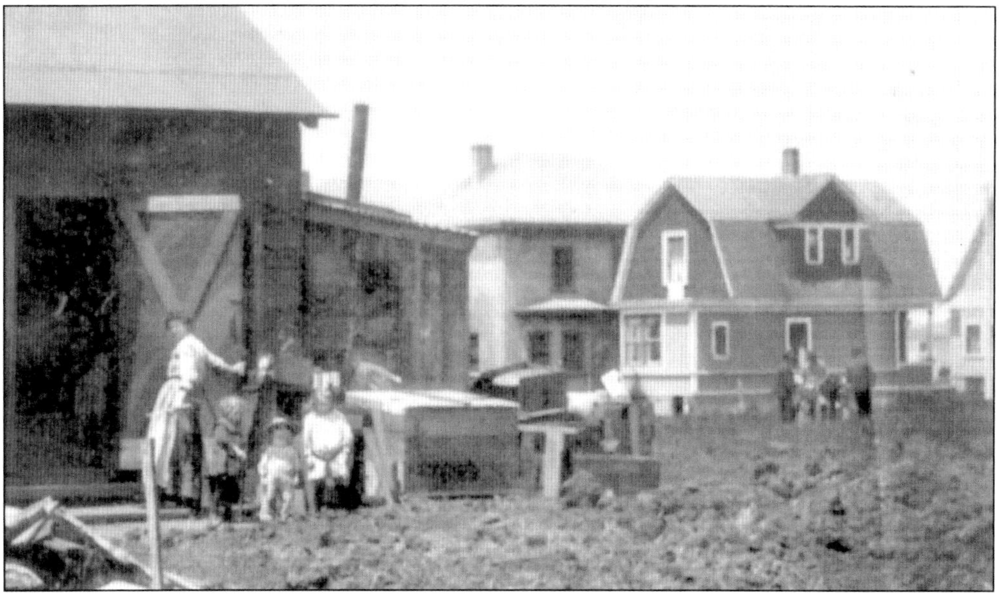

**HOME IN A BARN, 1906.** Thomas Russell's wife and children are shown here in of the barn on the farm where they lived from 1905 until 1907 while their house was being designed and constructed. Russell's wife, two children, and a neighbor child are shown by the barn door. Russell chose this building site because of good streetcar transportation to work in downtown Oakland. (Courtesy Kevin Flynn and Marilyn Citron.)

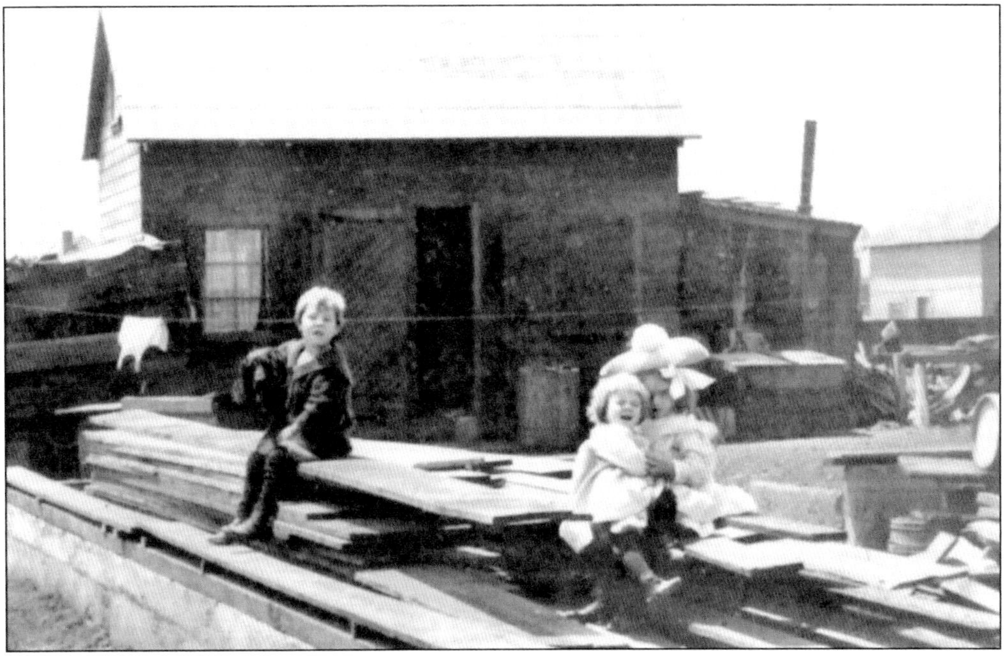

**RUSSELL CONSTRUCTION SITE, 1906.** The Thomas Russell daughters and a neighbor play on boards for construction of their new home on Hillegass Avenue near College Avenue. During construction, Thomas Russell's father, Edward, climbed onto the house roof to view the fires in San Francisco following the 1906 earthquake. He fell, later died, and his son, Thomas Russell, subsequently became president of Phoenix Iron Works. (Courtesy Kevin Flynn and Marilyn Citron.)

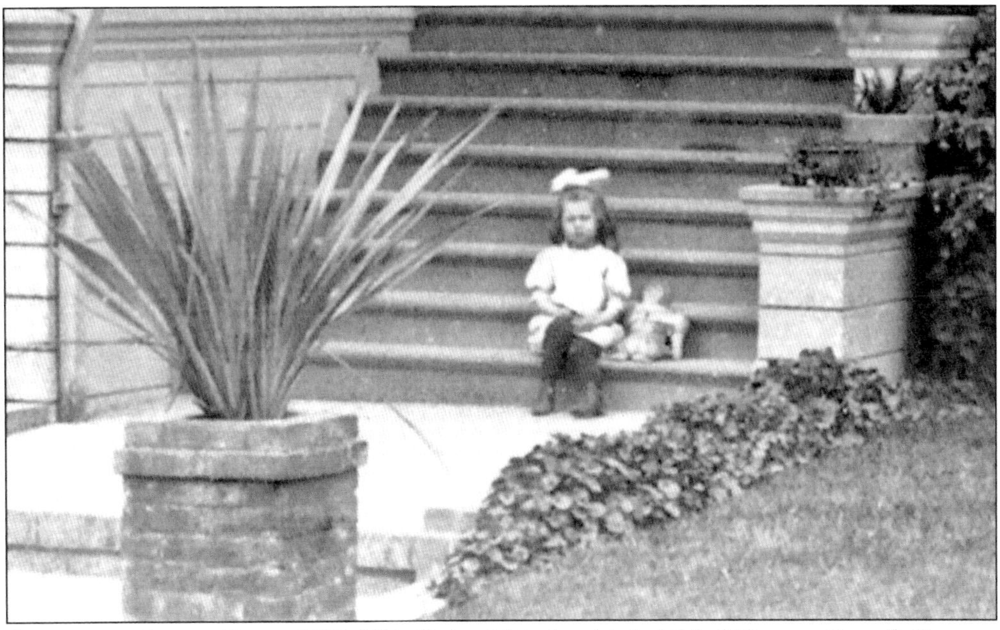

**GIRL WITH CLOTH DOLL, 1910.** This little girl is the third child of Thomas Russell. She was born while her parents were living in the barn shown on the opposite page and on the top of this page. She has her cloth doll beside her on the steps of her new home at Hillegass Avenue and Sixty-second Street in Rockridge. (Courtesy Kevin Flynn and Marilyn Citron.)

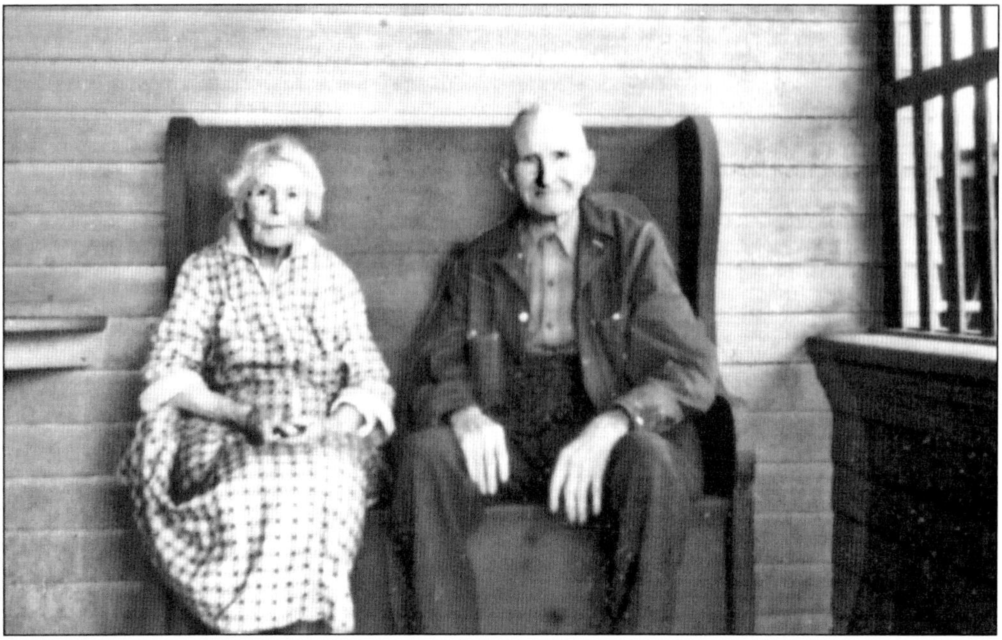

**The Russells on Their Porch, 1950s.** The Russells lived in their Hillegass home until their deaths. Then the house was occupied by two of their daughters until their deaths. The Russell house remained in the family for more than 70 years. (Courtesy Kevin Flynn and Marilyn Citron.)

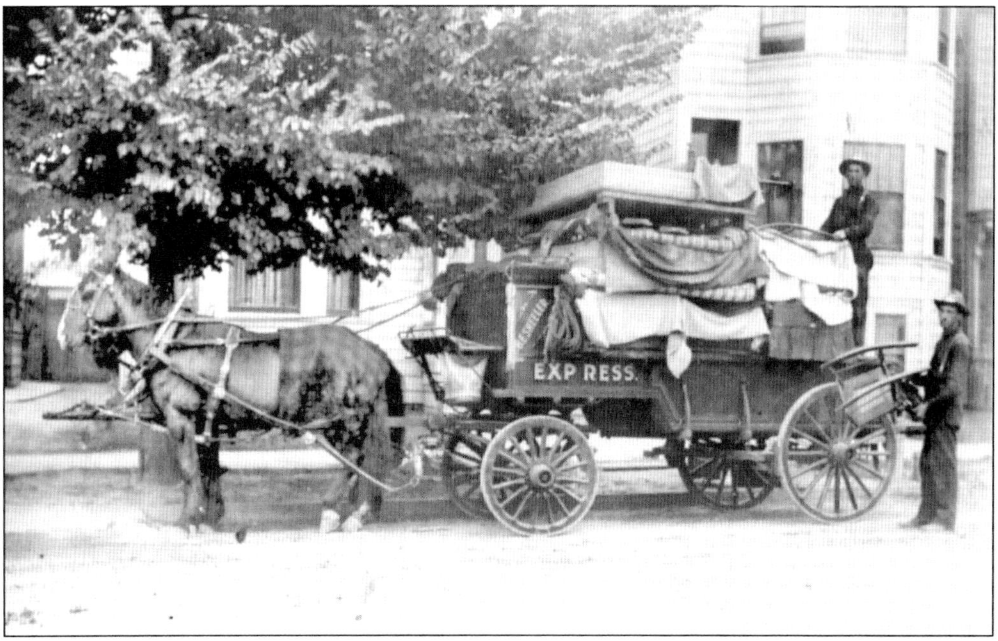


**Freighter in the Early 1900s.** After the 1906 earthquake, many refugees from San Francisco got off the ferry in Oakland and loaded their belongings onto a horse-drawn freighter such as this one operated by Bert Sheeler. More than 200,000 refugees came to the East Bay following the quake, many to Rockridge. Of these, 150,000 never returned home. Oakland's population increased from 67,000 in 1906 to 150,000 in 1915. The new population pressures spurred a building boom in Rockridge. (Courtesy Oakland History Room.)

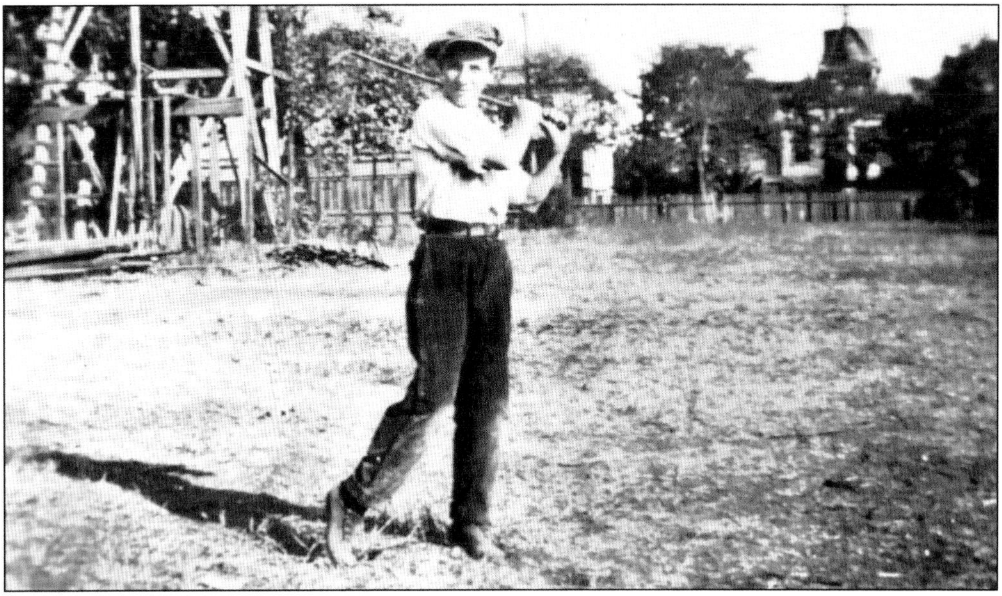

**Louis Siegriest, 1913.** Young Louis Siegriest, like many boys in Rockridge, worked as a caddy at the Claremont Country Club. After the 1906 earthquake, he climbed the water tower above the well in the backyard of his Miles Avenue home and reported seeing the fields of Rockridge covered with tents housing refugees from San Francisco as well as Rockridge residents who feared aftershocks. His family also slept in a tent in his yard after the 1906 earthquake. (Courtesy Louis Siegriest estate.)

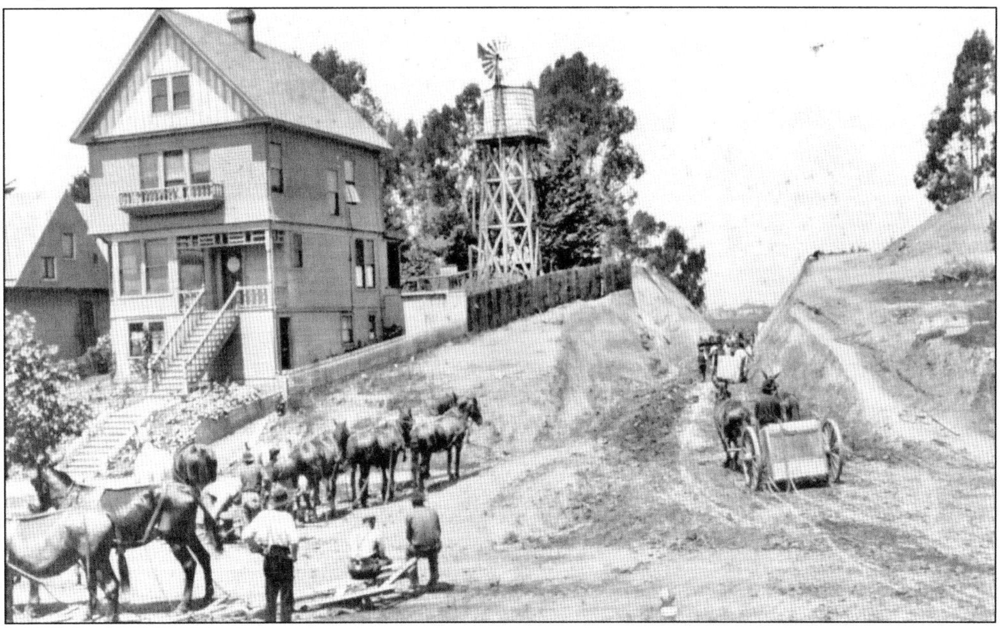

**Laying Streetcar Rails, 1904.** Here a crew is grading the road in preparation for laying streetcar rails. While this crew is working at Fortieth and Howe Streets just south of Rockridge, a similar crew laid rails on College Avenue in the same year for an electric streetcar line. This electric line replaced the horsecar line that was operating on College Avenue in the 1890s. (Courtesy Oakland History Room.)

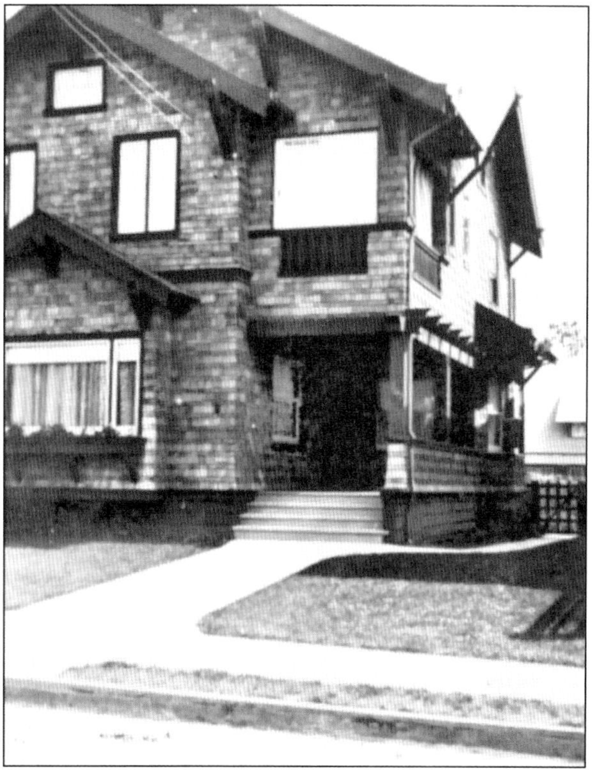

**HALLE HOUSE, C. 1912.** Rainsford Halle, owner of a composing room in San Francisco that set linotype for printing companies, escaped the 1906 quake and moved to this house just west of College Avenue in 1907. His San Francisco apartment was so badly damaged in the quake that he had to climb out the transom window over the front door to escape. When he entered the street, he was commandeered by soldiers and forced to fight fires for the rest of the day, then joined the soup line in the park. (Courtesy Neville Desouza and Bill Morrison.)

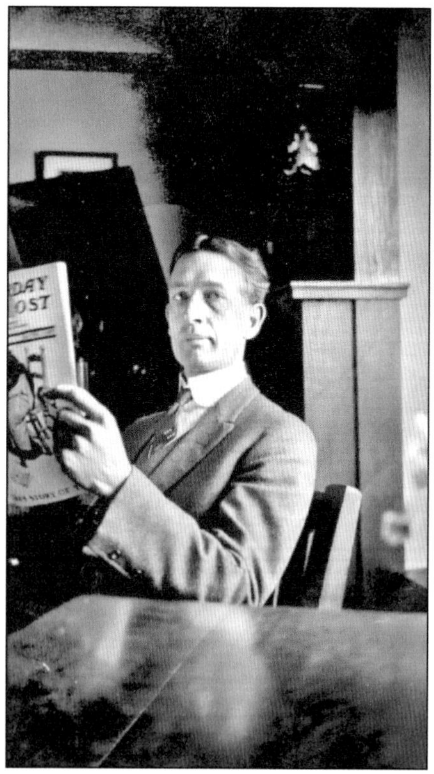

**ARTS AND CRAFTS INTERIOR, 1907.** Rainsford Halle sits reading the *Saturday Evening Post* in his dining room that has an arts and crafts design. The paneling is redwood, and a Tiffany-style, built-in, stained-glass sconce light can be seen behind him. Rainsford walked across open fields to catch the Key System train on Claremont Avenue for his daily commute to San Francisco. (Courtesy Neville Desouza and Bill Morrison.)

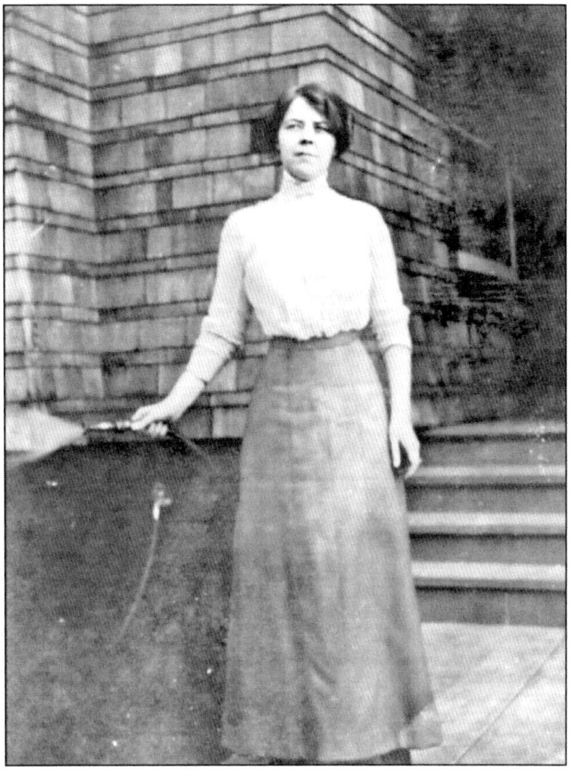

**WATERING THE LAWN, 1907.** Rainsford's wife, Hortense, is watering the lawn in their new home near Claremont Avenue, half a block below College Avenue. Their house had a sleeping porch in the back with many windows that brought in the summer evening breezes. (Courtesy Neville Desouza and Bill Morrison.)

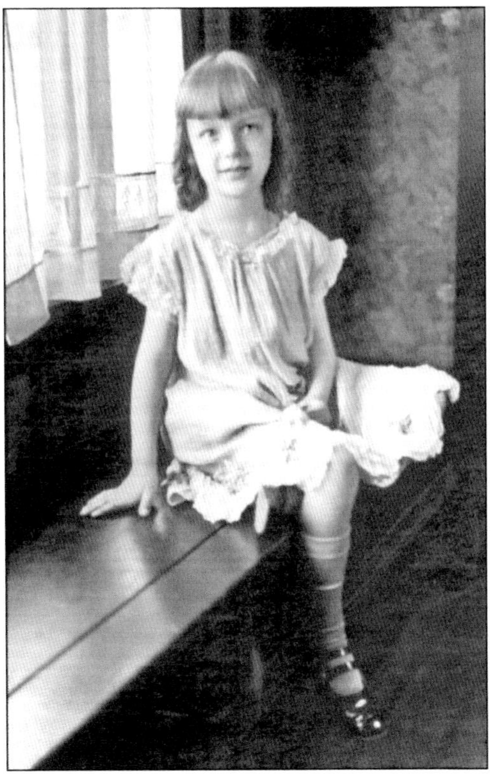

**HALLE DAUGHTER, C. 1912.** Virginia Halle sits on a windowsill in her Craftsman-style home with much interior natural wood. She is the daughter of Rainsford Halle, who moved to escape the devastation of the 1906 earthquake in San Francisco. Couples bought homes in Rockridge as a good place to raise children in weather that was warmer and less foggy than San Francisco. (Courtesy Neville Desouza and Bill Morrison.)

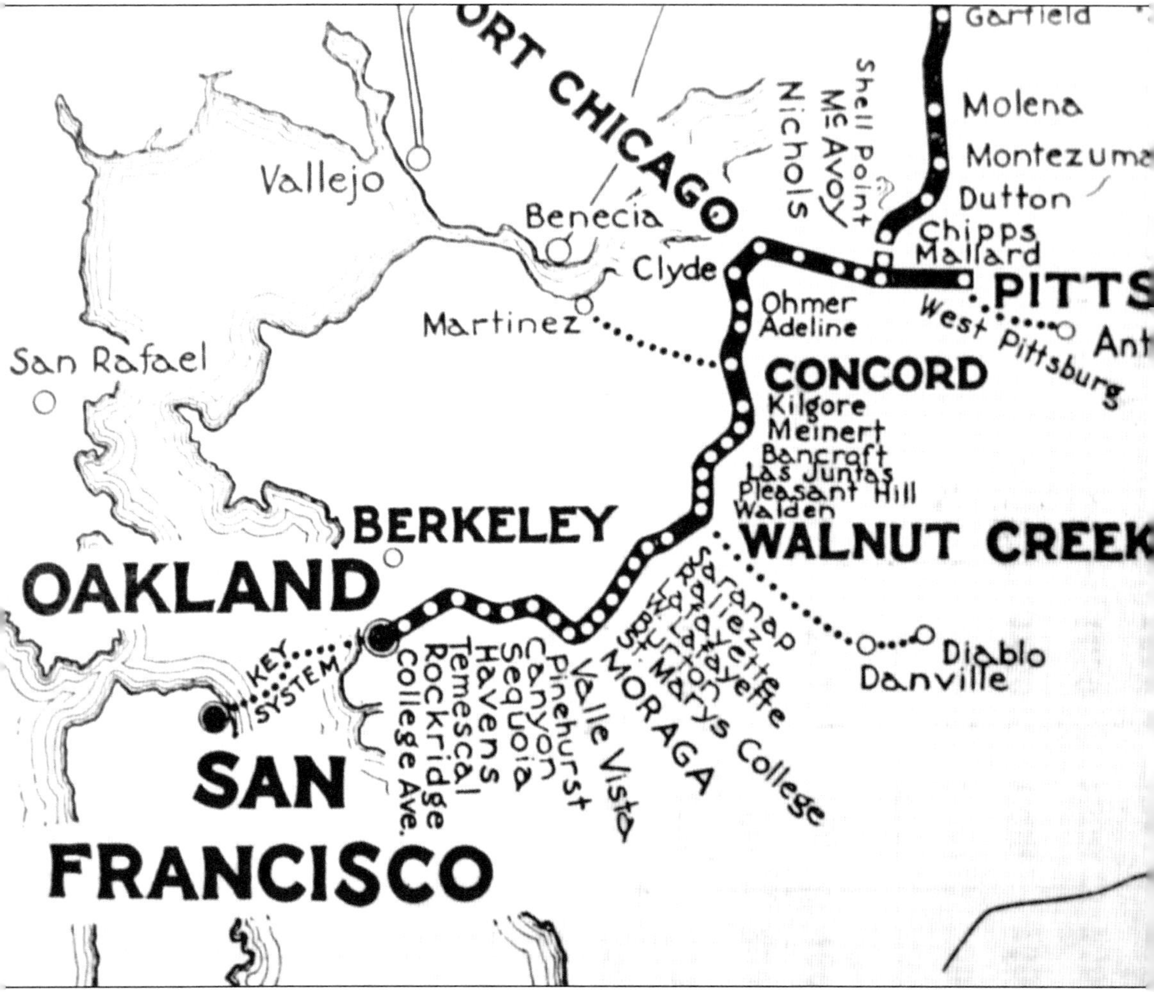


**MAP OF SACRAMENTO NORTHERN RAILROAD ROUTE, 1938.** The route of the Sacramento Northern Railroad is shown here. From Rockridge, a passenger could go east through Contra Costa County to Sacramento and on to Chico. Rockridge resident Meriam Combs remembers taking the Sacramento Northern Railroad each year to the state fair in Sacramento, a highlight of her year. Alternatively, a trip west takes Rockridge passengers along Shafter to the Fortieth Street depot and on to the Key System pier where they transferred to a ferry boat for the ride across the bay to San Francisco. (Courtesy John Harder.)

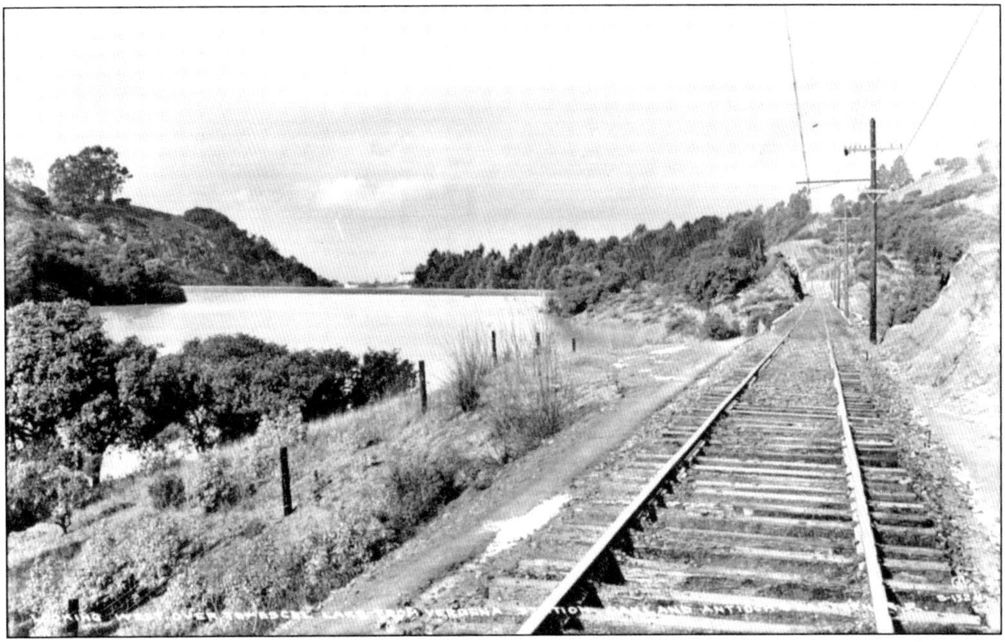

**Oakland and Antioch Railroad, c. 1914.** The next series of photographs traces the route of the Oakland and Antioch Railroad, later the Sacramento Northern Railroad, as it approached Rockridge, picked up passengers, and took them to San Francisco. Here the track runs by Lake Temescal coming from Contra Costa County heading toward Rockridge. (Courtesy Ray Raineri, Vernon Sappers photograph, Cook and Cook collection.)

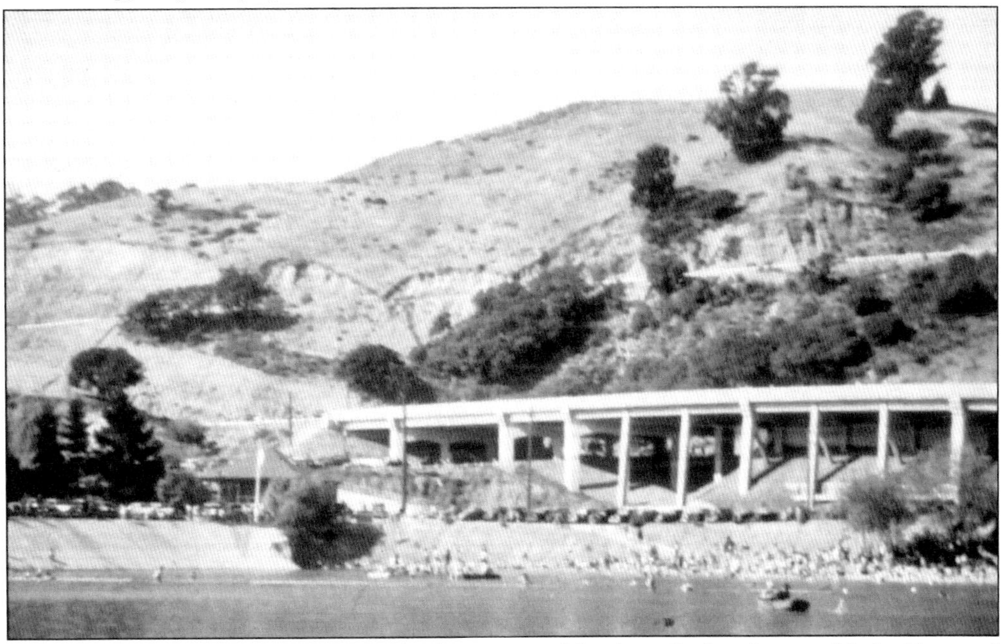

**Trestle across Lake Temescal.** The Sacramento Northern Railroad crossed Lake Temescal on a trestle at the eastern end of Rockridge. The train came from Sacramento and was heading for Rockridge and connections to San Francisco. The rail tunnel (different from the Caldecott Tunnel) through the Oakland hills to Contra Costa County opened in 1913. (Courtesy J. Kent.)

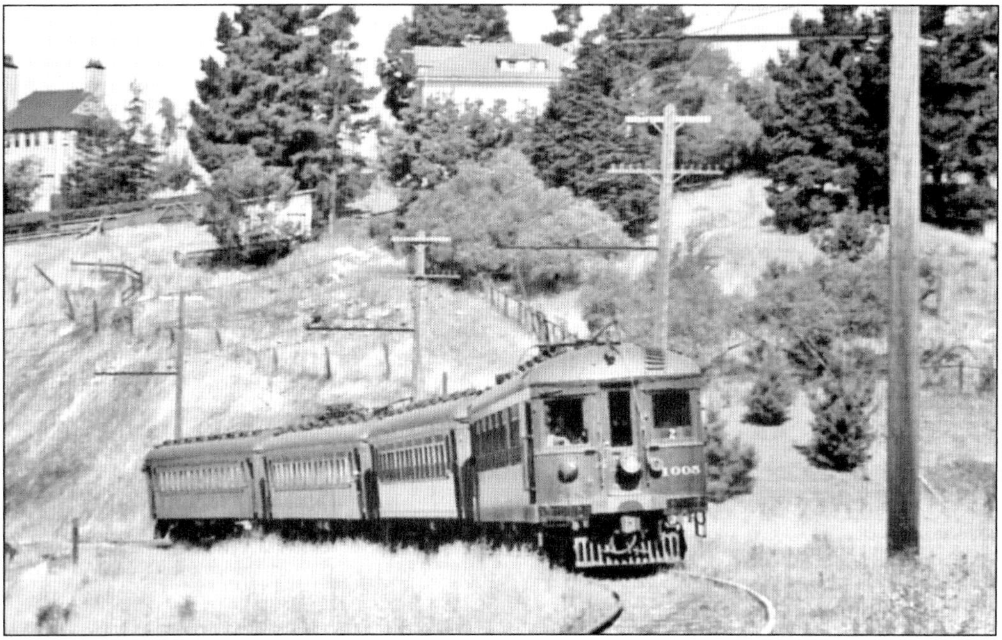

**ROCKRIDGE GRADE, 1939.** The Sacramento Northern electric passenger train is coming down the Rockridge grade after leaving Lake Temescal with the next stop Rockridge. The maximum speed the Sacramento Northern Railroad allowed engineers to run trains on this grade was 22 miles per hour. The last Sacramento Northern revenue passenger train ran between Pittsburg and Rockridge in 1941. (Courtesy John Harder, Ralph Demoro photograph.)

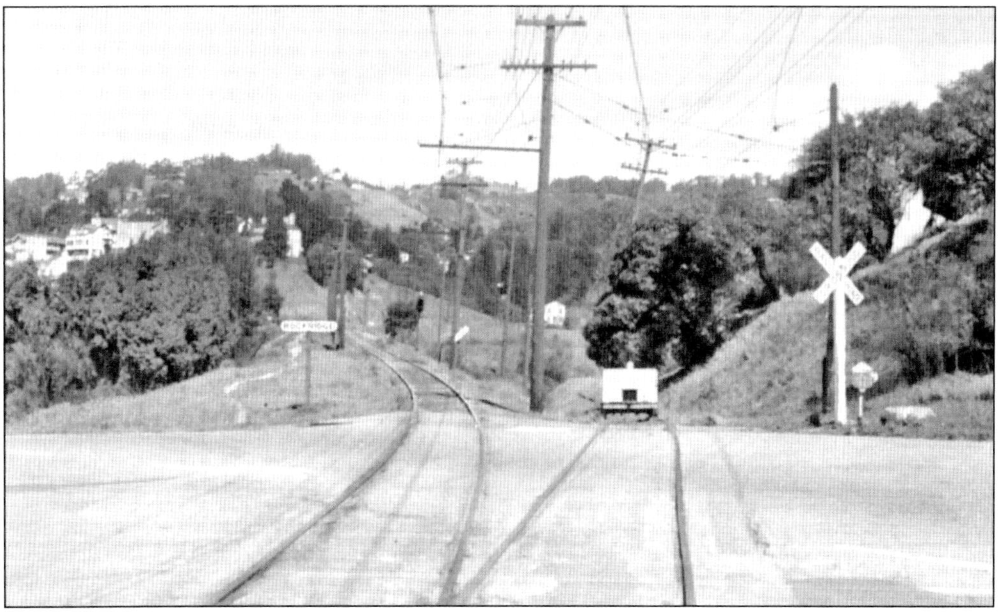

**SACRAMENTO NORTHERN SPUR, LATE 1940S.** The tracks of the Sacramento Northern electric railroad ran behind Chabot School, where a spur with a bumper can be seen on the right of the photograph. The sign on the left says "Rockridge." The railroad originally had plans to put a train yard here, but objections from Rockridge neighbors led the railroad to scuttle the plan. The view is looking east toward Lake Temescal. (Courtesy John Harder, John Harder photograph.)

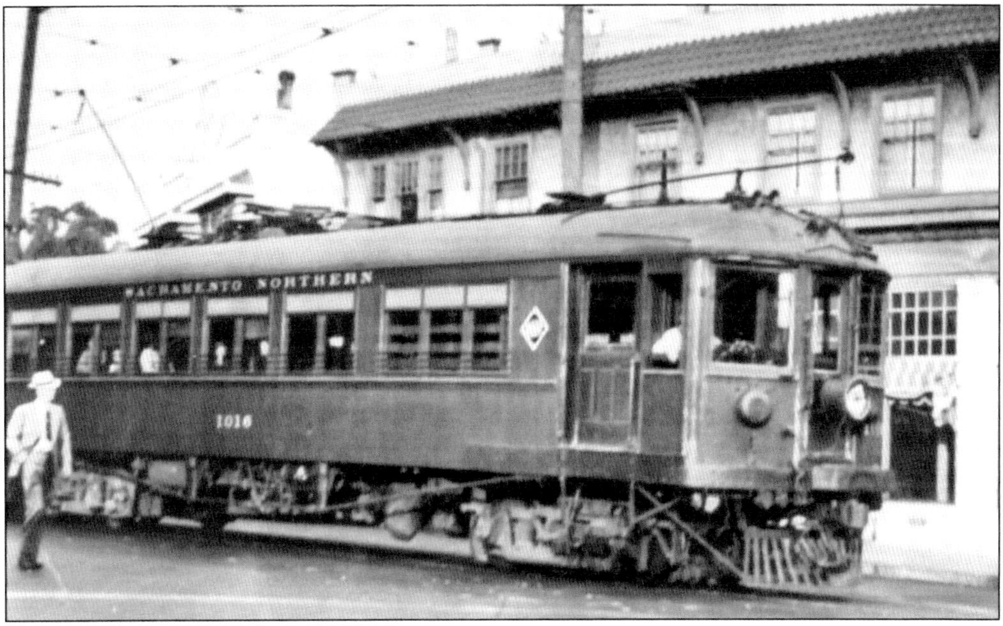


**College Avenue Interurban Stop.** A Sacramento Northern train stops at the southeast corner of College Avenue and Shafter (now Miles Avenue) to pick up passengers in Rockridge. Disembarking passengers can transfer here to the No. 6 streetcar line that runs down College Avenue. The first Rockridge branch library was housed in a building behind the train. The building was demolished in the 1960s to make way for the Grove Shafter Freeway and Bay Area Rapid Transit (BART). (Courtesy Ray Raineri.)

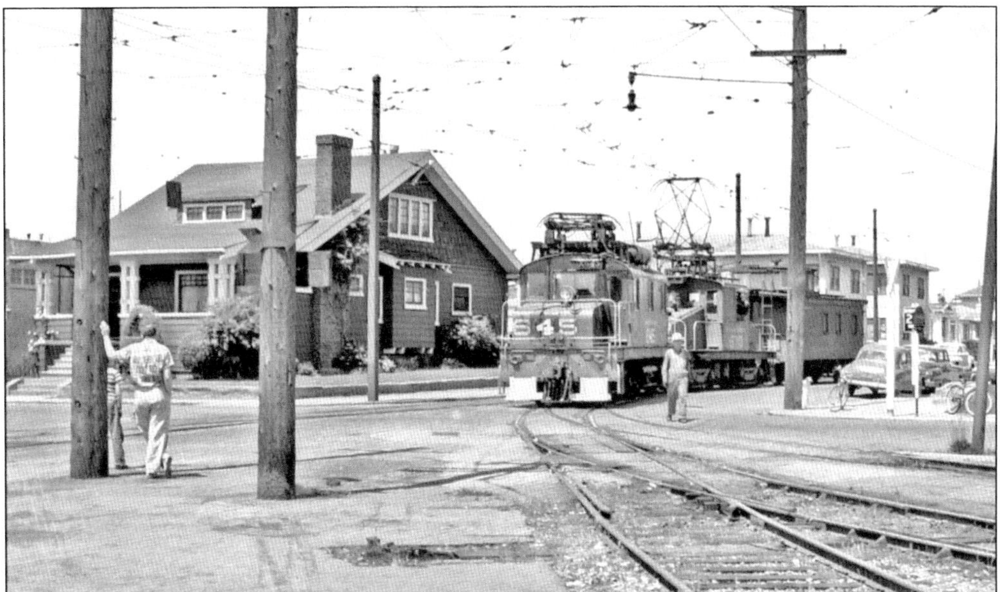

**Sacramento Northern at Forty-First Street.** After crossing College Avenue, Sacramento Northern trains traveled down Shafter Avenue (when Shafter Avenue used to cross College Avenue). These electric freight motors are rounding the corner at Forty-first Street approaching the throat of the freight yards. (Courtesy John Harder.)

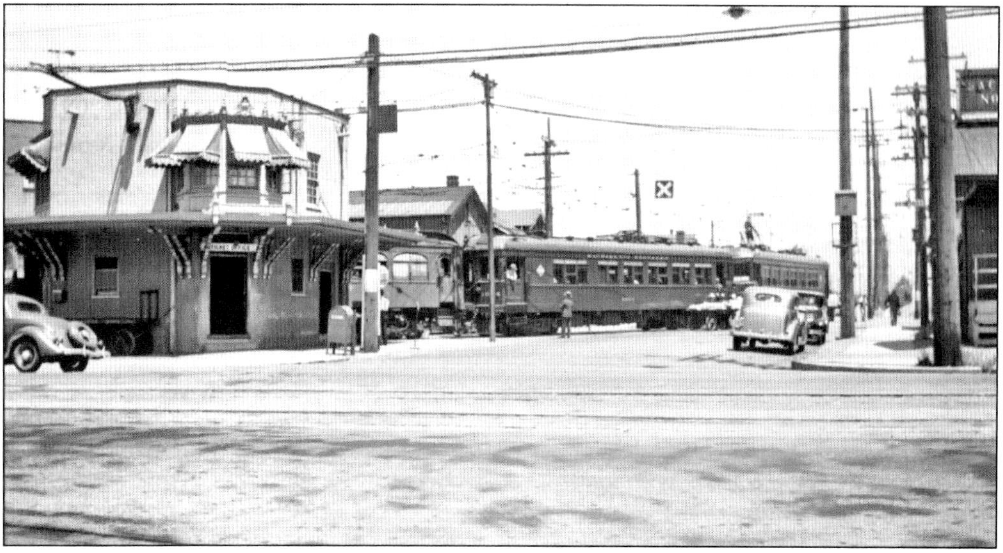

**FORTIETH STREET STATION, 1936.** A Sacramento Northern train is switching into the Fortieth Street depot yards from Shafter Avenue. The building at the left is the depot waiting room. (Courtesy John Harder.)

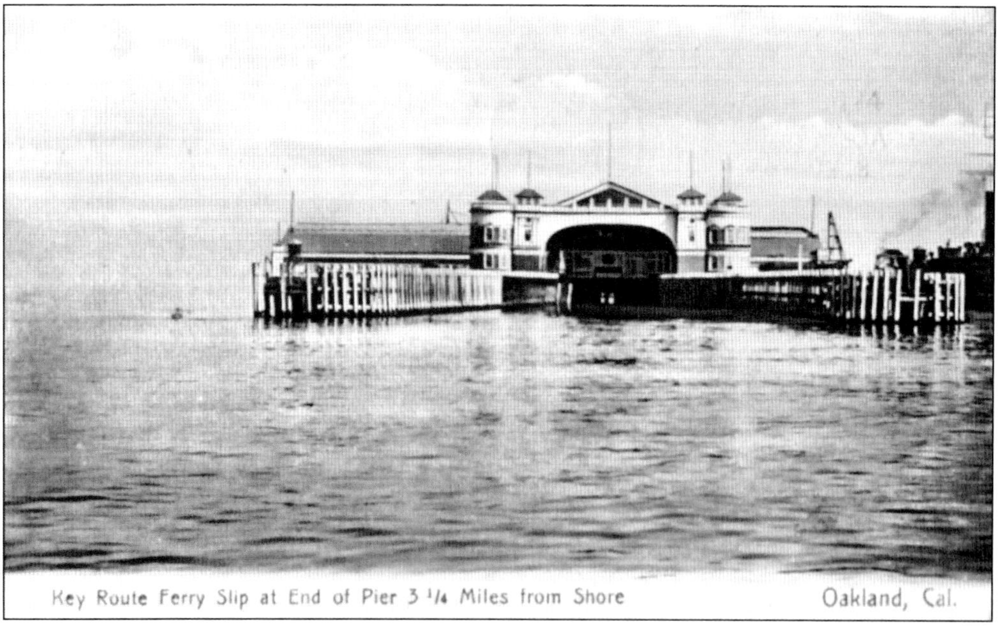


**FERRY SLIP, 1908.** Ferries took Oakland passengers to San Francisco as early as the 1850s. This postcard shows the terminal on the Key System pier. When this postcard was postmarked in 1908, Rockridge passengers could catch a trolley from College Avenue and, with transfers, arrive at this ferry slip for their commute to San Francisco. (Courtesy Oakland History Room, postcard by Cook and Cook, Oakland.)

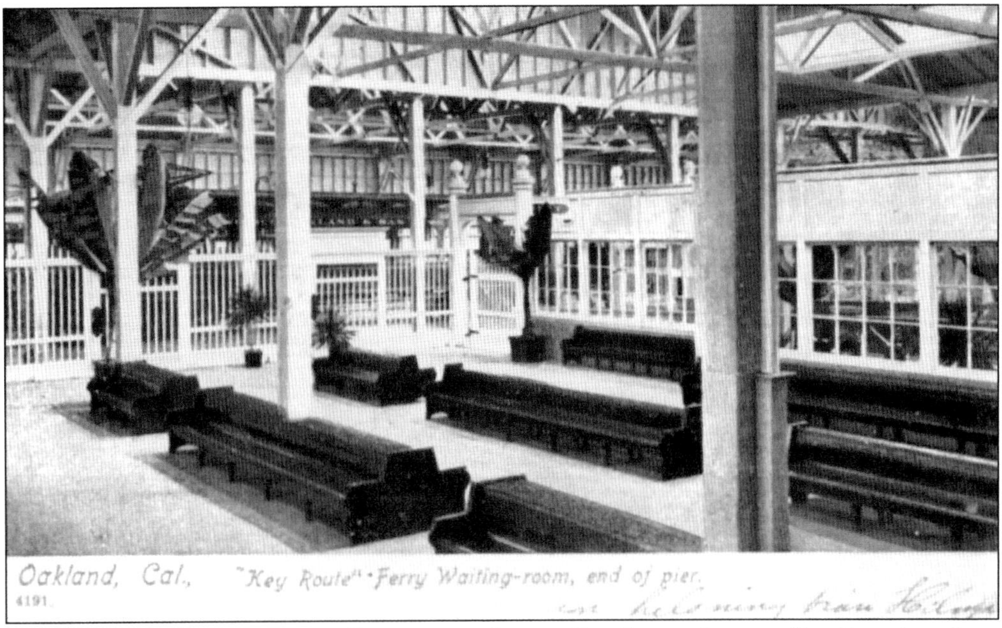


**FERRY WAITING ROOM, 1908.** Passengers taking a Key System ferry to San Francisco from Oakland had a comfortable waiting room on the Key System pier. This postcard with a 1908 postmark shows the interior of the waiting room at the end of a pier that extended three-and-a-quarter miles from shore into the bay. (Courtesy Oakland History Room, postcard by Paul C. Koeber Company, New York.)

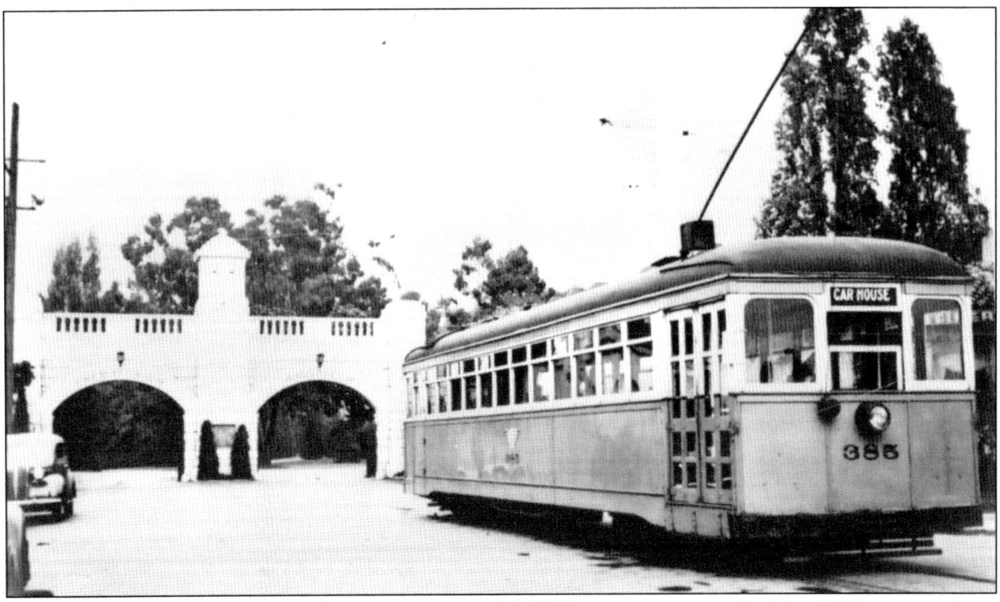


**MOUNTAIN VIEW CEMETERY STREETCAR, C. 1936.** This streetcar on the No. 27 Cemetery Line operated between 1903 and 1940, running for one long block along Piedmont Avenue between Pleasant Valley Road and the Mountain View Cemetery gates, 0.18 miles. Cemetery visitors could take the Piedmont Avenue streetcar, exit before it turned on Pleasant Valley Road toward Piedmont, then board the cemetery line for the rest of the trip to the cemetery gates. (Courtesy Ray Raineri, Ted Wurm collection.)

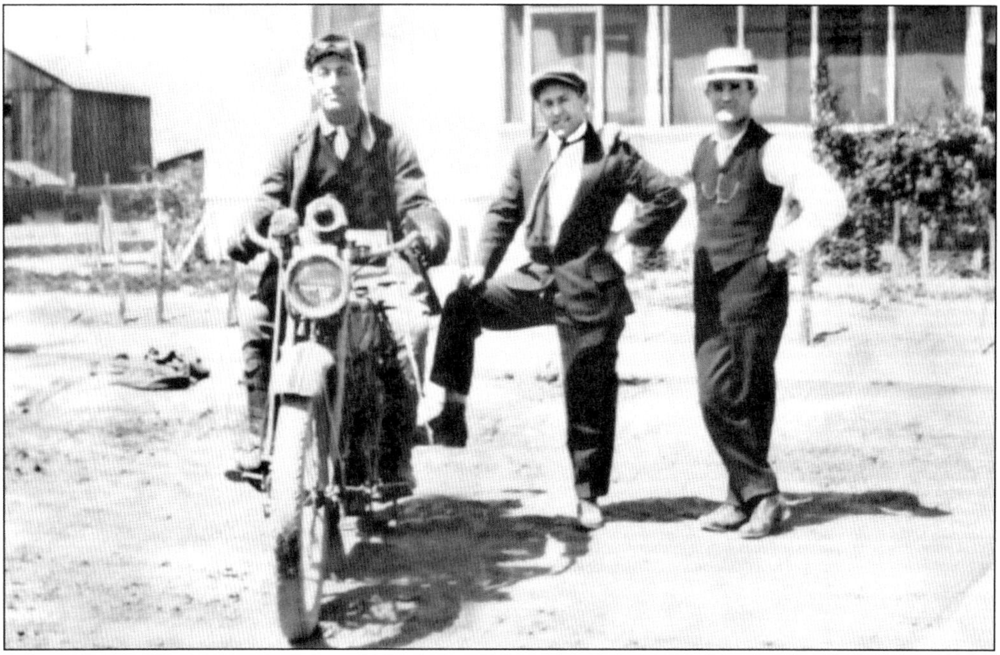

**MOTORCYCLE.** Some men in Thelma Milliff's family proudly show off their new form of motorized transportation. This photograph was taken in 1915 on Desmond Street. Roads in Rockridge were increasingly being paved between 1910 and 1920 with gravel from the Bilger Quarry. Trains were starting to face competition from autos. (Courtesy John Coffin and Jo Coffin.)

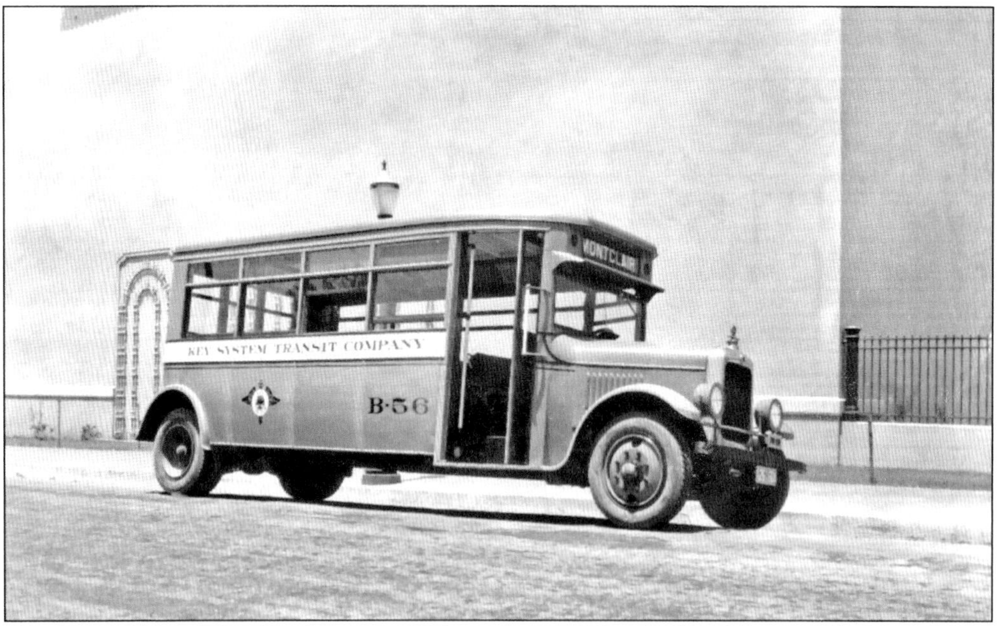


**KEY SYSTEM BUS.** This bus shown in 1925 was operated by the Key System and was similar to the Rockridge busses. The arrival of buses and privately owned automobiles made the settlement of the Rockridge hills possible. Eventually neighbors would lobby that trains in an urbanizing Rockridge created a hazard for cars, pedestrians, and children, and a movement would develop to end street rail transportation in Rockridge and elsewhere. (Courtesy John Harder.)

## *Three*

# DEVELOPMENT

Rockridge experienced a house-building boom after the 1906 earthquake. Within 10 years, Oakland's population more than doubled to 150,000. Newcomers gravitated to neighborhoods with good transportation. A flurry of annexations nearly tripled the area of the city. Annexations followed housing booms on the outskirts, such as the home building rush that took place in 1907 and 1908 along Lawton Street and Kales Avenue, between College Avenue and Broadway. The College Avenue area was annexed in 1897, the Broadway area in 1909.

Rock Ridge was appropriated as a brand name in 1909 when the Rock Ridge Properties development opened. The Realty Syndicate, a consortium of land developers, bought and subdivided a large tract in the Rockridge hills that ran from Broadway to Lake Temescal and from the Claremont Country Club to Ocean View Drive. The land in the Rockridge hills, a stiff walk from streetcar lines, had remained largely undeveloped until population pressure and the coming of the automobile created a market for middle-class homes there in the second decade of the 20th century. The Laymance Real Estate Company sold lots for home building sites.

The development was right in tune with hot trends in the design of middle-class automobile suburbs. The orderly grid gave way to curving streets respecting the hilly contour. Grand entry pillars on Broadway made the sprawling development seem cohesive and somewhat exclusive. In order to attract upscale buyers concerned with maintaining property values in the days before city zoning laws, Laymance placed a wide range of restrictions in deeds. Besides notorious clauses meant to exclude certain racial groups—struck down in 1948 by the U.S. Supreme Court—deeds controlled the scale of front lawn setbacks, the height of fences, and the quality of house construction. Buyers were forbidden to cut down palm trees, which lined the Rockridge Boulevard entrance. Lots were restricted to residential use. Fresh in mind was the incident involving Rockridge metallurgist Charles Butters, manufacturer of zinc dust on his estate nearby. One day, his factory blew up, and debris flew two blocks around to the outcry of neighbors.

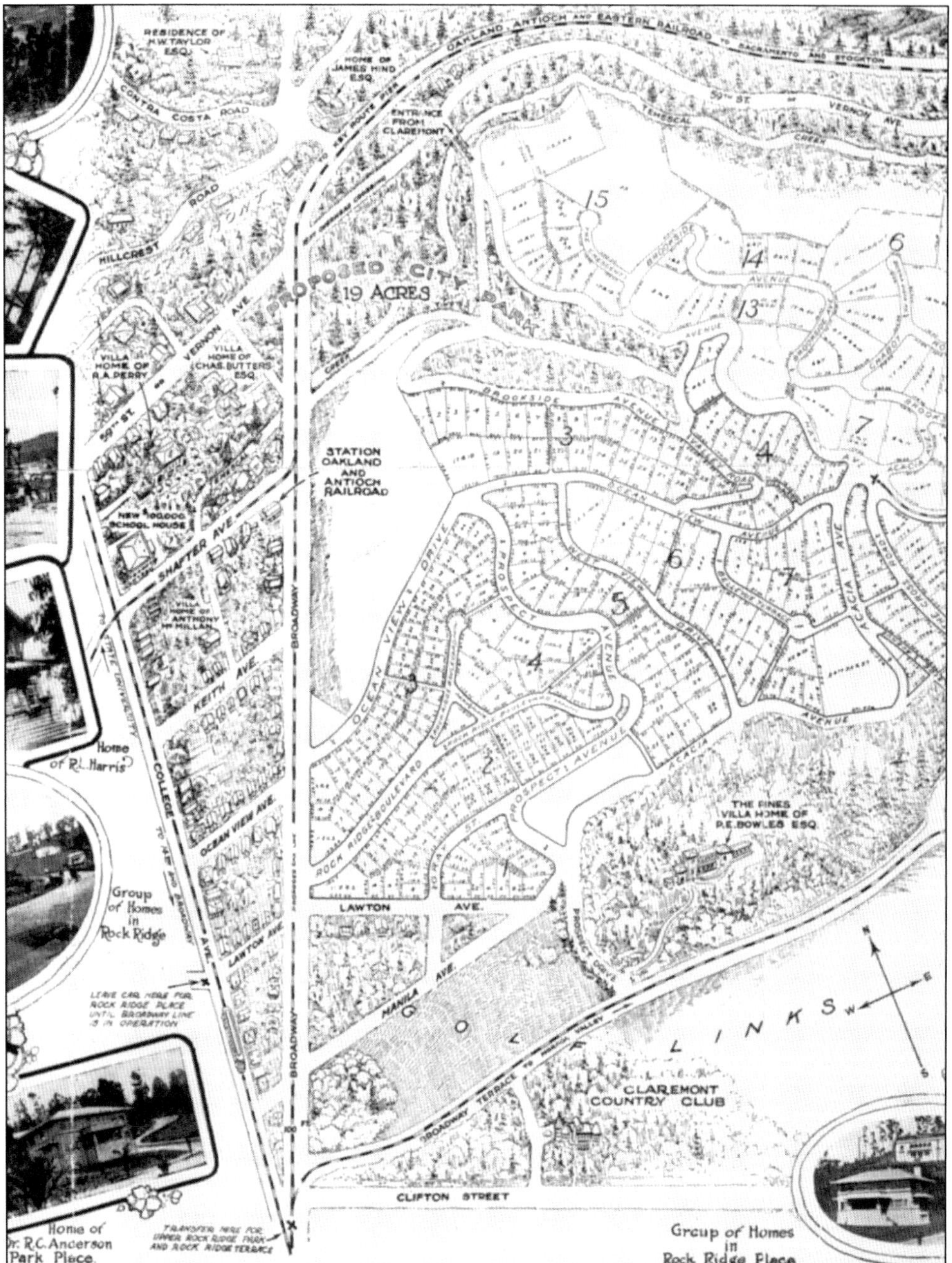


**MAP OF ROCK RIDGE PROPERTIES, 1912.** This Laymance Company map shows the Rock Ridge (two words) Properties Development, which sold lots as home building sites. This large development east of Broadway opened in 1909, just three years after refugees from the 1906 earthquake put pressure on Rockridge to grow. At the far left is College Avenue, which forms a pie wedge with Broadway. Prospective buyers were advised to take the No. 6 streetcar on College Avenue to Lawton Avenue and disembark. Then they were to walk up Lawton Avenue, cross Broadway, and wait at the Renaissance Gates at Rockridge Boulevard, where a touring car would pick them up and drive them to see lots for sale. (Courtesy Ray Raineri and Tom Wolf.)

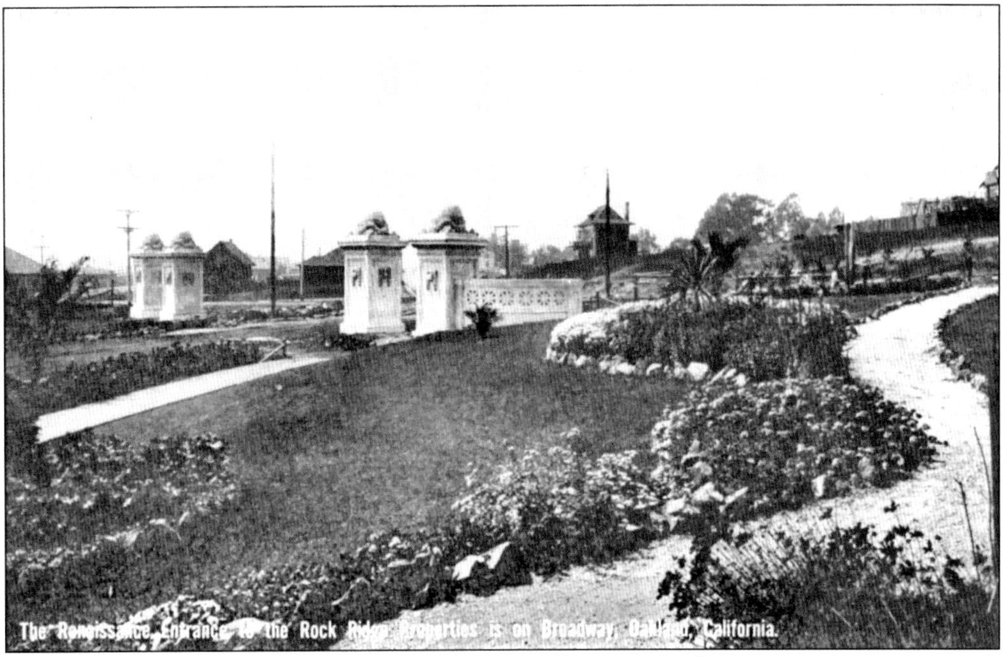


**RENAISSANCE GATES, C. 1910.** This view looks southwest at the Renaissance Gates that mark the entrance to Rock Ridge Properties. The gates stand on Broadway at Rockridge Boulevard. Rock Ridge Properties stretched 1.5 miles uphill from Broadway to above Lake Temescal and from the Claremont Country Club north to Ocean View Drive. Lots were marketed by the Laymance Company. (Courtesy Edmund Clausen.)

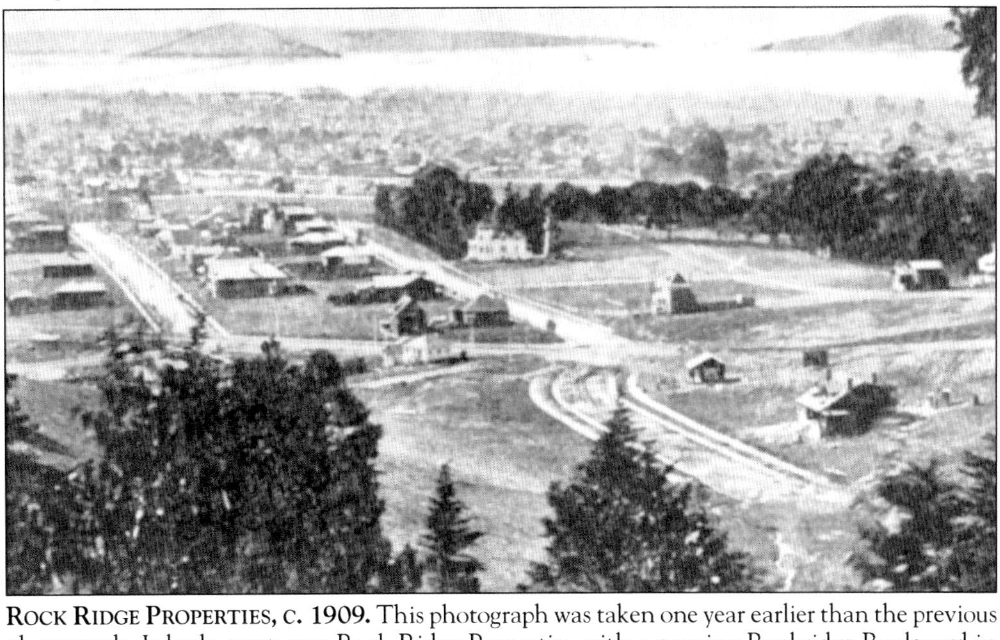

**ROCK RIDGE PROPERTIES, C. 1909.** This photograph was taken one year earlier than the previous photograph. It looks west over Rock Ridge Properties with a curving Rockridge Boulevard in the foreground that dead ends at Broadway, still a dirt road. The Renaissance Gates have not yet been built at Broadway. A farmhouse is on the north side of Lawton Avenue west of Broadway in front of a stand of trees. (Courtesy Edmund Clausen.)

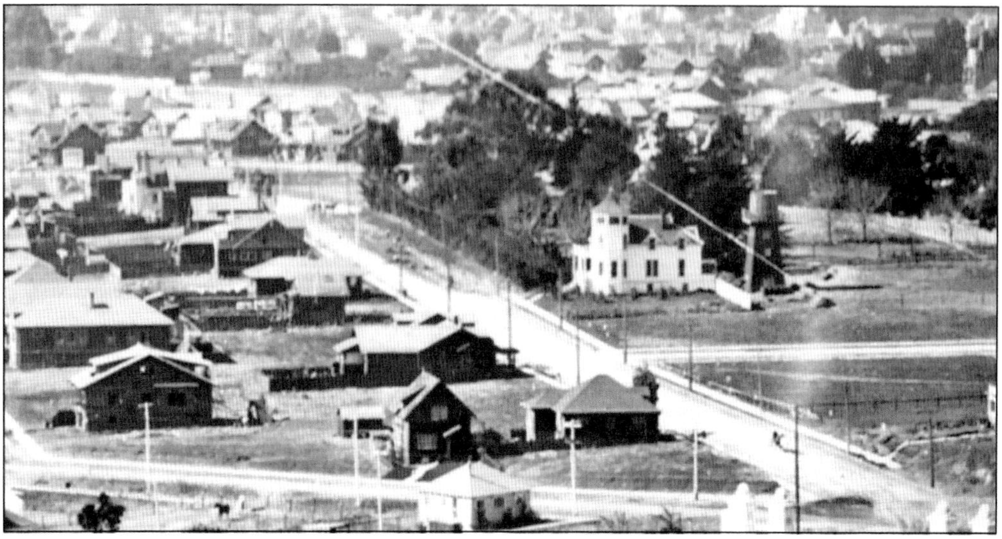

**LAWTON FARMHOUSE, C. 1910.** This farmhouse stands on the north side of Lawton Avenue between Broadway and College Avenue. College Avenue crosses Lawton Avenue just beyond the stand of trees. Broadway runs horizontally across the bottom of the photograph. The farmhouse has a water tower and windmill pump in the backyard. On the south side of Lawton Avenue, farmland was subdivided for individual houses after the 1906 earthquake. (Courtesy Oakland History Room and Alan Simpson.)

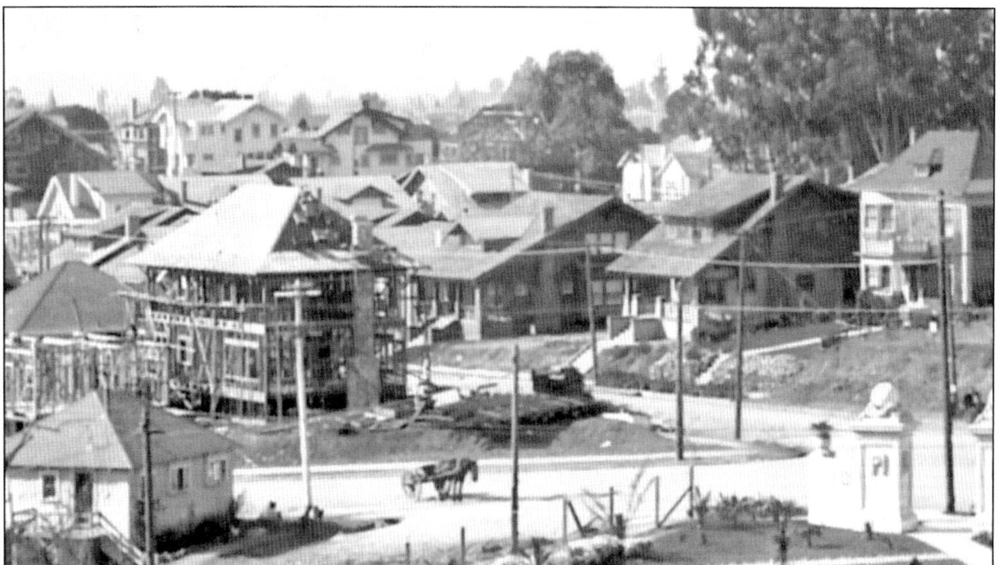

**CONSTRUCTION ON LAWTON AVENUE, 1912.** Intensive home building was taking place around Lawton Avenue and Broadway in 1912. The photograph looks northwest at Lawton Avenue across Broadway from the Renaissance Gates. A horsecart is on Broadway at the bottom center of the photograph. (Courtesy Ray Raineri.)

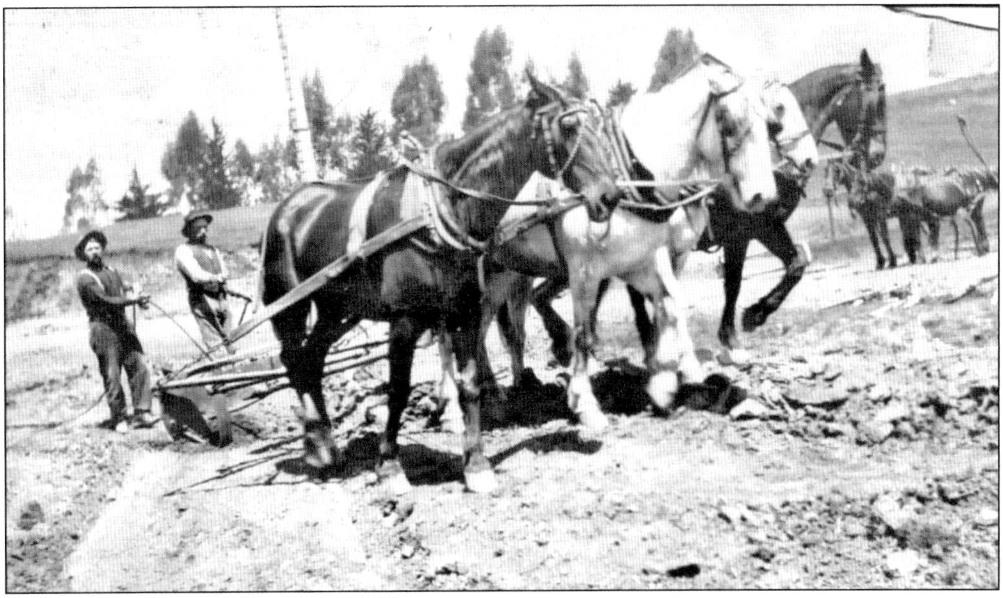

**Grading Street, c. 1910.** Horses helped grade the streets in Rock Ridge Properties in preparation for paving, which was a luxury in 1910. Water mains were laid under the streets. Lot purchasers no longer had to put in a well with a windmill. The Laymance Company advertised that as soon as a lot was purchased, water lines would bring Lake Temescal water directly to the homesite. (Courtesy Oakland History Room.)

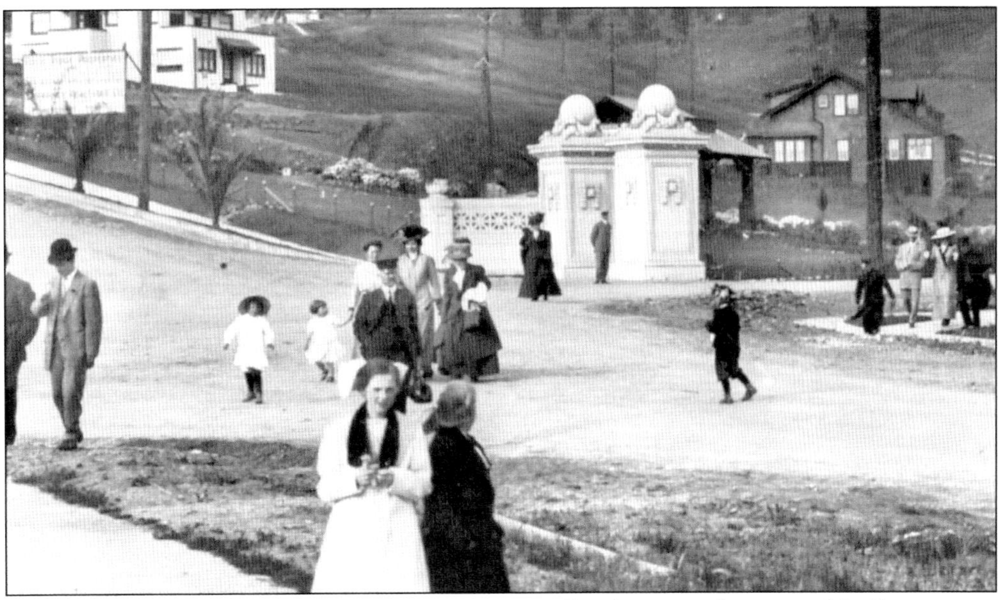

**Families Leaving Rock Ridge Properties, c. 1911.** Families are walking out of the Renaissance Gates onto Broadway after shopping for a homesite. Rock Ridge Properties advertised that their homesites would retain their value because of deed restrictions. (Courtesy Ray Raineri, Vernon Sappers collection.)

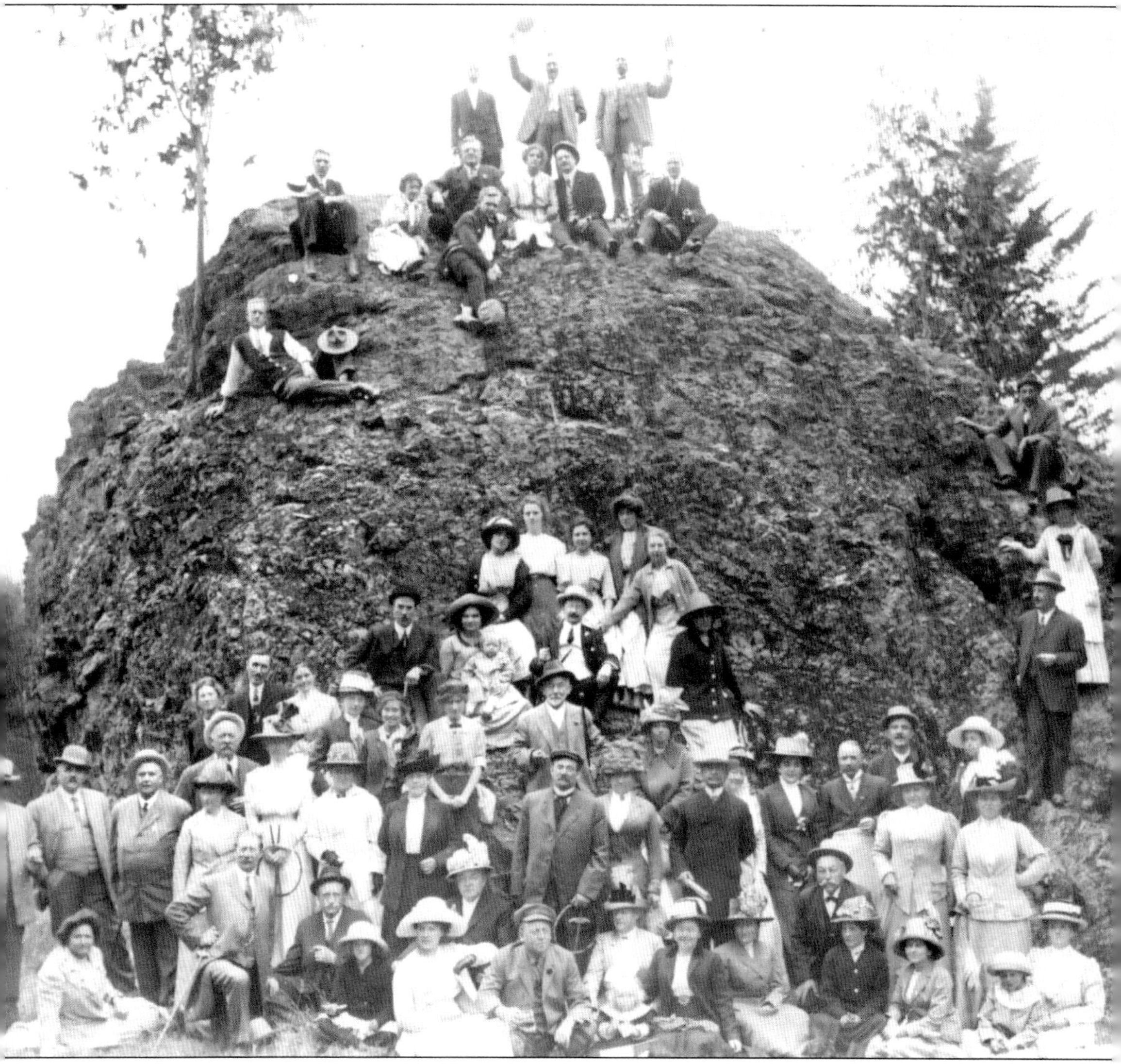

**CACTUS ROCK, C. 1912.** The Laymance Company used this promotional photograph of Cactus Rock on Acacia Avenue to enhance the legend that Rockridge got its name from this rock. The area that contained the rock originally belonged to Horatio Livermore. In some stories, Livermore's wife, Helen, named the area Rock Ridge (two words) after this rock in the 1870s. (Courtesy Oakland History Room.)

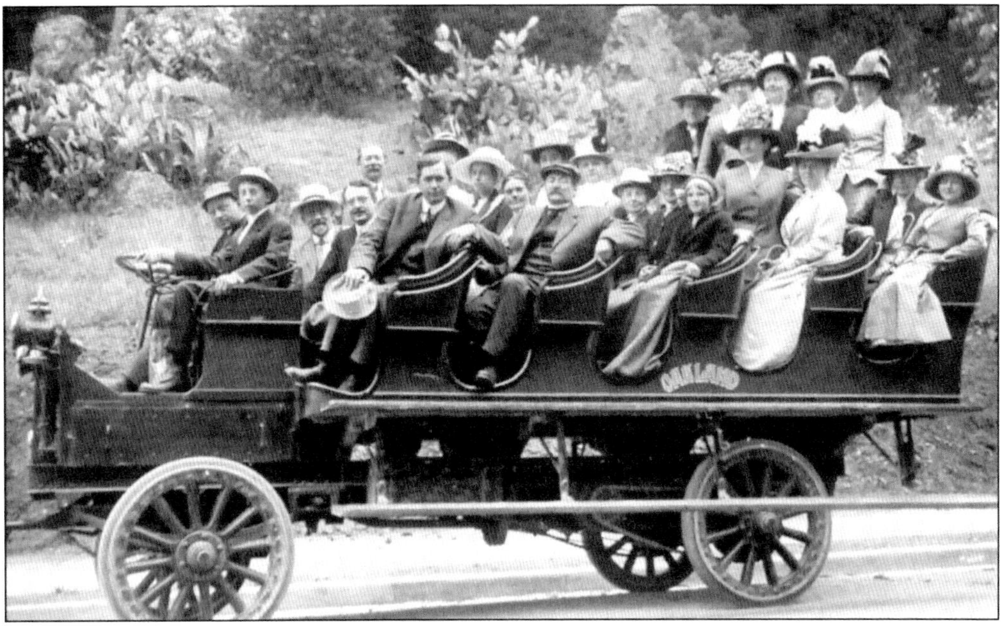

**LAYMANCE COMPANY TOURING CAR, C. 1912.** A driver is showing lots in Rock Ridge Properties to prospective buyers. This is a promotional photograph used in Laymance Company advertisements. Many of the people in the car can also be located on the previous promotional photograph of Cactus Rock. (Courtesy of Oakland History Room.)

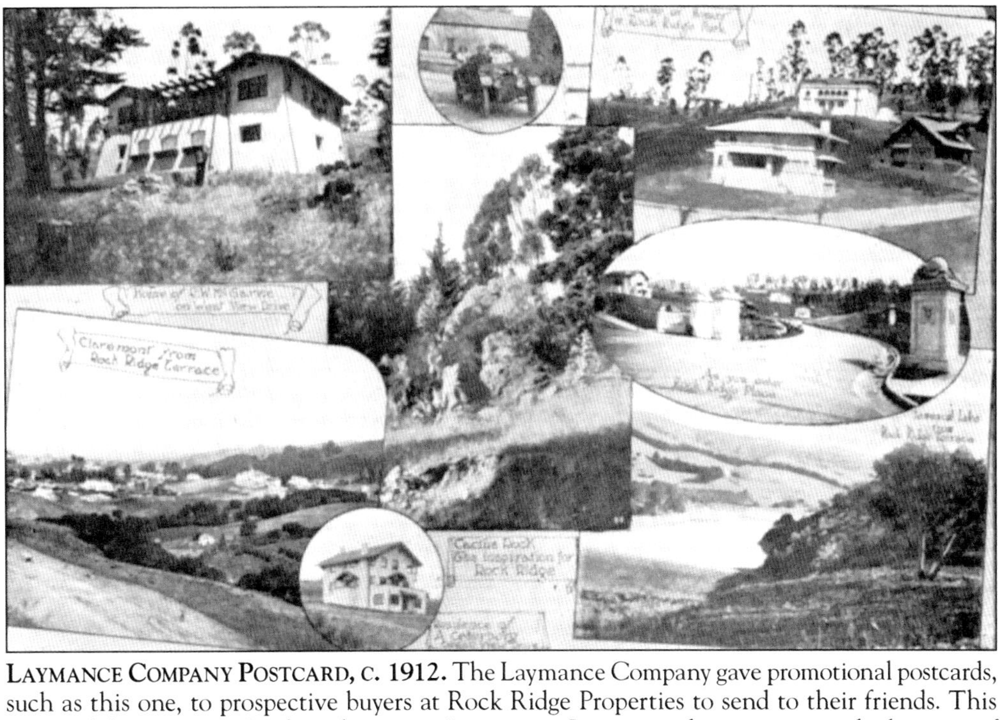


**LAYMANCE COMPANY POSTCARD, C. 1912.** The Laymance Company gave promotional postcards, such as this one, to prospective buyers at Rock Ridge Properties to send to their friends. This postcard shows Cactus Rock in the center. Laymance Company advertising gives the location of Cactus Rock as Acacia Avenue, and a similar-looking rock can still be seen on that street. This postcard reads, "Cactus Rock, the Inspiration for Rock Ridge." (Courtesy Edmund Clausen.)

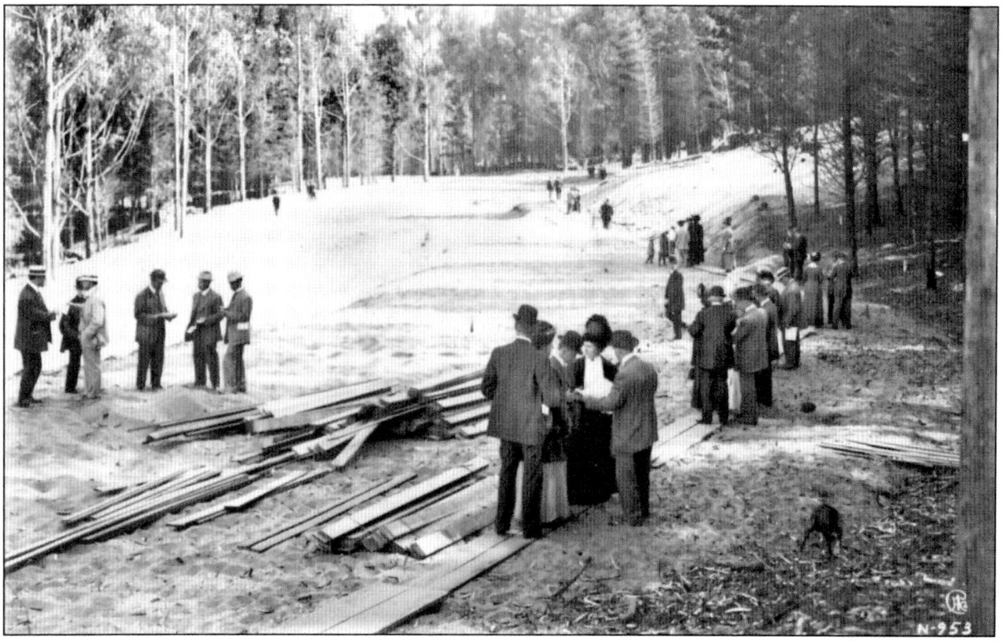


**CHOOSING A SITE, C. 1910.** Shoppers are looking at home building sites to purchase in Rock Ridge Properties. The development was opened for sale in three stages. The first was Rock Ridge Park, shown here, halfway up the hill from Broadway. Next Rock Ridge Place opened adjacent to Broadway and the Renaissance Gates. Last to open was Rock Ridge Terrace at the top of the hill. (Courtesy Oakland History Room.)

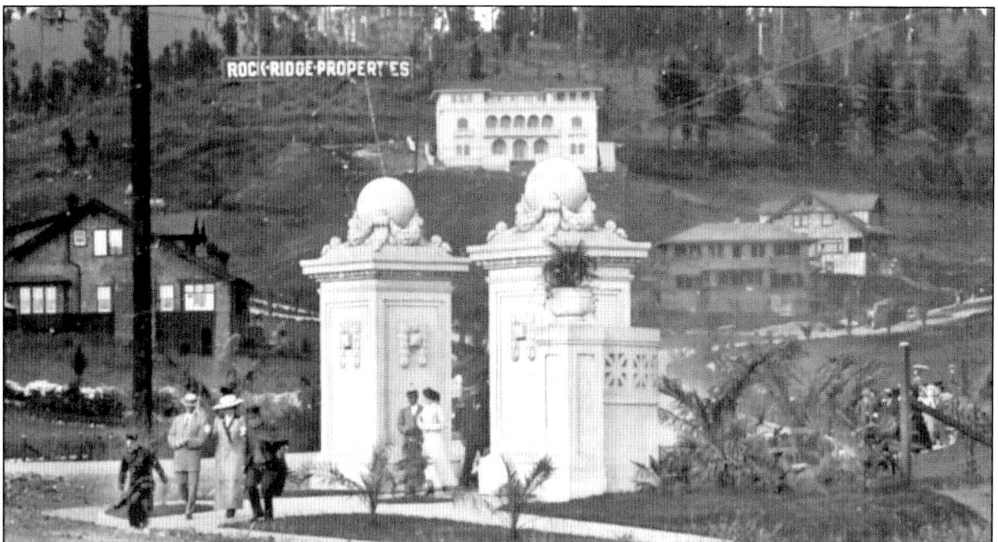

**RENAISSANCE GATES, C. 1910.** Behind the Renaissance Gates is the Enslen mansion in Rockridge Park. James Enslen was involved in the development of irrigation projects that made agriculture in the central valley possible. Some wealthy buyers, such as Enslen, purchased several lots and built street-side mansions without the large tract of land typical of previous Rockridge mansions. The Enslen home was later demolished and the land subdivided for smaller houses. (Courtesy Ray Raineri, Vernon Sappers Collection.)

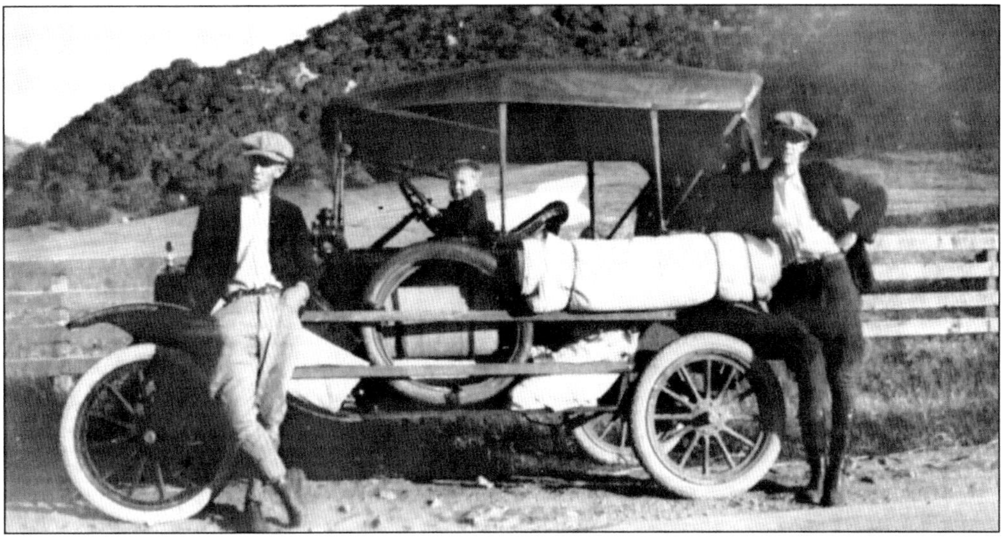

**Louis Siegriest Road Trip, c. 1917.** The automobile transformed Rockridge, making suburban living more desirable. Louis Siegriest (left) and Dewey Westaway have left from Siegriest's Miles Avenue home for a road trip. Siegriest's nephew, Charles Brown, sits in the car. (Courtesy Louis Siegriest estate.)

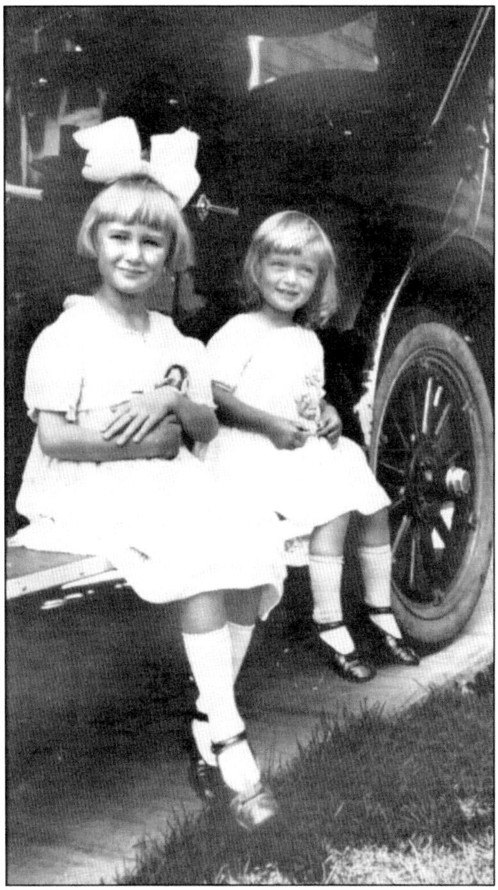

**Sisters on a Running Board, c. 1911.** The arrival of automobiles made homesites in the Rockridge hills accessible and desirable. The automobile made it easy to climb hills that presented an arduous task for horses drawing a carriage. By 1911, cars could be seen all around Rockridge in both hilly and flat areas. Here Margaret Halle and her younger sister, Virginia, sit on the running board of the family car at their home west of College Avenue. (Courtesy Neville Desouza and Bill Morrison.)

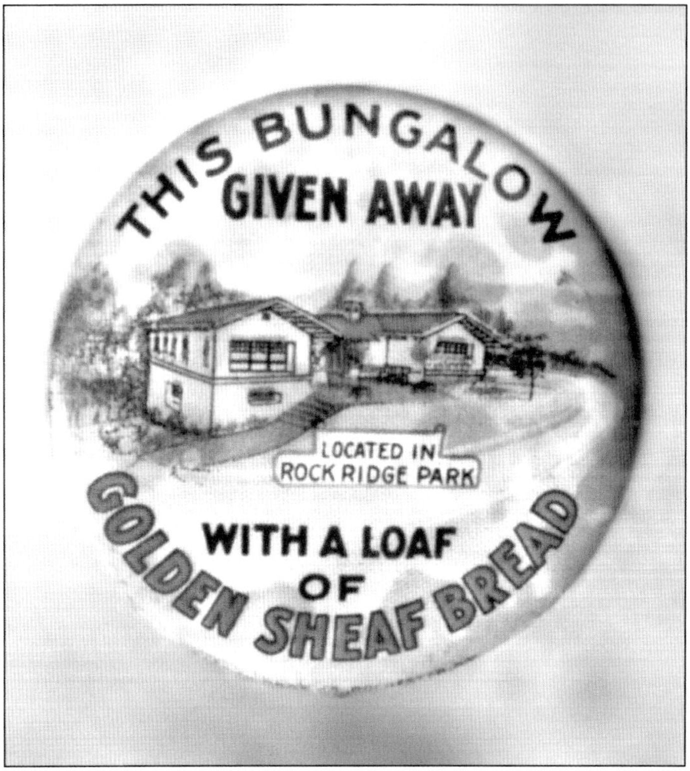


**PROMOTIONAL BUTTON, C. 1910.** The button reads, "This bungalow given away in Rock Ridge Park." The free house shown on this button was in the first stage of the Rock Ridge Properties development. The rest of the button reads, "With a Loaf of Golden Sheaf Bread." Customers could obtain a button and entry into the contest with the purchase of a loaf of bread. (Courtesy Ray Raineri.)

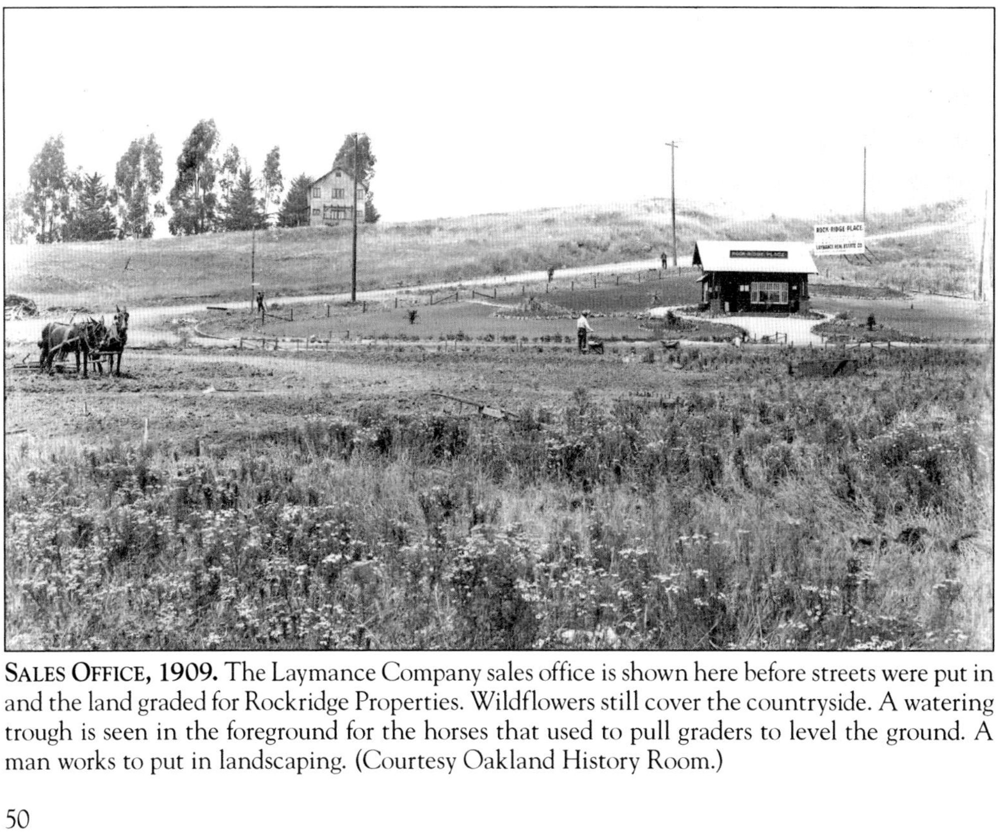

**SALES OFFICE, 1909.** The Laymance Company sales office is shown here before streets were put in and the land graded for Rockridge Properties. Wildflowers still cover the countryside. A watering trough is seen in the foreground for the horses that used to pull graders to level the ground. A man works to put in landscaping. (Courtesy Oakland History Room.)

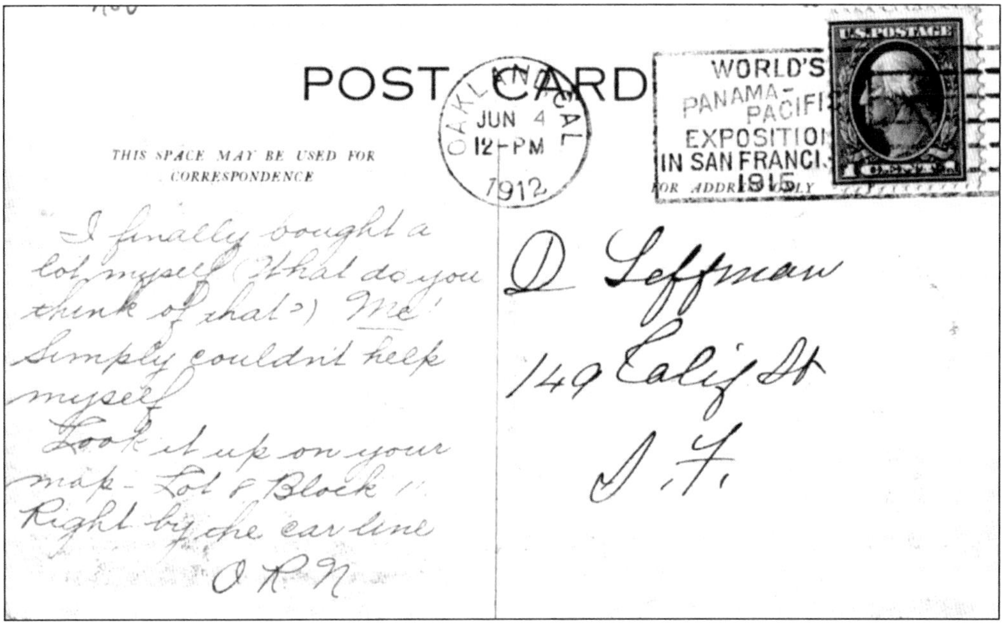


**POSTCARD FROM LOT BUYER, C. 1912.** The Laymance Company produced postcards for homesite buyers to send to their friends. This postcard message says that the sender has just bought a Rock Ridge lot "right by the car [trolley] line." It was sent to San Francisco, as were a number of the surviving postcards, probably indicating that Laymance was interested in advertising to San Franciscans who may have been disillusioned after the 1906 earthquake. (Courtesy Edmund Clausen.)

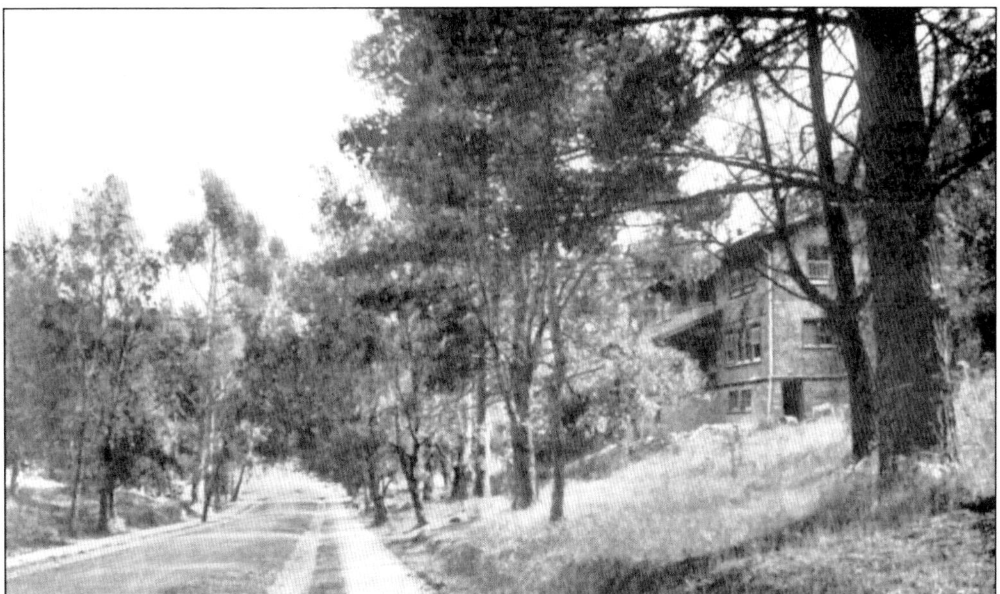


**BROADWAY TERRACE, C. 1909.** This postcard shows the view of Broadway Terrace looking east from the Claremont Country Club toward the Rock Ridge Park homesite development. The photograph was taken when Broadway Terrace was still unpaved and the rails had not yet been laid for the Rock Ridge line streetcar up Broadway Terrace. (Courtesy Edmund Clausen.)

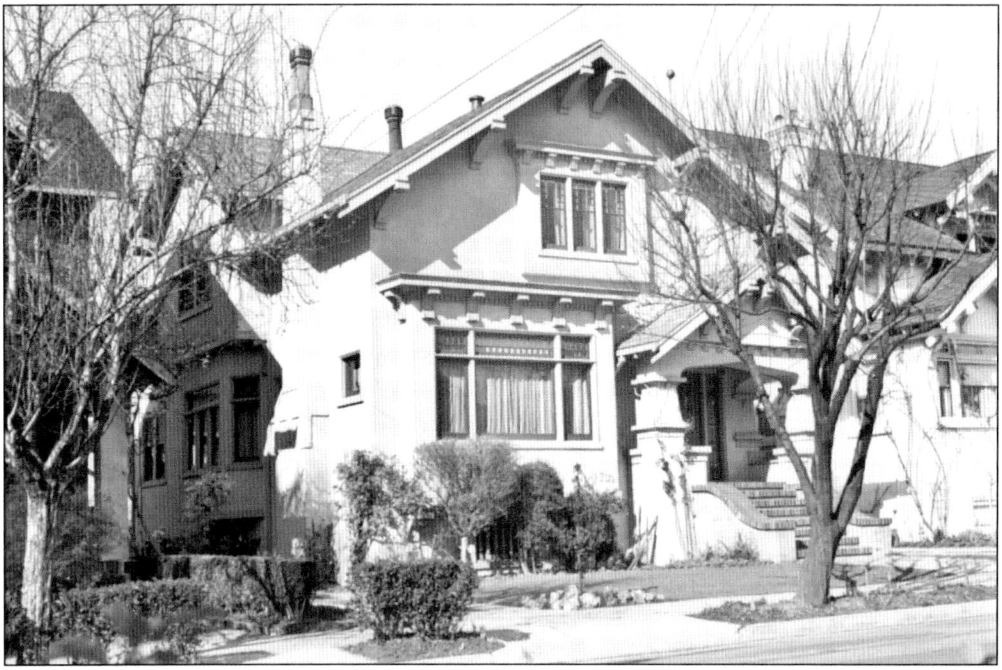

**ROCK RIDGE PARK HOME.** The Rock Ridge Properties development appealed to more than tycoons who built mansions. A large number of middle-class families bought lots and built new stucco homes. Here the Larkins home on Ocean View is seen in a 1940 photograph. (Courtesy William Larkins.)

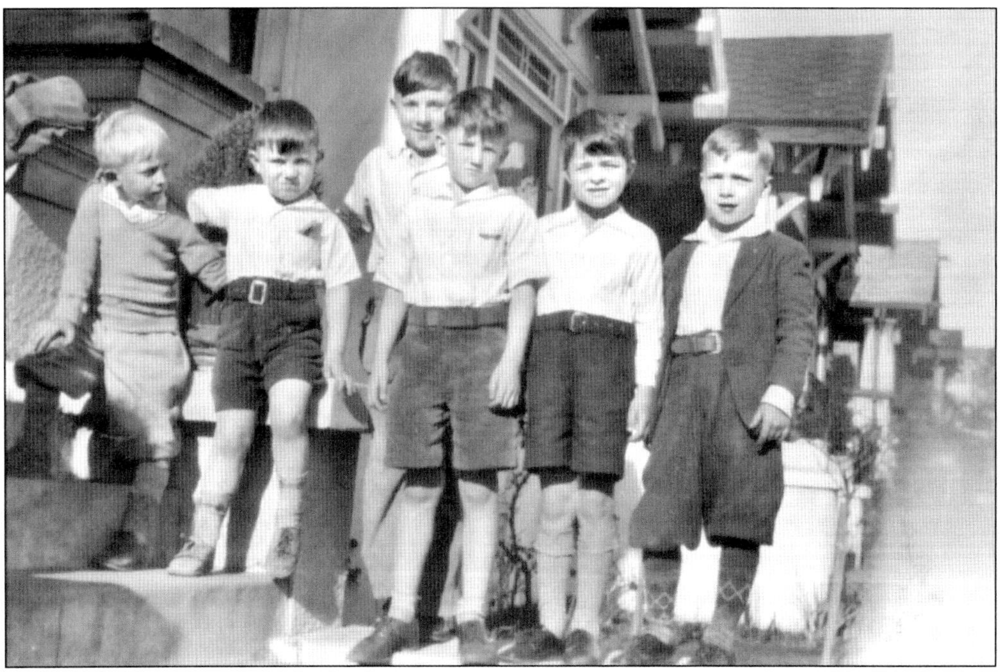

**BOYS ON OCEAN VIEW DRIVE, 1933.** Rock Ridge was a place to raise families. Here a group of boys on Ocean View Drive plays on the steps of the Larkins home, shown in the previous photograph. John Larkins is the boy second from the left. (Courtesy William Larkins.)

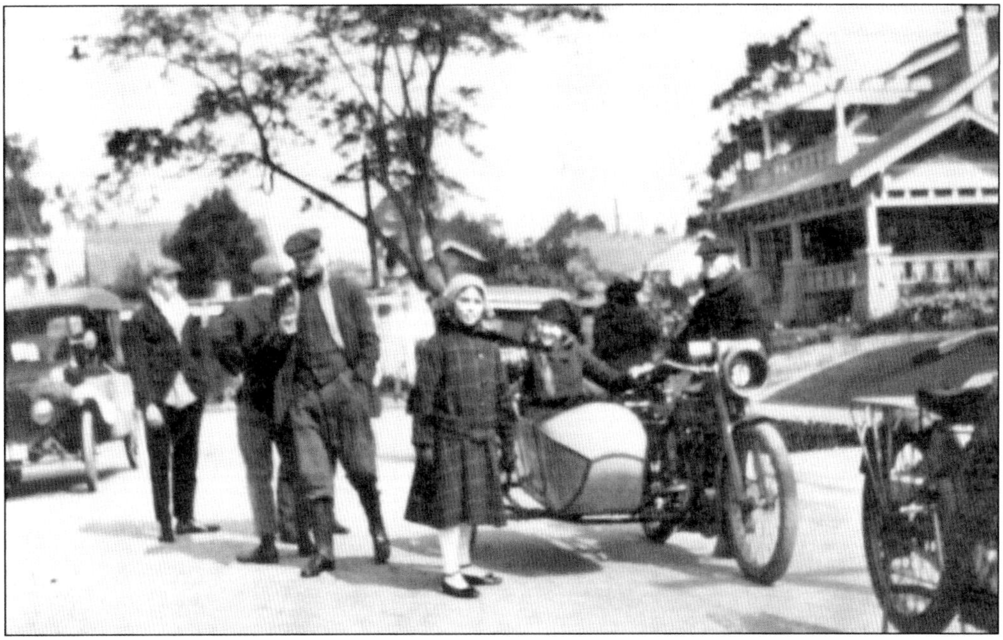

**DESMOND STREET BUNGALOW, 1915.** A bungalow can be seen here in the Arts and Crafts style with wooden exterior and a large front porch on Desmond Street below College Avenue. The family of Thelma Milliff is proud of their new motorcycle with side passenger seat, which neighbors have come to admire. (Courtesy John and Jo Coffin.)

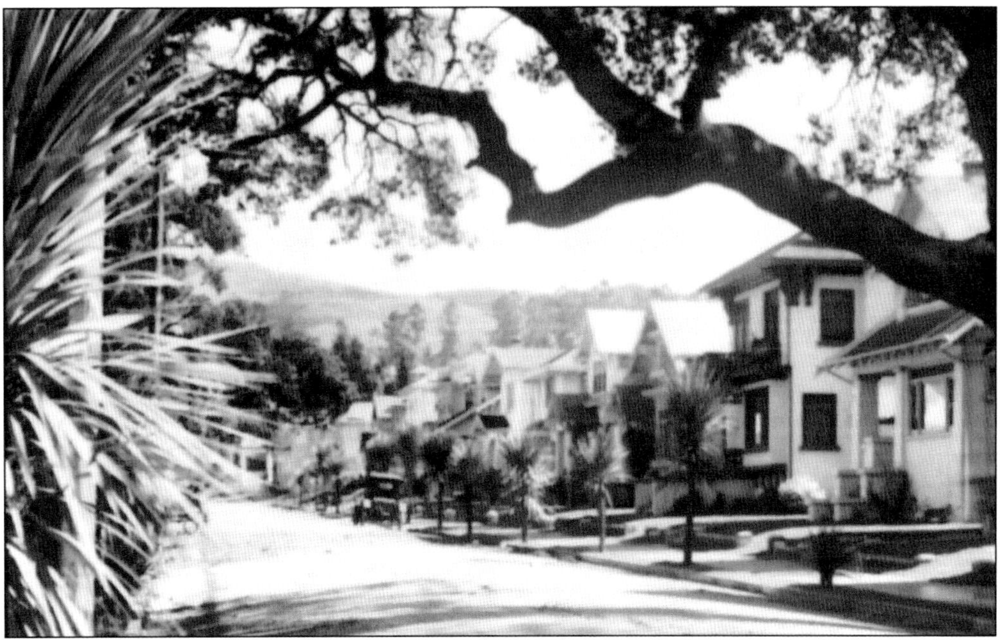

**KEITH AVENUE, C. 1910.** This view of Keith Avenue looks from Broadway toward College Avenue. These houses were built with garages that were part of the housing design. Garages were no longer just a barn in which to store the car. Driveways between houses provided off-street parking and gave a separation between houses that offered a sense of space lacking in many San Francisco row homes. (Courtesy Oakland History Room.)

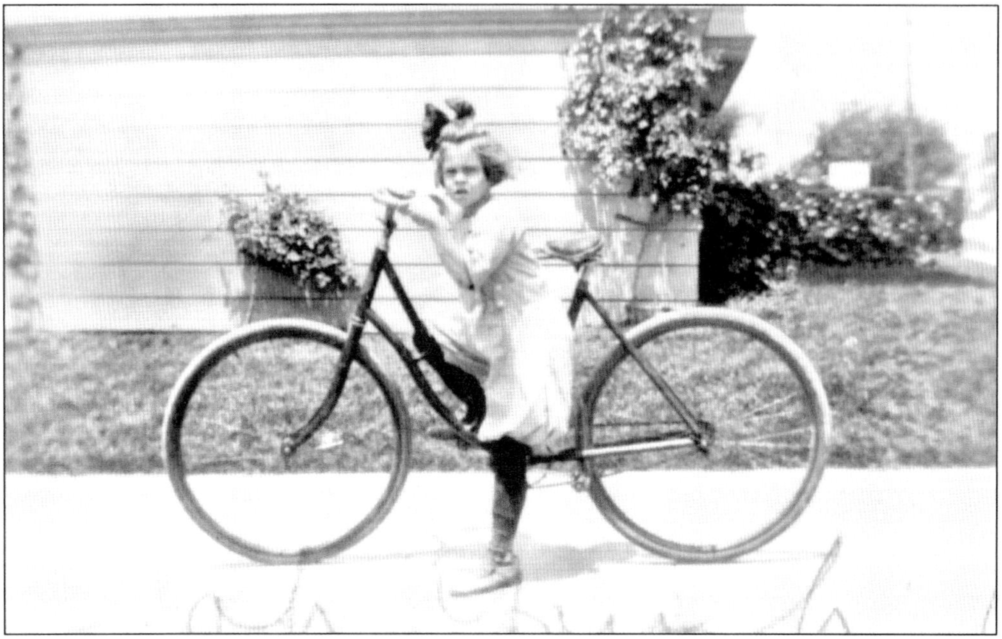

**GIRL ON SIXTY-SECOND STREET, C. 1911.** This girl is enjoying suburban living west of College Avenue. She is the daughter of Thomas Russell, who was president of the Phoenix Iron Works. (Courtesy Kevin Flynn and Marilyn Citron.)

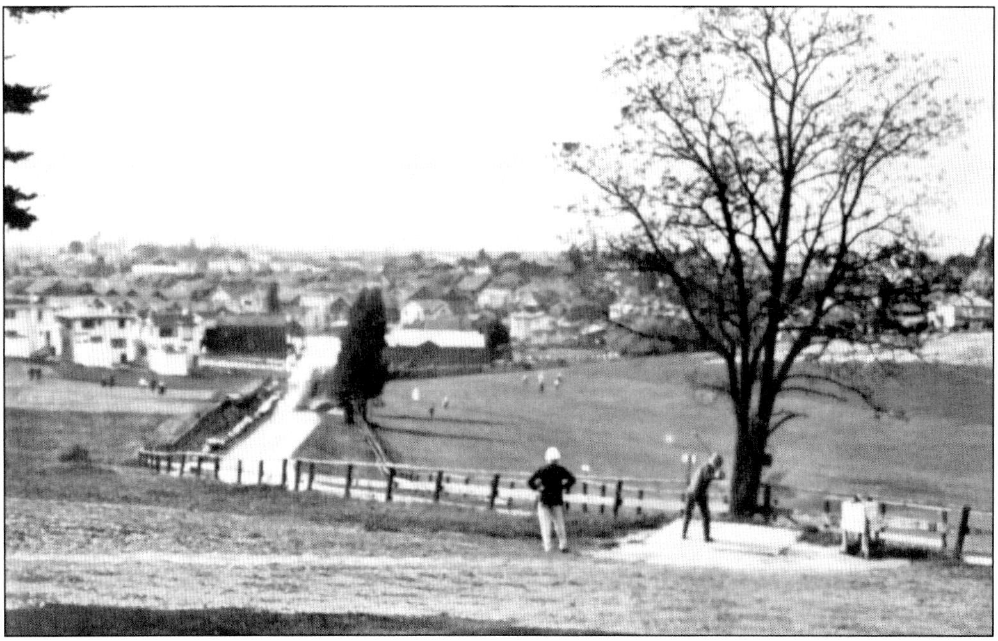

**GOLFER, 1915.** This view of the Claremont Country Club looks west toward Clifton Street and shows the development west of Broadway in 1915. The wooden box beside the golfer contains wet sand that the golfer mounds to make a tee. Wooden tees were not yet used. (Courtesy Claremont Country Club.)

**HOMEMADE SCOOTER, C. 1933.** This scooter belonged to John Larkins, who is shown riding it on Ocean View Drive. The scooter was the 1930s version of a modern skateboard. Roller-skate wheels were attached to a wooden structure to make a scooter, popular with youngsters. (Courtesy William Larkins.)

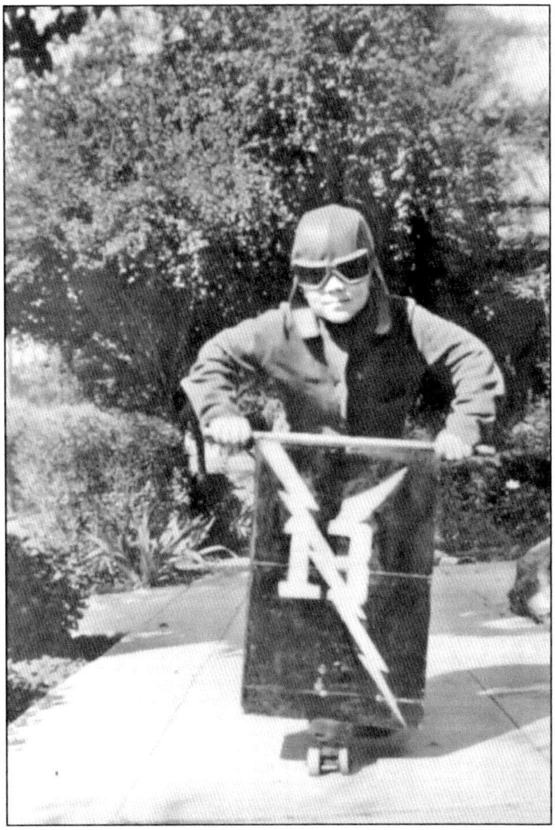

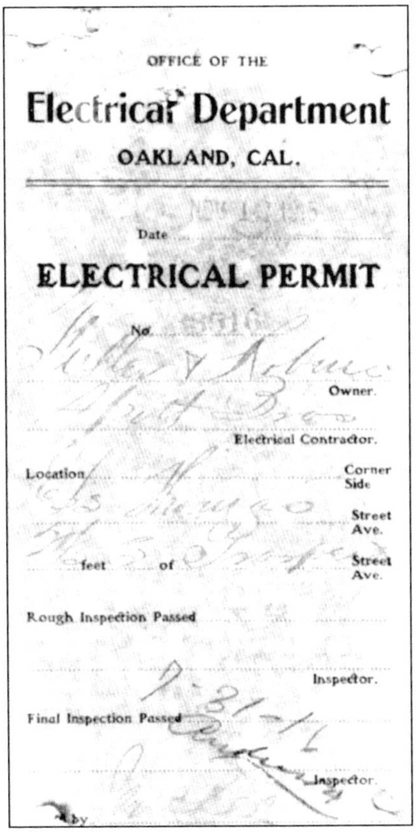

OFFICE OF THE

**Electrical Department**

OAKLAND, CAL.

Date

**ELECTRICAL PERMIT**

No.

Owner.

Electrical Contractor.

Location — Corner / Side

Street / Ave.

feet of — Street / Ave.

Rough Inspection Passed

Inspector.

Final Inspection Passed

Inspector.

by

**ELECTRICAL PERMIT, 1915.** This electrical permit was found in a Thomas Avenue house. The date shows that electrical work began during construction in 1915 and was completed in 1916. Thomas Avenue was part of the Country Club Terrace development that also included Belgrave Place and Carlton Street. The land belonged to the University of California, then to the Claremont Country Club before it was developed into housing. (Courtesy David and Christine Wright.)

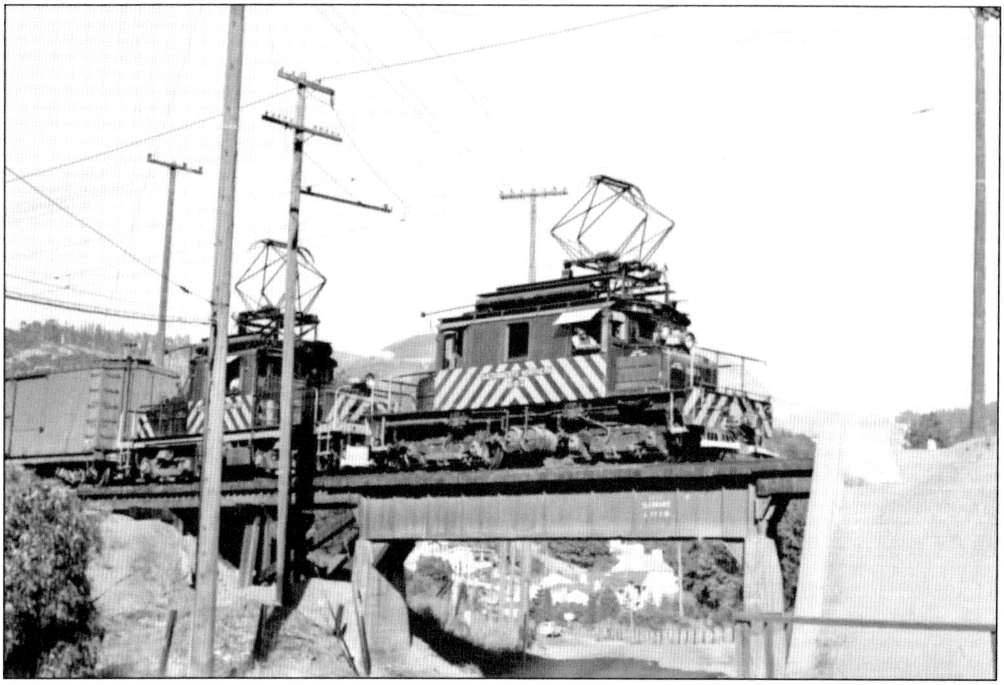

**SACRAMENTO NORTHERN FREIGHT ENGINE.** The trestle in this 1940 photograph was located just east of Chabot School in Rockridge. In 1911, the electric Oakland, Antioch, and Eastern Railroad (later the Sacramento Northern Railroad) began construction of a link between Oakland and Contra Costa County. The route ran through Rockridge along Shafter Avenue. The rail tunnel through the Oakland hills to Contra Costa County was completed in 1913. (Courtesy William Larkins.)

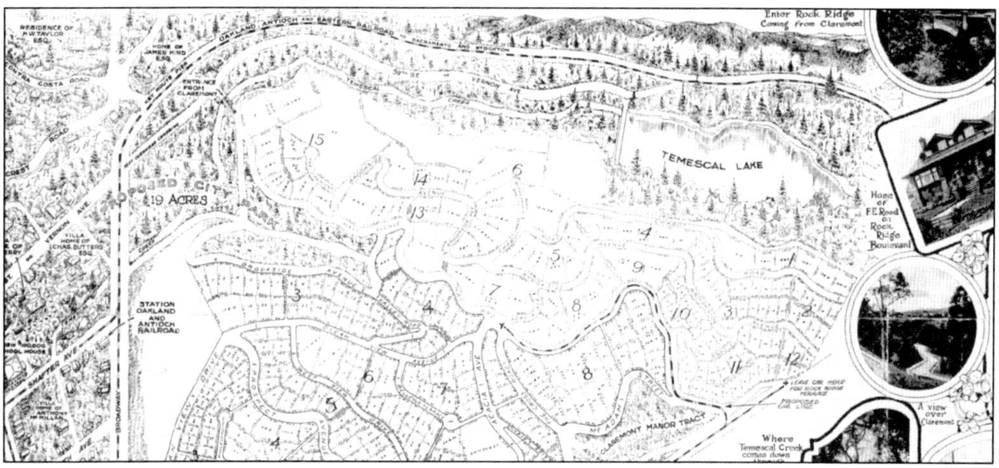


**MAP OF RAILROAD ROUTE, C. 1912.** This Laymance Company map shows the route of the Oakland, Antioch, and Eastern Railroad, which later became the Sacramento Northern Railroad. It ran up Shafter and stopped to pick up passengers at College Avenue and then at Broadway. It then continued up Shafter Avenue (now Miles Avenue), crossing Vernon Avenue (now Chabot Road) and continuing above the eastern edge of the Rock Ridge Properties section known as Rock Ridge Terrace, and then passing Lake Temescal. (Courtesy Ray Raineri and Tom Wolf.)

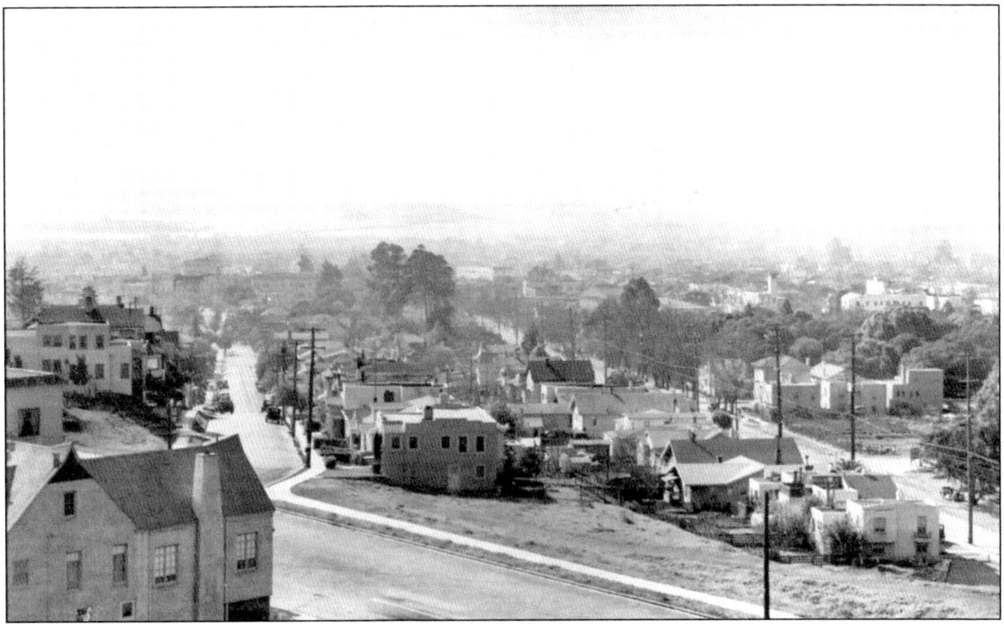

**KEITH AND SHAFTER AVENUES, C. 1920.** This strip of land between Keith Avenue and Shafter Avenue (now Miles Avenue) became the right-of-way for BART and the Grove Shafter Freeway in the 1960s. The houses in this photograph were removed to make way for freeway and BART construction. This resulted in a considerable loss of housing stock in Rockridge but added convenient transportation. (Courtesy John Bosko.)

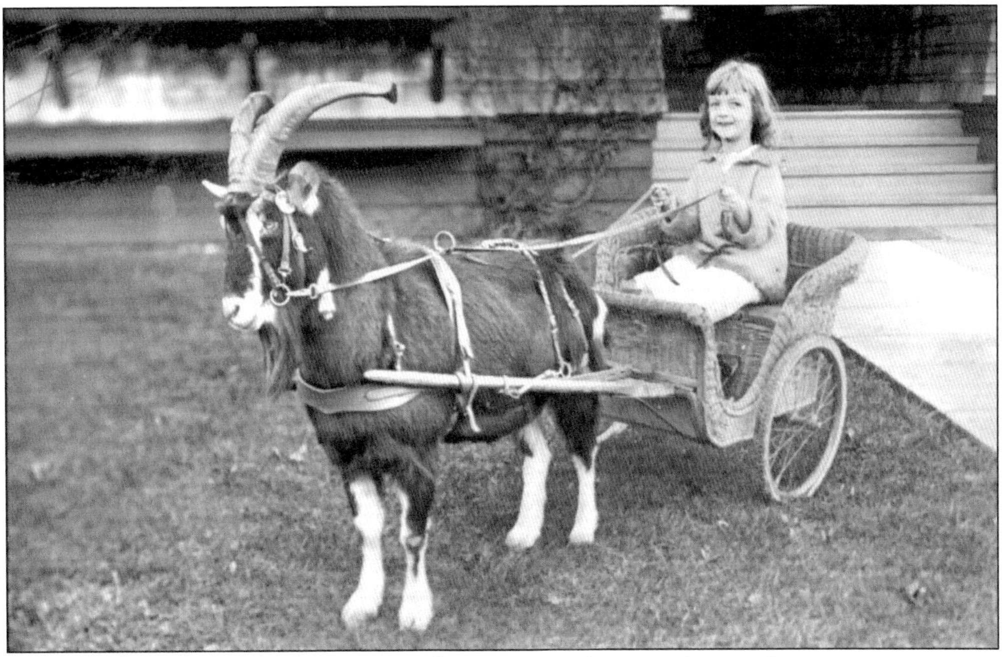

**GOAT GIRL, C. 1910.** It was common for itinerant photographers to bring a goat cart to a neighborhood, knock on suburban doors, and photograph neighborhood children in the goat cart for a fee. Here Virginia Halle, the daughter of Rainsford Halle, rides in a goat cart west of College Avenue. (Courtesy Neville Desouza and Bill Morrison.)

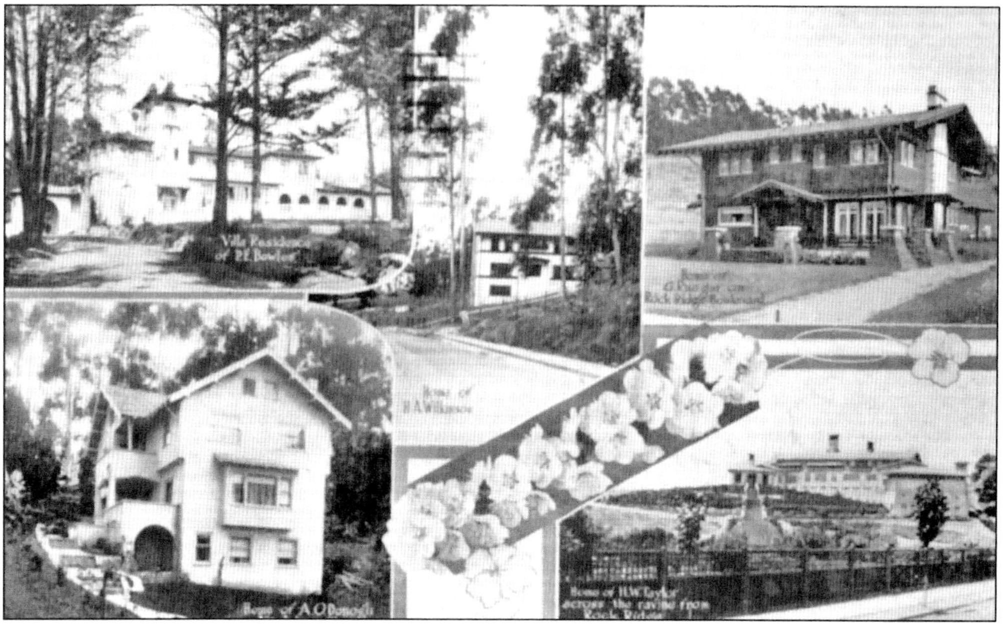

**LAYMANCE COMPANY POSTCARD, C. 1912.** This postcard used for advertising Rock Ridge Properties promoted the development by showing that wealthy families lived in Rockridge. In the upper left-hand corner is a photograph of the P. E. Bowles estate. Bowles made his money in banking and bought part of the Livermore estate that fronted on Broadway Terrace just east of the Claremont Country Club. (Courtesy Edmund Clausen.)

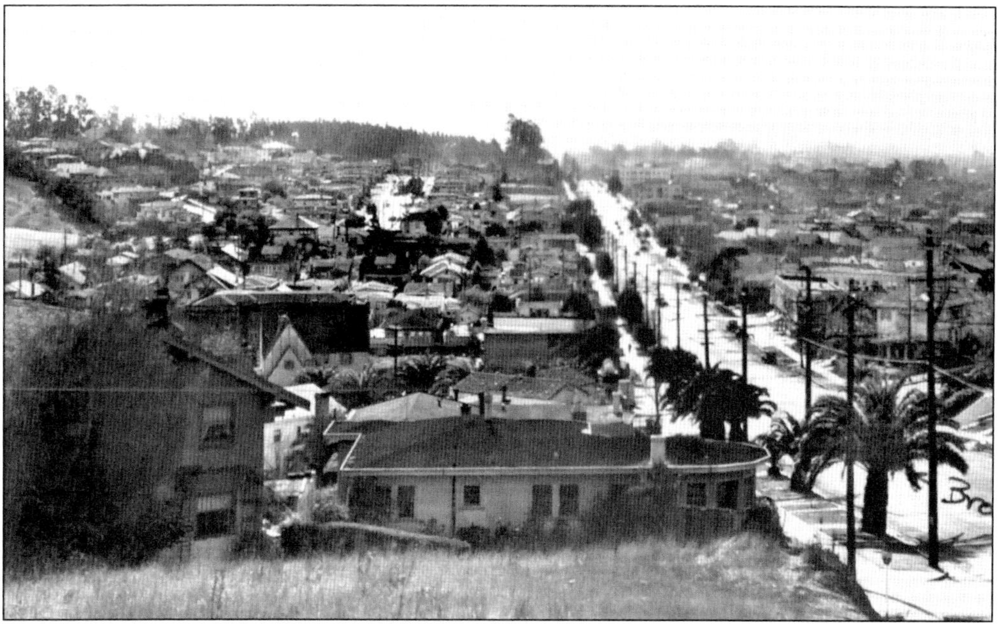

**BROADWAY, C. 1920.** This photograph looks south down Broadway from Ocean View Drive to Broadway Terrace. This area around Broadway was annexed to the City of Oakland in 1909, the same year that the stretch of Broadway between Broadway Terrace and Ocean View Drive was paved. Broadway is lined with palm trees, which were considered exotic in the early 1900s. (Courtesy John Bosko.)

# *Four*

# TRANSITIONS

Rockridge underwent important transitions that helped shape its unique character. In the late 19th and early 20th centuries, the Rockridge hills had a scattering of big estates owned largely by tycoons who had made their fortunes in mining and other earth-moving trades. In response to the pressure to build more housing after the 1906 earthquake, some of the estates were subdivided into lots for middle-class houses. Two important exceptions were the Perry mansion that became Saint Albert's Priory and the Livermore estate that was converted into the Claremont Country Club. These two institutions retained open space in Rockridge, along with settings that can still give a whiff of the former estates of the moneyed, while the Priory grounds also exist as an impressive preserve of the primitive Temescal Creek.

A major force in the transformation of Rockridge was the Vernon Rockridge Improvement Club, established in 1910 by a group of businessmen. Operating from a clubhouse on College Avenue, the club campaigned to get schools, open a firehouse, and close saloons. Claremont Elementary School and Oakland Technical High School both opened in the decade following the club's organization. The Rockridge Saloon on Broadway, a popular watering hole for Bilger Quarry workers, was closed down when Oakland Tech opened down the street. Rockridge was no longer a sparsely settled hinterland of farmhouses, saloons, and estates. By 1910, it was a community of middle-class and affluent families that demanded schools and disdained saloons.

The improvement club had the city's ear. When the Oakland, Antioch, and Eastern Railroad proposed extending a rail line through Rockridge, the club supported the proposal. Here the businessmen of College Avenue came into conflict with the owners of large estates. Raymond Perry and Charles Butters, whose estates backed up to the proposed train route, publicly opposed the railroad project as a nuisance. The club prevailed, and the railroad that eventually became the Sacramento Northern Railroad began construction through Rockridge in 1911 with stops on College Avenue and Broadway.

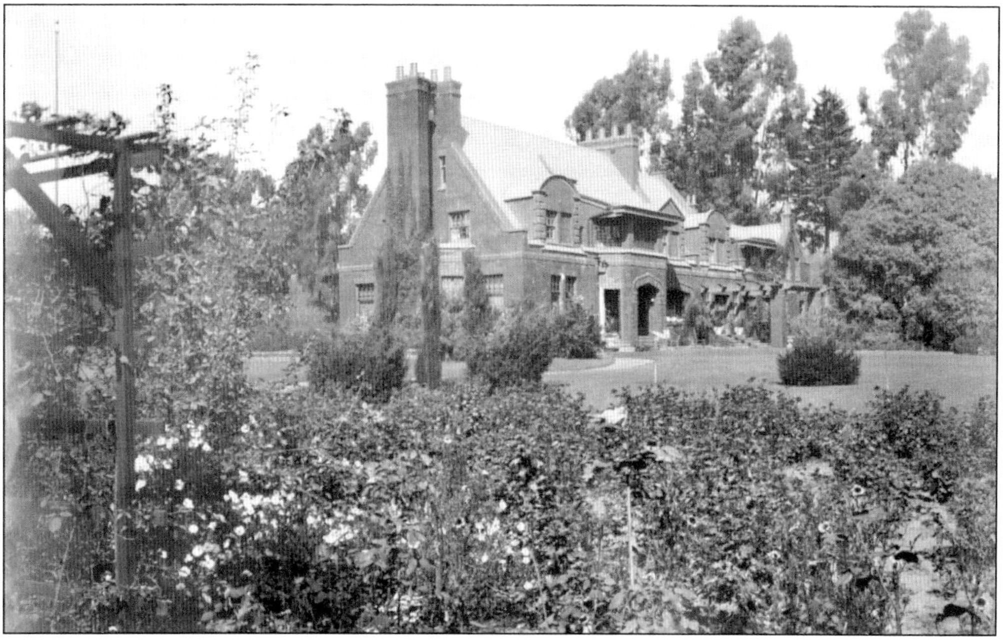

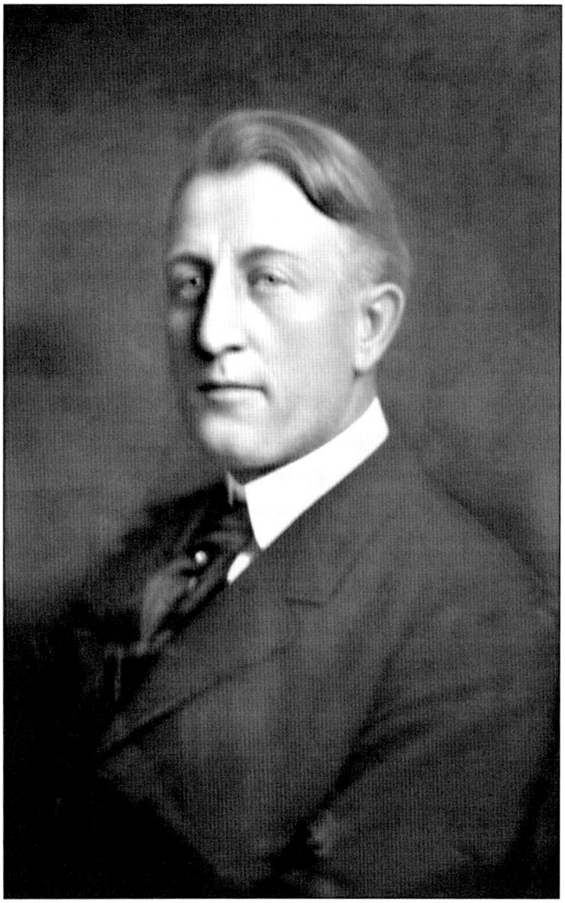

**PERRY MANSION, c. 1912.** The Perry mansion was built in 1910 on Chabot Road. In the left foreground are rose arbors reaching over a pathway, reminiscent of the 19th-century Roselawn estate, near property purchased by Raymond Perry to build this mansion. This property was one of several that made a transition from 19th-century country estate to another use in the 20th century. The Perry estate became St. Albert's Priory. (Courtesy Patricia Browne Arthur.)

**PERRY PORTRAIT, c. 1915.** Raymond Perry made his fortune dredging ports. He was a dredging engineer who developed a hydraulic dredge that changed dredging methods. Perry owned or ran companies that dredged most of the ports in the United States, including Pearl Harbor and Puget Sound. He also dredged the Oakland slip for the Key System ferry. (Courtesy Patricia Browne Arthur.)

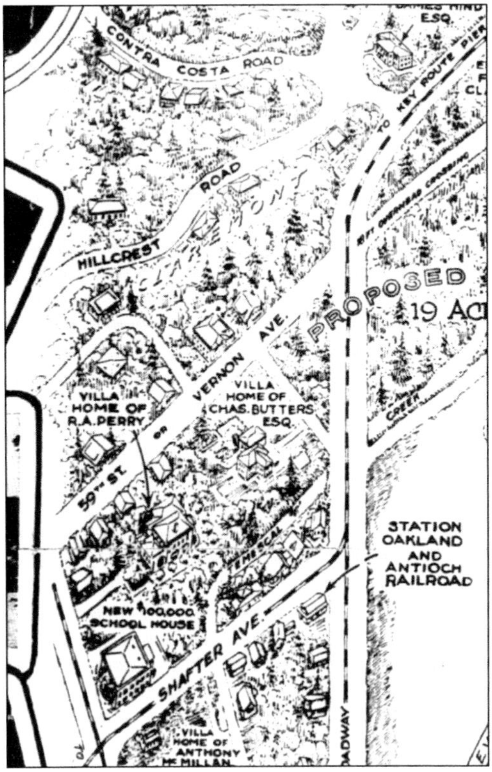


**MAP OF PERRY ESTATE, 1912.** This map by Laymance Real Estate Company shows Broadway on the right with the station for the Oakland, Antioch, and Eastern Railroad (precursor to the Sacramento Northern Railroad) marked at the corner of Shafter Avenue and Broadway. On the left is College Avenue, and just south of Fifty-ninth Street or Vernon Avenue (now Chabot Road) is the mansion of Raymond Perry. (Courtesy Ray Raineri and Tom Wolf.)

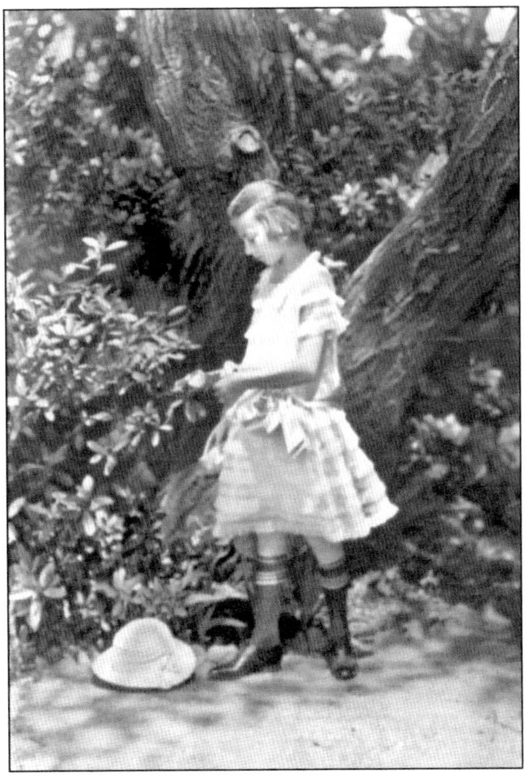

**ALOHA PERRY, C. 1917.** Aloha, daughter of Raymond and Winifred Perry, is standing by one of the many trees on the Perry estate with her hat lying on the ground. Aloha is said to have acquired her name because her mother, Winifred, became pregnant in Hawaii when Raymond was working on a dredging project. (Courtesy Patricia Browne Arthur.)

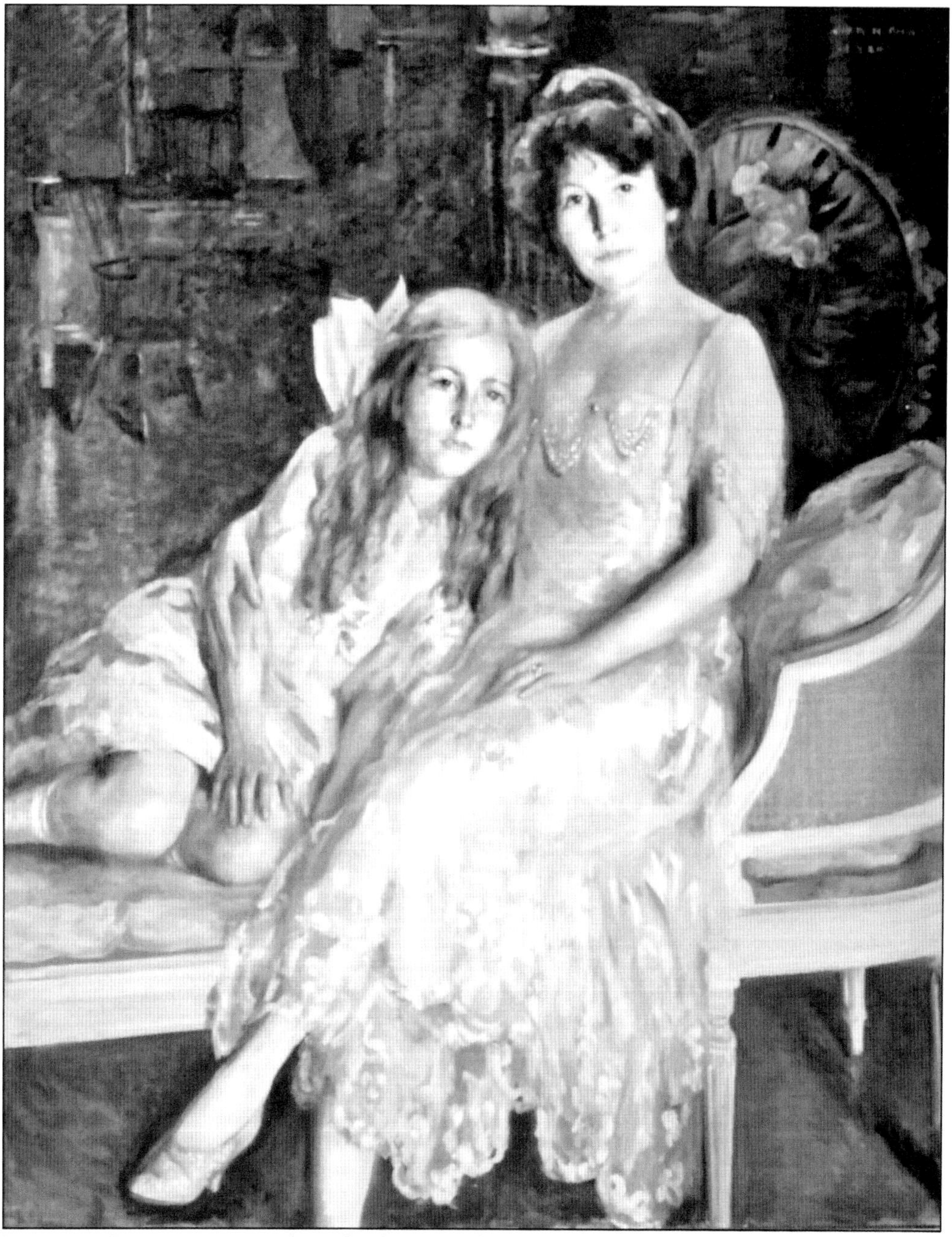

**WINIFRED PERRY, C. 1920.** The wife of Raymond Perry, Winifred, and their daughter, Aloha, are shown in this oil painting by John Rich. The Perrys were a prominent family in Rockridge, and Winifred's parties and teas were often covered in the *Oakland Tribune* in the 1920s. (Courtesy Patricia Browne Arthur.)

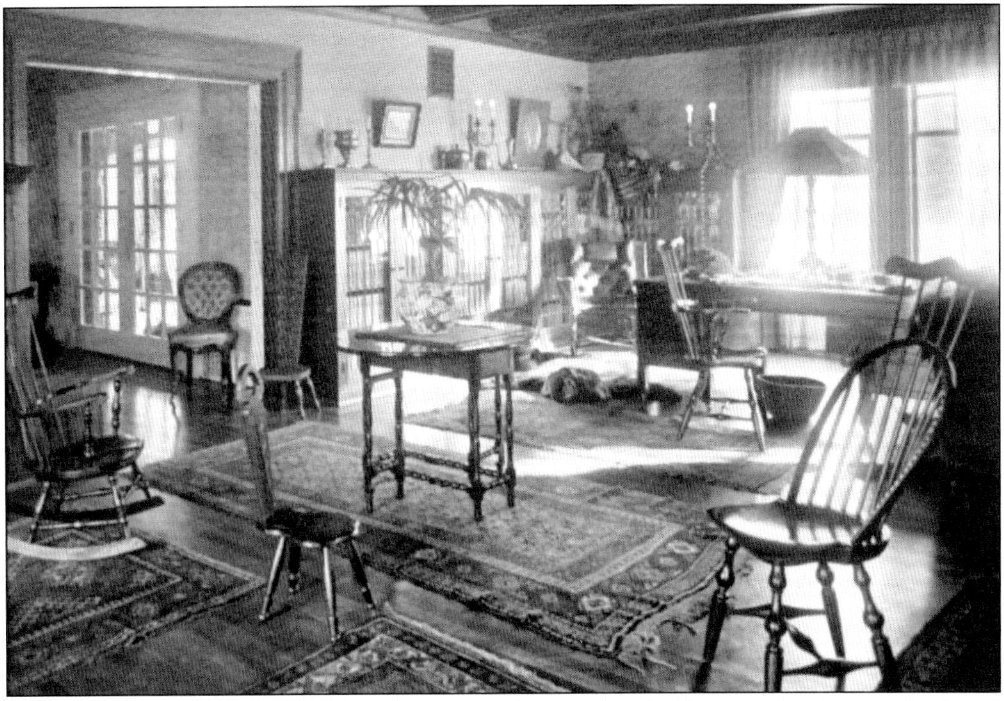

**PERRY LIBRARY, C. 1915.** The Perry home was decorated with Victorian furniture and oriental rugs. A bit of the still-wild West can be seen in the bearskin rug in the back left corner of the room. Another bearskin rug decorated the living room. (Courtesy Patricia Browne Arthur.)

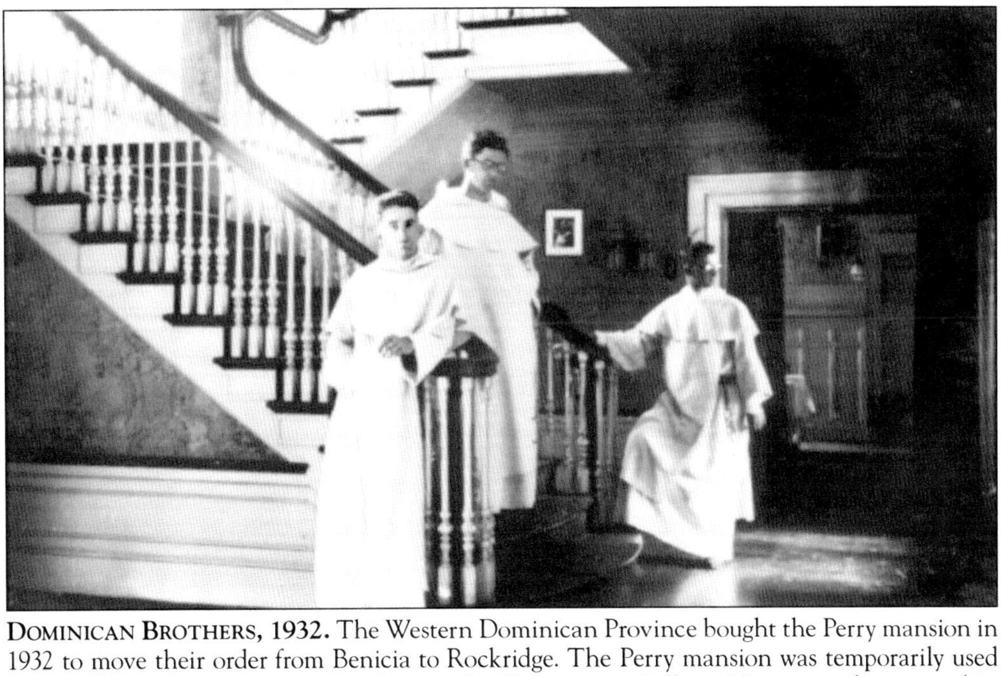

**DOMINICAN BROTHERS, 1932.** The Western Dominican Province bought the Perry mansion in 1932 to move their order from Benicia to Rockridge. The Perry mansion was temporarily used as St. Albert's Priory, housing brothers at the Dominican College. Here some friars stand in the entryway of the Perry mansion soon after its purchase. (Courtesy and copyright © Western Dominican Province.)

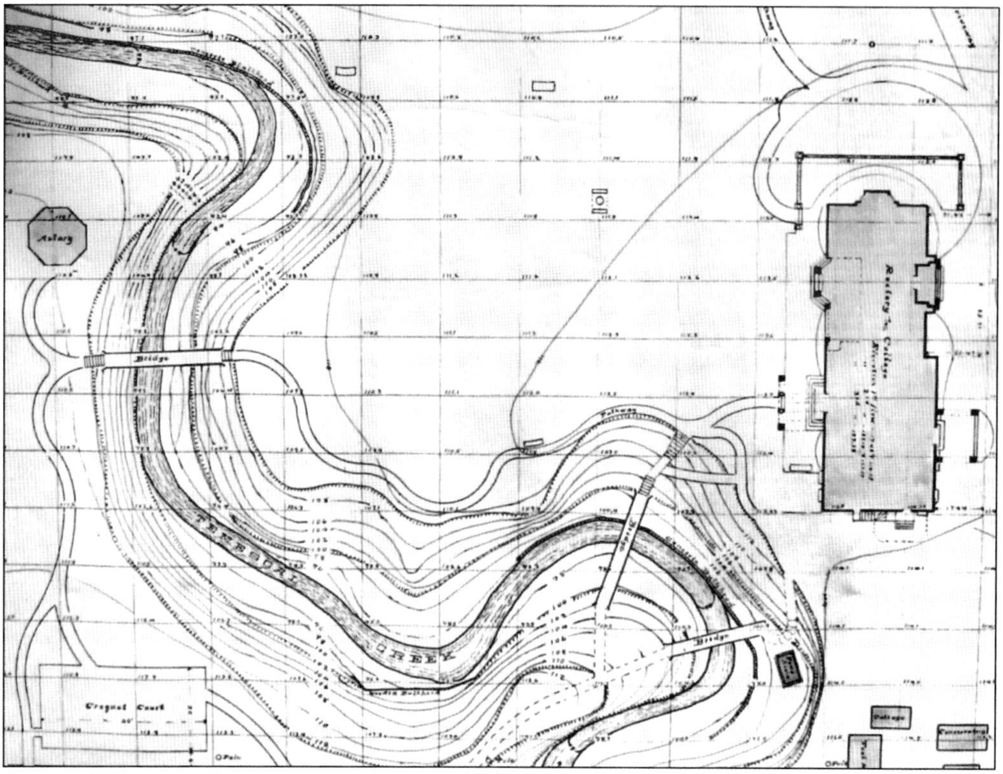


**MAP OF TEMESCAL CREEK, 1932.** This map shows a drawing of the proposed new building for St. Albert's Priory beside Temescal Creek, which ran through the Perry estate. Temescal Creek was put underground in 1917 in most of Rockridge as part of a flood control project, but the creek is preserved aboveground at the priory. (Courtesy and copyright © Western Dominican Province.)

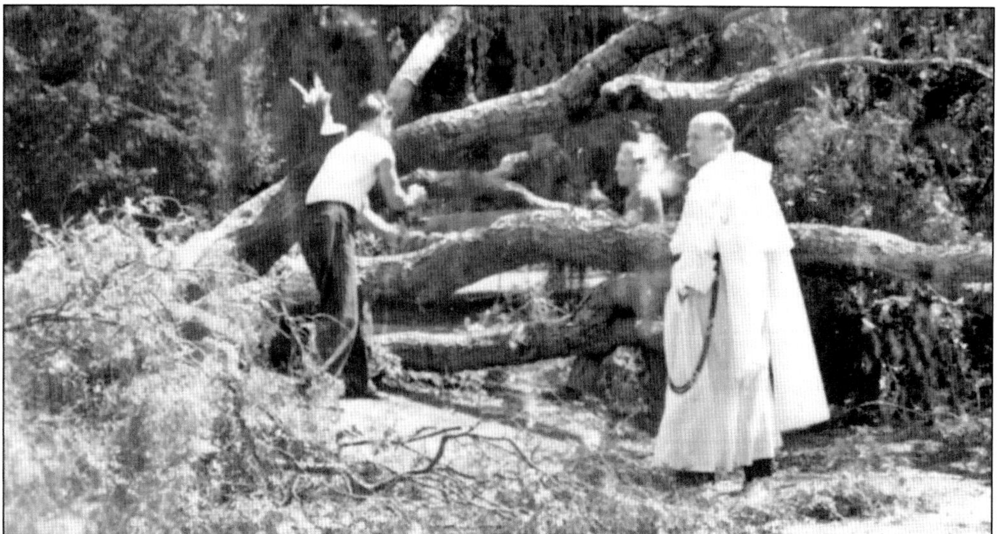

**CLEARING LAND, 1932.** Construction of the new priory required some clearing of land. Here Dominican brothers work on the grounds. (Courtesy and copyright © Western Dominican Province.)

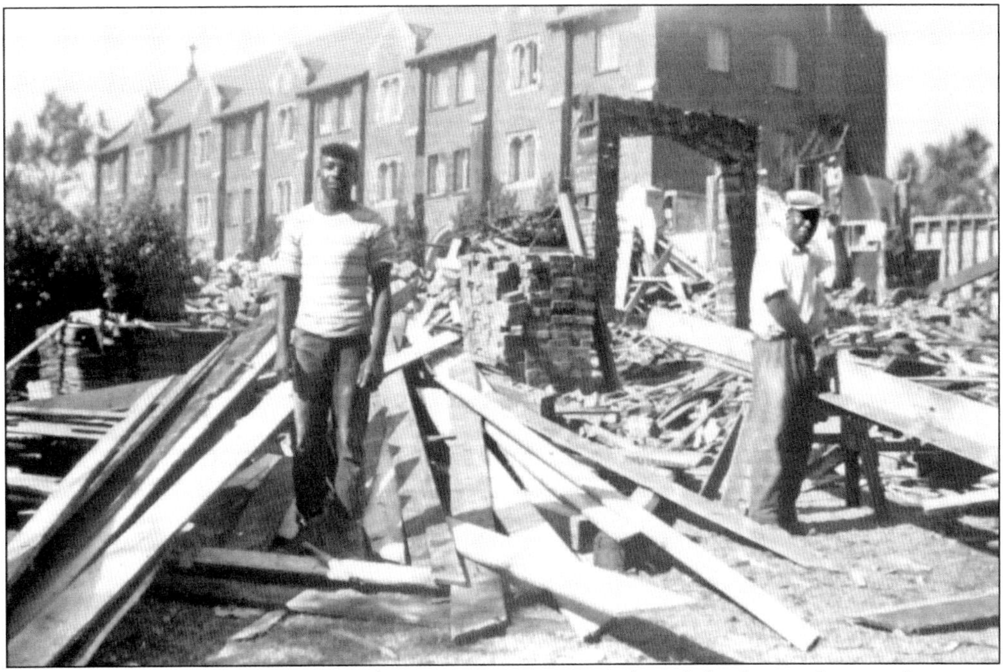

**NEW PRIORY BUILDING, 1949.** The Perry mansion was demolished to make way for a new priory building with more space and new plumbing and electrical systems. The first building of St. Albert's Priory can be seen in the background, and the mansion demolition appears in the foreground. (Courtesy and copyright © Western Dominican Province.)

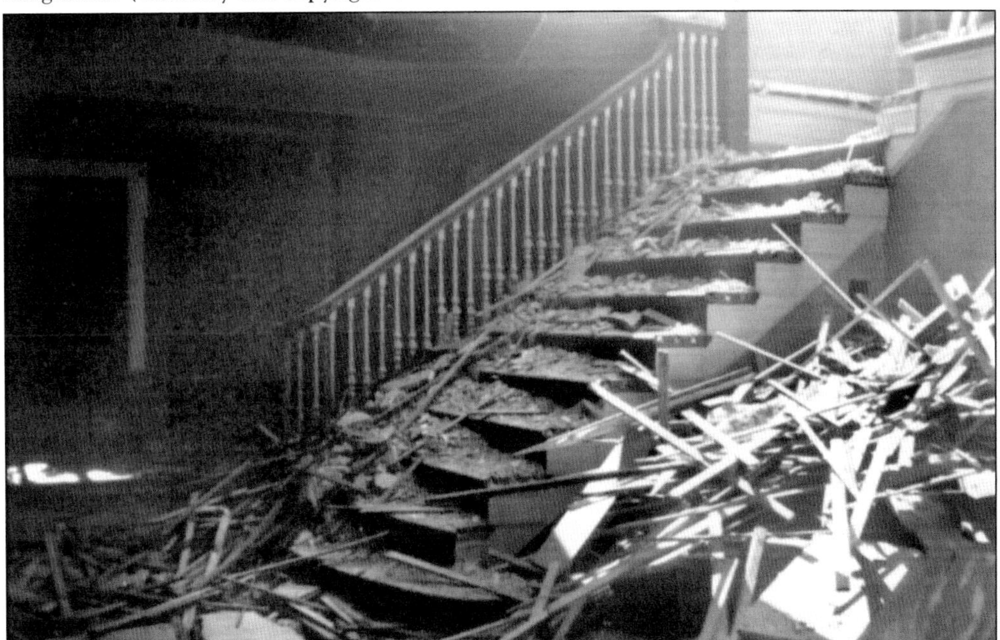

**STAIRWELL DEMOLITION, 1949.** The Perry mansion was demolished to provide space for the new priory facilities. Here demolition has begun on the stairwell in the entryway of the Perry mansion. (Courtesy and copyright © Western Dominican Province.)

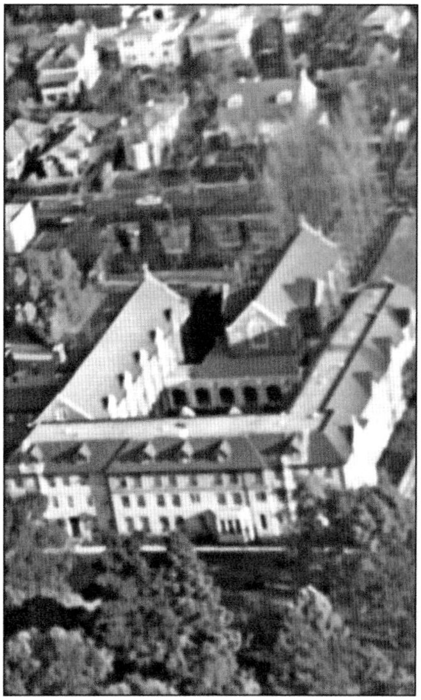

**St. Albert's Priory, 1960s.** This aerial view was taken at the time that BART construction was beginning in the 1960s. The priory allowed the land of the Perry estate to remain intact with its many trees and open space. Without the priory, this land would most likely have been bought by developers for housing. (Courtesy and copyright © Western Dominican Province.)

**Livermore Mansion, 1891.** Here the Livermore mansion is in the process of being transformed into the clubhouse for the Claremont Country Club. When the City of Oakland wanted Oakland Golf Club land for a park, the club reorganized as the Claremont Country Club and purchased part of the Livermore estate. The mansion was moved across Broadway Terrace. (Courtesy Claremont Country Club.)

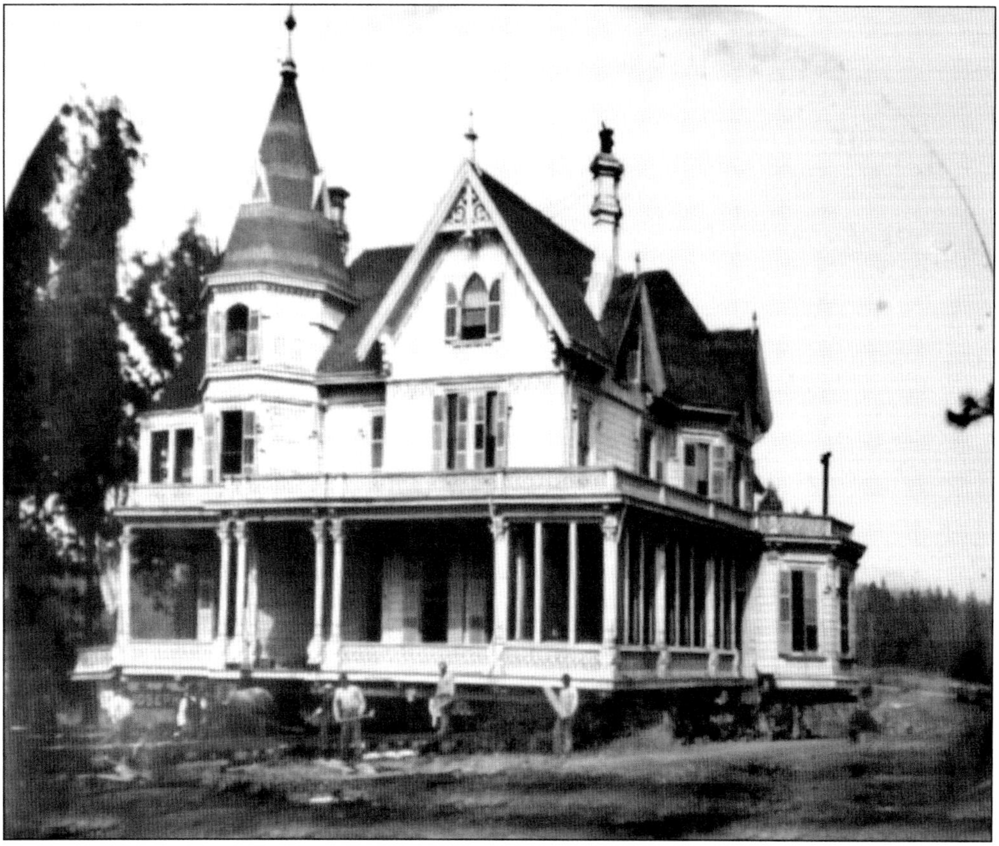

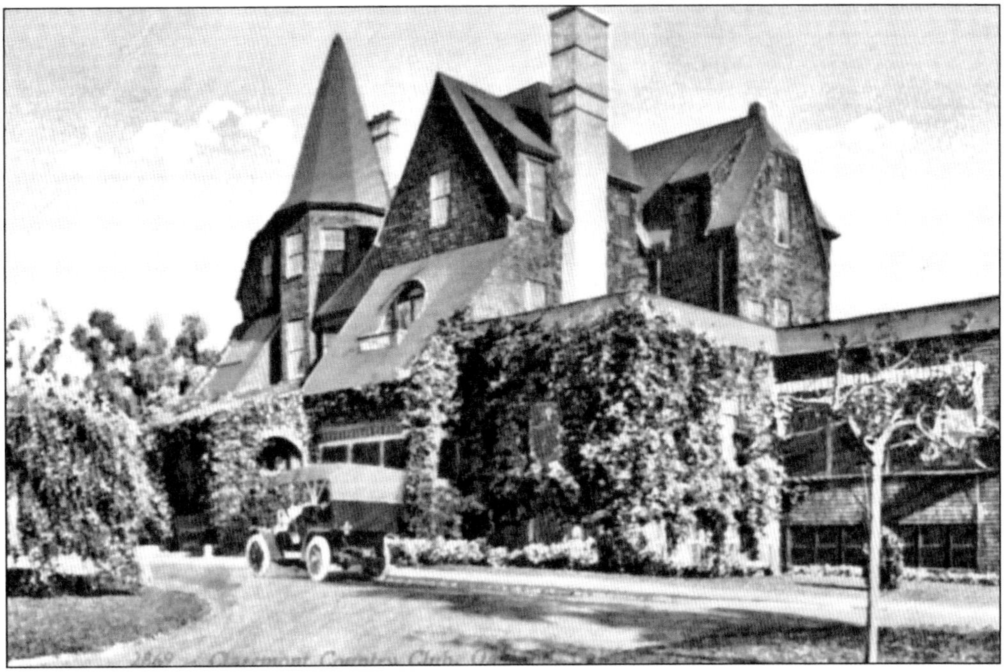

**CLAREMONT COUNTRY CLUB, C. 1920.** The 38-room Livermore Mansion was refurbished after its move across Broadway Terrace and served as the clubhouse of the Claremont Country Club until it burned in 1927. (Courtesy Claremont Country Club.)

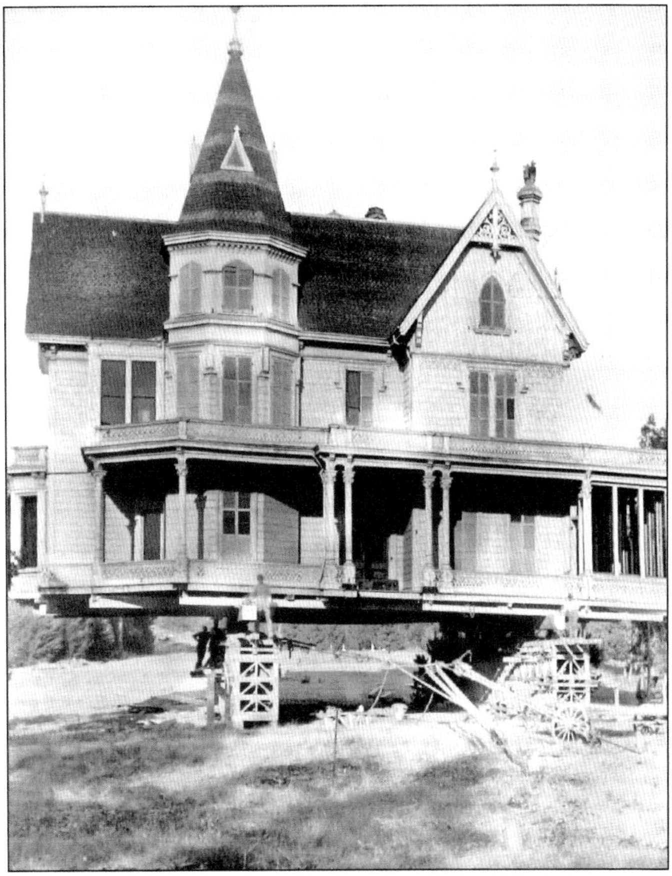

**MOVING THE LIVERMORE MANSION.** The Claremont Country Club had the old Livermore Mansion raised up and moved across McAdam Street (now Broadway Terrace) in 1891. Logs were placed under the mansion so that they would roll when teams of strong horses pulled the mansion across the street to become the new clubhouse. (Courtesy Claremont Country Club.)

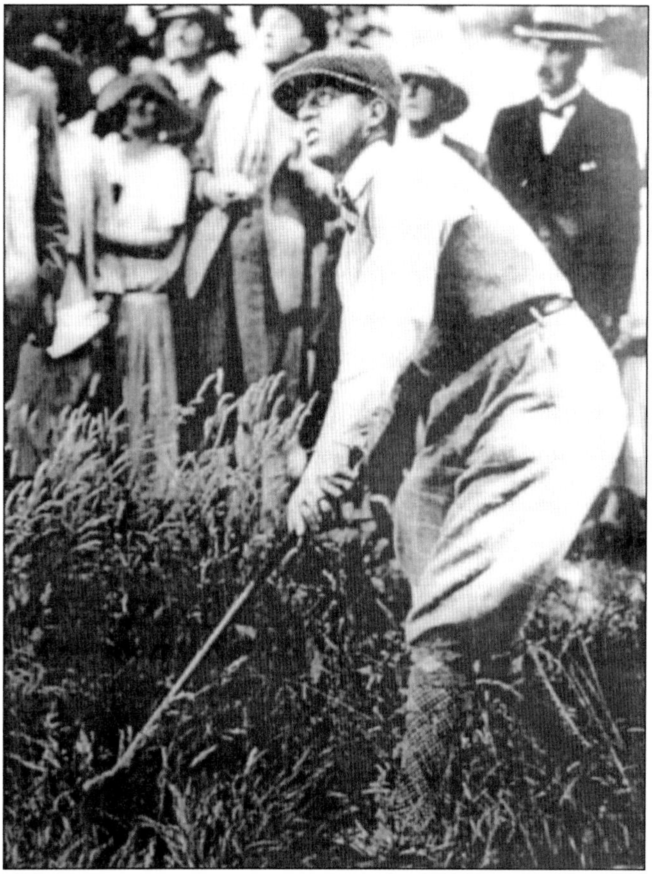

**MacDonald Smith.** MacDonald Smith, youngest son of Claremont Country Club golf pro George "Pop" Smith, won the Oakland Open Golf Tournament in 1910. He later won the U.S. Open three times. (Courtesy Claremont Country Club.)

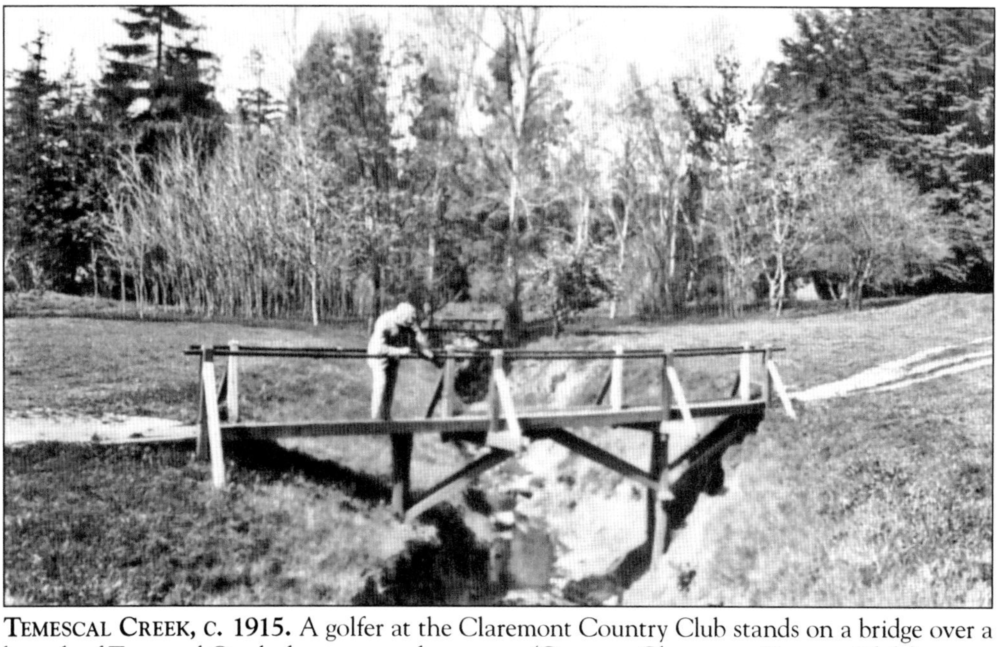

**Temescal Creek, c. 1915.** A golfer at the Claremont Country Club stands on a bridge over a branch of Temescal Creek that runs to the quarry. (Courtesy Claremont Country Club.)

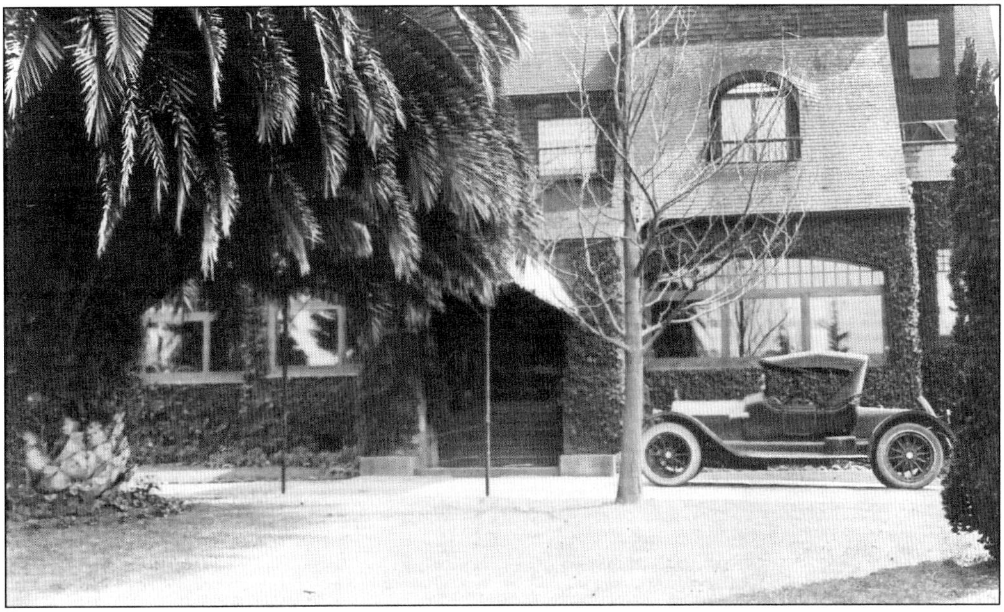

**Claremont Country Club Entrance, c. 1920.** The old Livermore Mansion, which was serving as the clubhouse for the Claremont Country Club, had this graceful entrance. The large palm tree in the front was one of many on the Livermore estate planted in the late 19th century. Palm trees were considered exotic and were popular with Victorians. (Courtesy Claremont Country Club.)

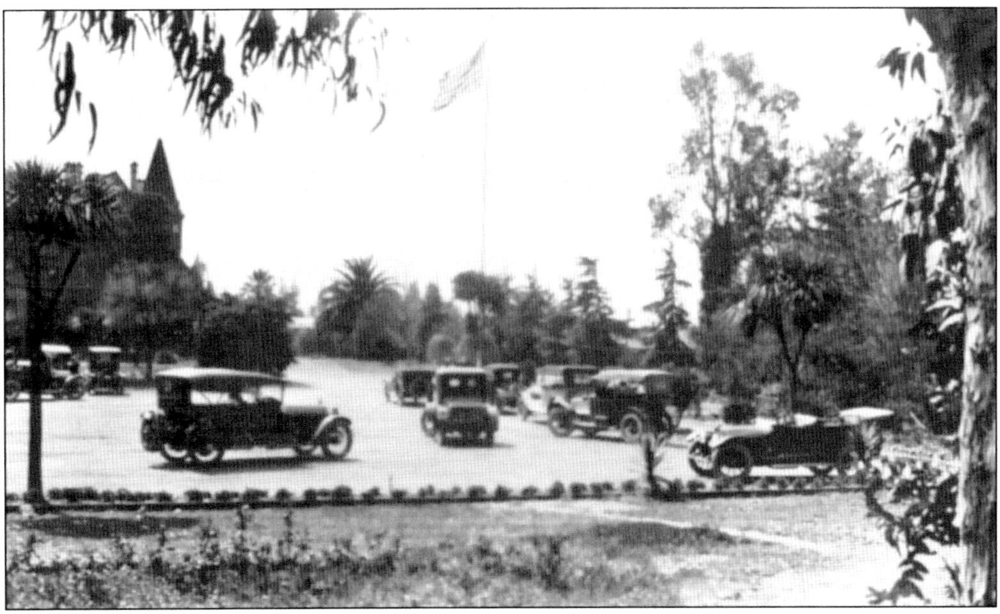

**Parking Lot, 1920s.** The parking lot of the Claremont Country Club was near the club's Clifton Street entrance near Broadway. While some earlier golfers arrived by streetcar, by the 1920s, most members arrived at the club by car and parked in this parking lot. (Courtesy Claremont Country Club.)

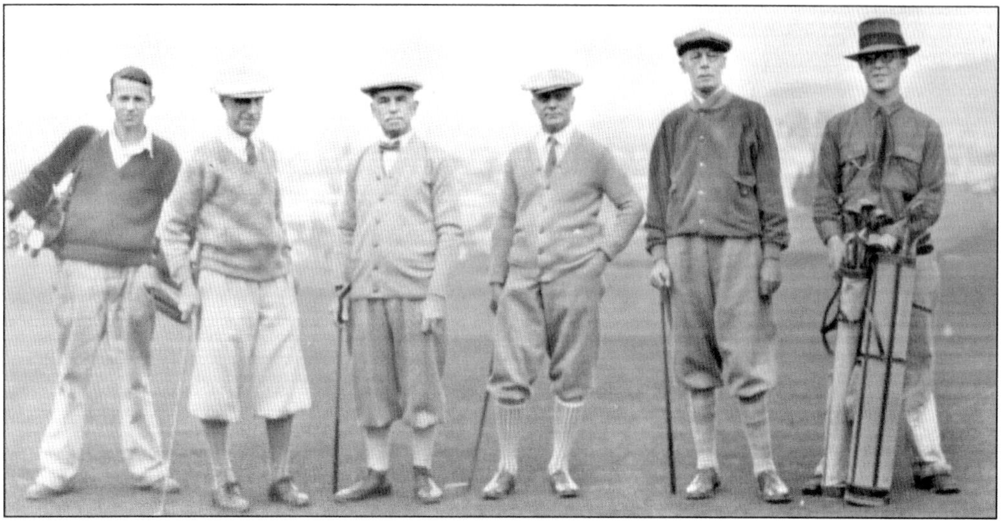

**CLAREMONT COUNTRY CLUB GOLFERS, 1938.** In the Great Depression decade of the 1930s, the number of games played at the Claremont Country Club declined by half. The Oakland Open golf tournament of 1937 at the country club drew 12,000 spectators. Only one-fourth (3,000) paid the admission of $3. Nonetheless, the club broke even and covered expenses, which was considered a success in an era of economic hard times. (Courtesy Claremont Country Club.)

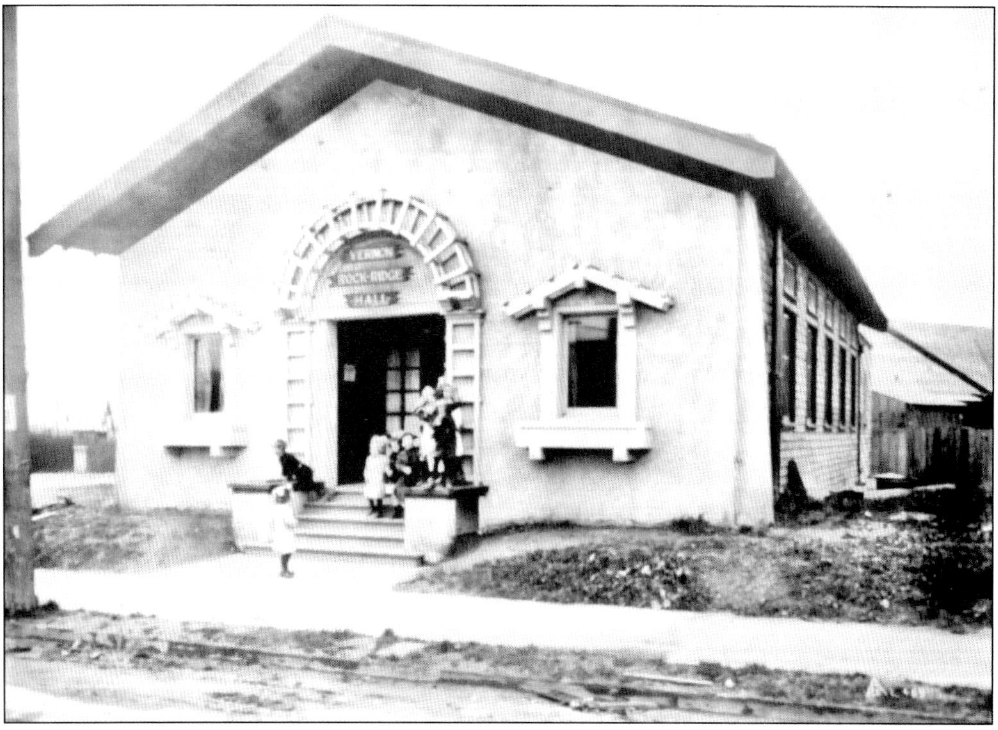


**VERNON ROCKRIDGE IMPROVEMENT CLUB, C. 1911.** Rockridge businessmen established the Vernon Rockridge Improvement Club (the predecessor of Rockridge Community Planning Council or RCPC) and built this clubhouse on College Avenue in 1910. The club lobbied the City of Oakland for street lighting, sidewalks, schools, a firehouse, a library, and the removal of saloons. (Courtesy Jennifer Dowling.)

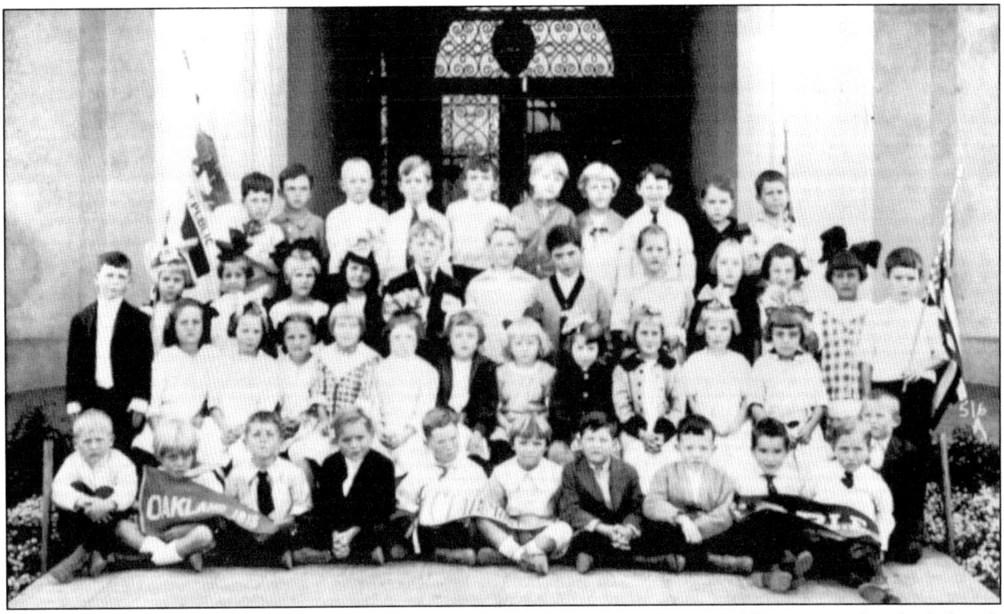


**CLAREMONT GRADE SCHOOL, C. 1918.** The first-grade class poses at Claremont Grade School, which opened in 1918 at College Avenue and Birch Court. The grate above the front door is now preserved in the courtyard of Claremont Middle School on the same site. The school replaced a one-room schoolhouse located at the intersection of College and Claremont Avenues. (Courtesy Ray Raineri.)

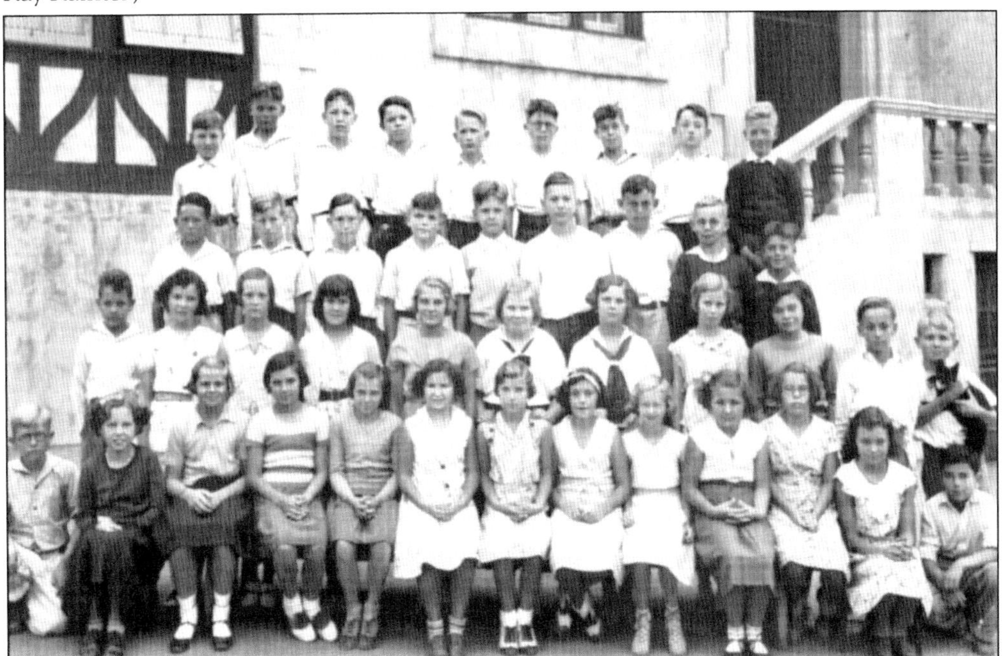

**CHABOT ELEMENTARY SCHOOL, 1933.** The sixth-grade class at Chabot Elementary School is shown with aviation historian William Larkins (fourth row, far left). When enrollment at Claremont School increased, the lower grades were split off in 1924 to form the Claremont School Annex, which later became Chabot School. (Courtesy William Larkins.)

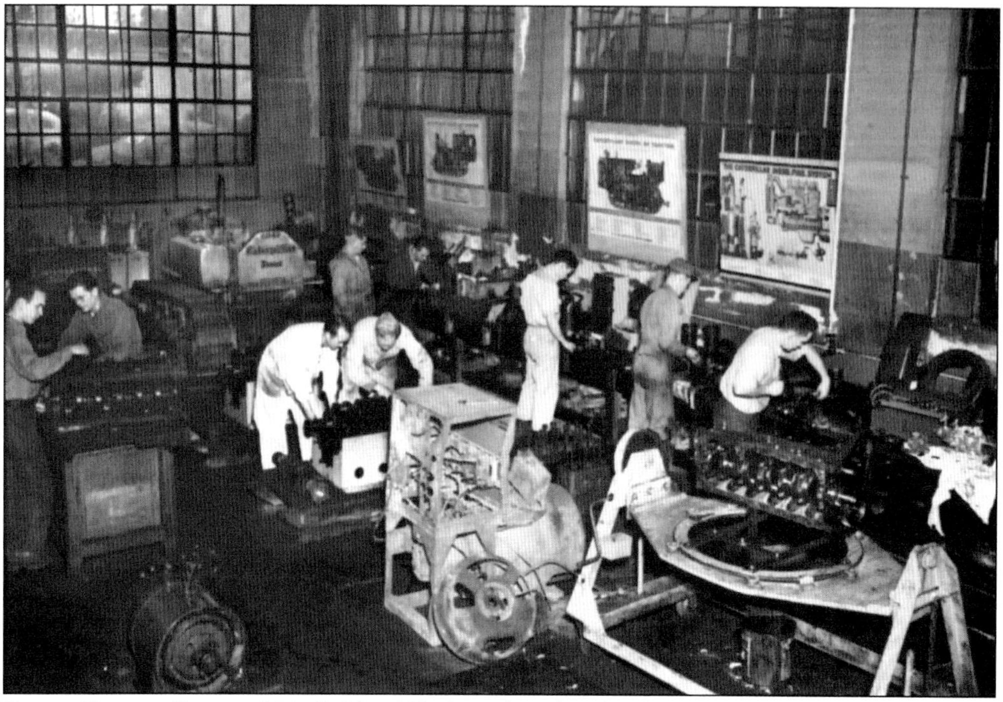

**DIESEL ENGINE CLASS, 1930.** Oakland Technical High School was dedicated in 1914 and opened in 1917. The philosophy of Oakland Tech was to prepare students for skilled jobs after graduation as well as to provide a well-rounded education. (Courtesy Oakland History Room.)

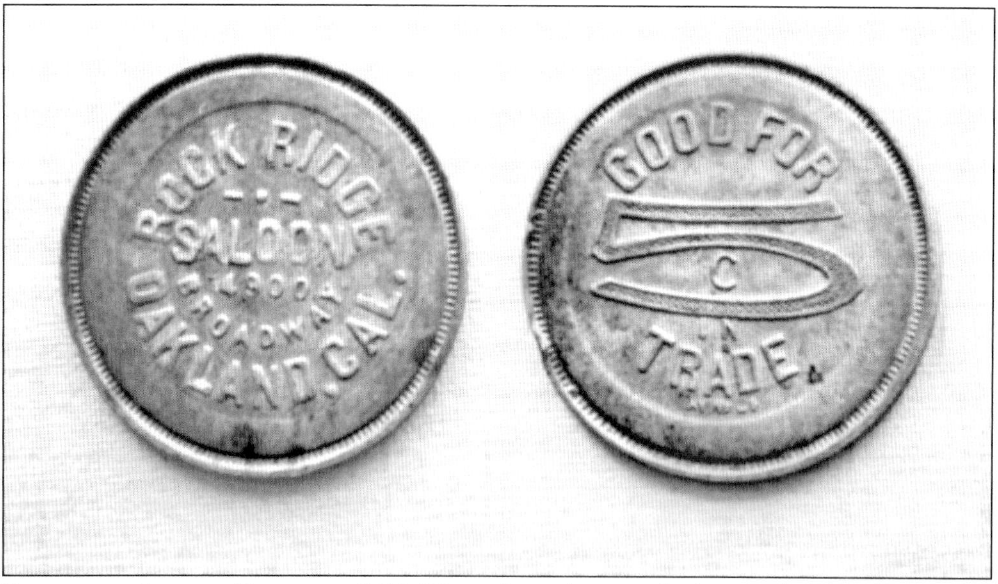


**ROCKRIDGE SALOON TOKEN, C. 1910.** This token, photographed on both sides, entitled the holder to a 5¢ beer at the Rockridge Saloon. Urged on by the Vernon Rockridge Improvement Club, the city council forced the Rockridge Saloon at 4900 Broadway to move when Oakland Tech opened down the street. Tokens were used to encourage repeat business. The Rockridge Saloon served primarily quarry workers, many of whom lived at the quarry dormitory. (Courtesy Ray Raineri.)

**Kid's Day, 1925.** Oakland Technical High School held an annual "Kid's Day" in the 1920s when students could dress up like younger children. Here two freshmen dress up like their younger sisters. (Courtesy Oakland History Room.)

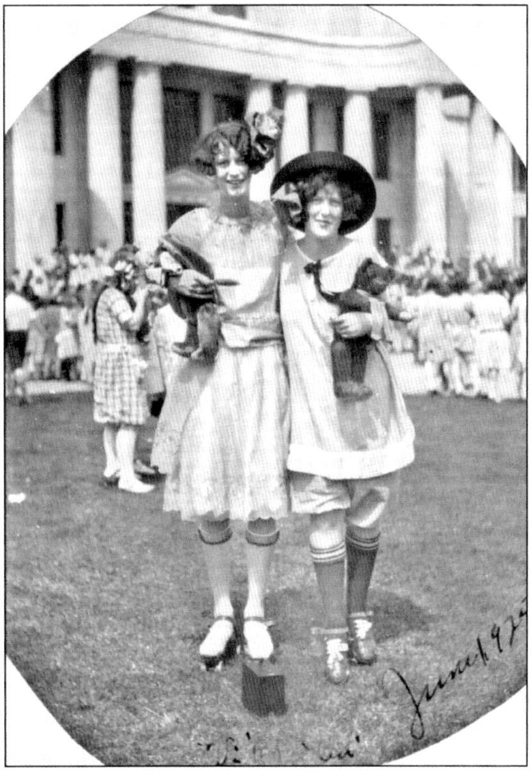

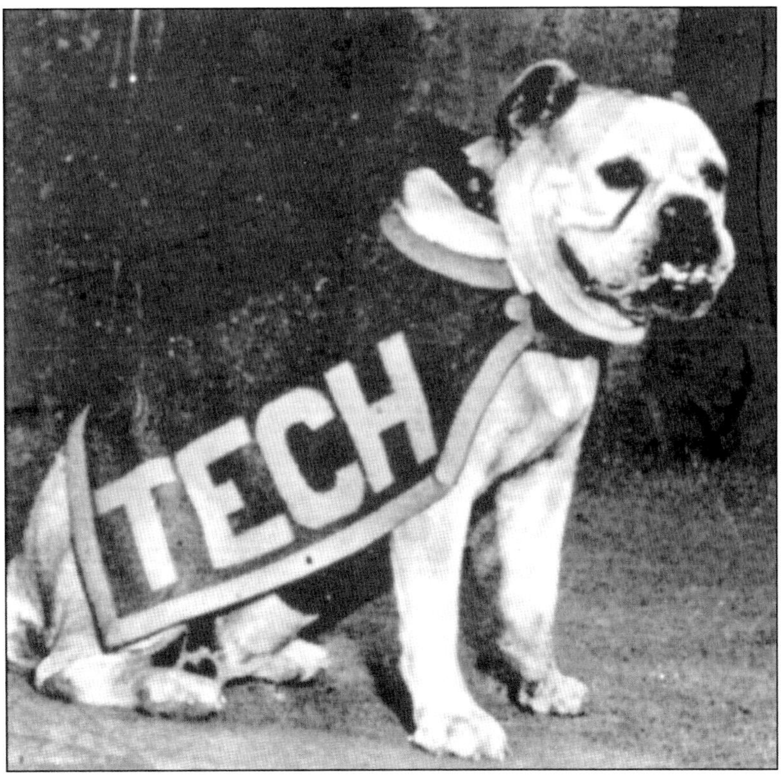


**Mascot, 1946.** Here a bulldog, the Oakland Technical High School mascot, is dressed in a specially designed "Tech" banner in 1946. (Courtesy Barbara Maltvy Follini.)

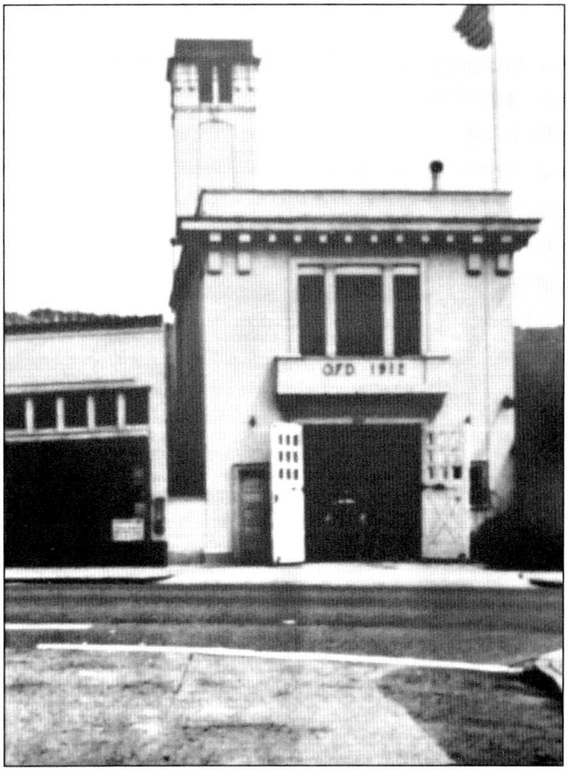


**ROCKRIDGE FIREHOUSE, 1948.** When the Vernon Rockridge Improvement Club was formed in 1910, it lobbied for a firehouse in Rockridge. This one was built in 1912 at 5800 College Avenue at the intersection of Birth Court. Originally occupied by Chemical Engine No. 1, it became the home of Engine No. 19 in 1924. This firehouse was closed when a new one was built in 1962 at 5766 Shafter Avenue (now Miles Avenue). (Courtesy Jennifer Dowling.)

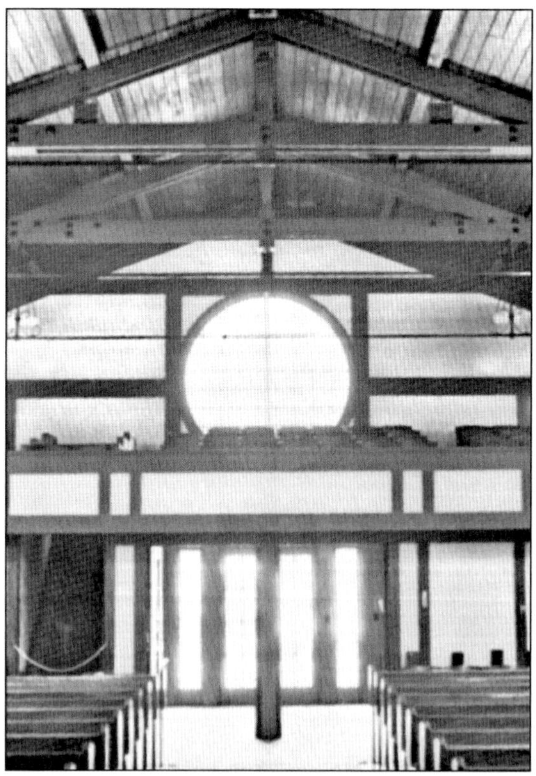

**COLLEGE AVENUE PRESBYTERIAN CHURCH.** Here we see the interior sanctuary of the College Avenue Presbyterian Church looking toward the choir loft and rose window. The College Avenue Presbyterian Church site on College Avenue was purchased in 1913, and architect Julia Morgan designed the church. (Courtesy College Avenue Presbyterian Church.)

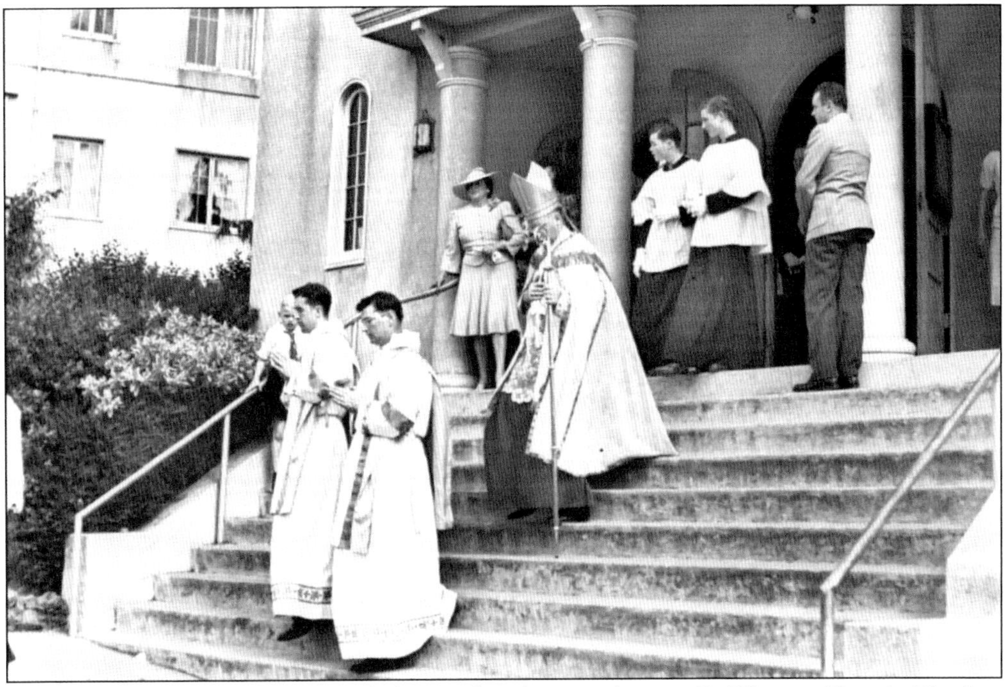

**St. Theresa Church, 1940s.** A bishop and acolytes are leaving St. Theresa Church. The first St. Theresa Church opened in 1925 at 5637 Manila Avenue before moving father up into the Rockridge hills in 1951. (Courtesy William Larkins.)

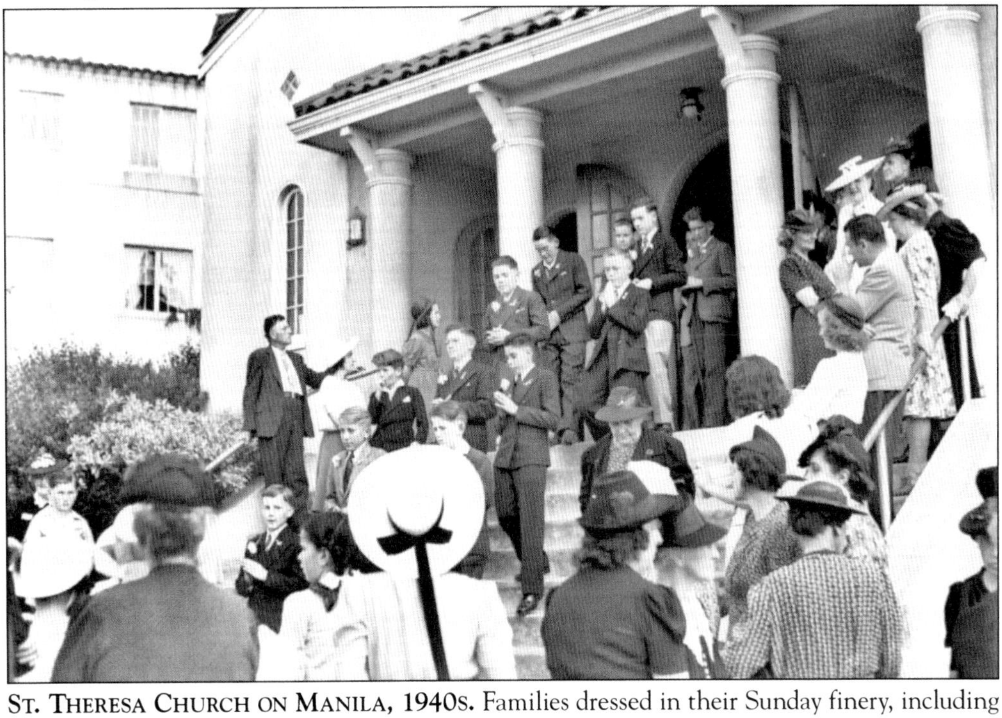

**St. Theresa Church on Manila, 1940s.** Families dressed in their Sunday finery, including ladies' hats, watch as youth leave St. Theresa Church on Manila. This is a First Communion class leaving the church. (Courtesy of William Larkins.)

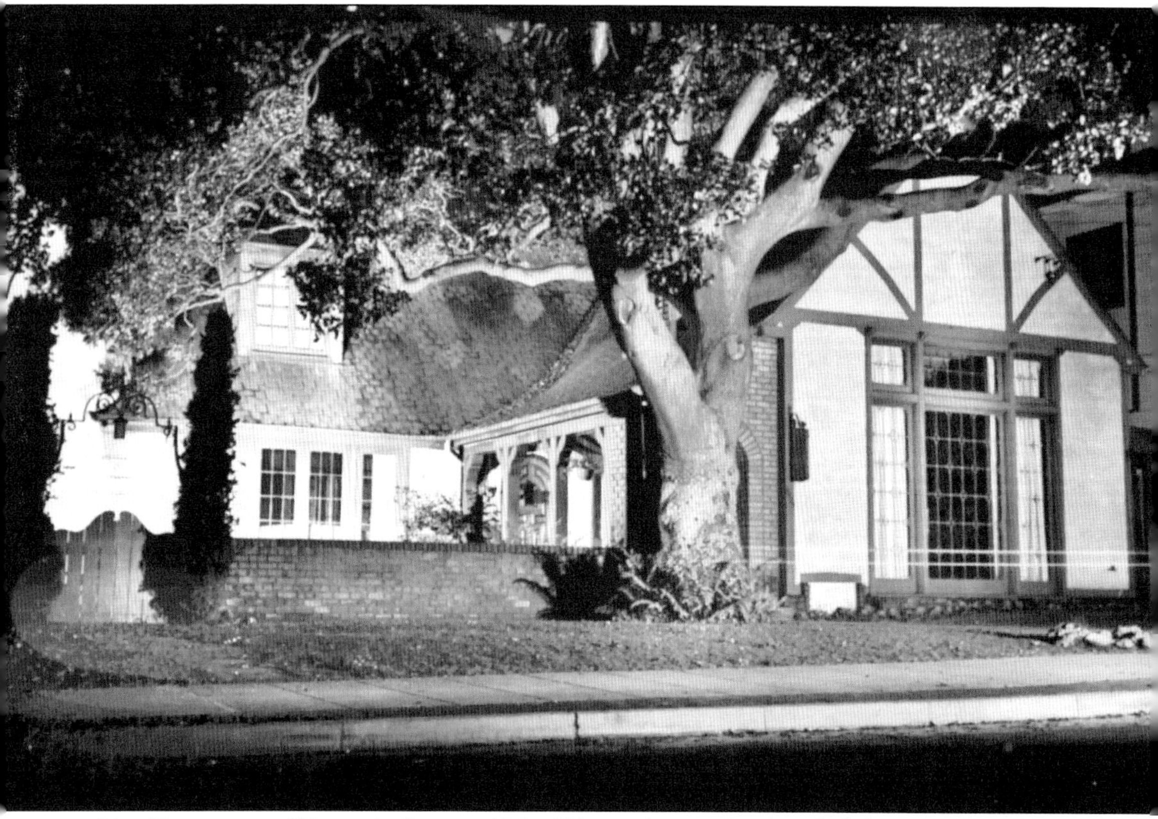

**THE ROCKRIDGE WOMEN'S CLUB, 1950S.** Wives of men who founded the Vernon Rockridge Improvement Club began their own Rockridge Women's Club in 1910. This clubhouse at 5682 Keith Avenue was demolished in the 1960s to make way for BART and the Grove Shafter Freeway. In the 1930s through the 1950s, women's clubs provided intellectual stimulation for women across the country as well as in Rockridge. (Courtesy William Larkins.)

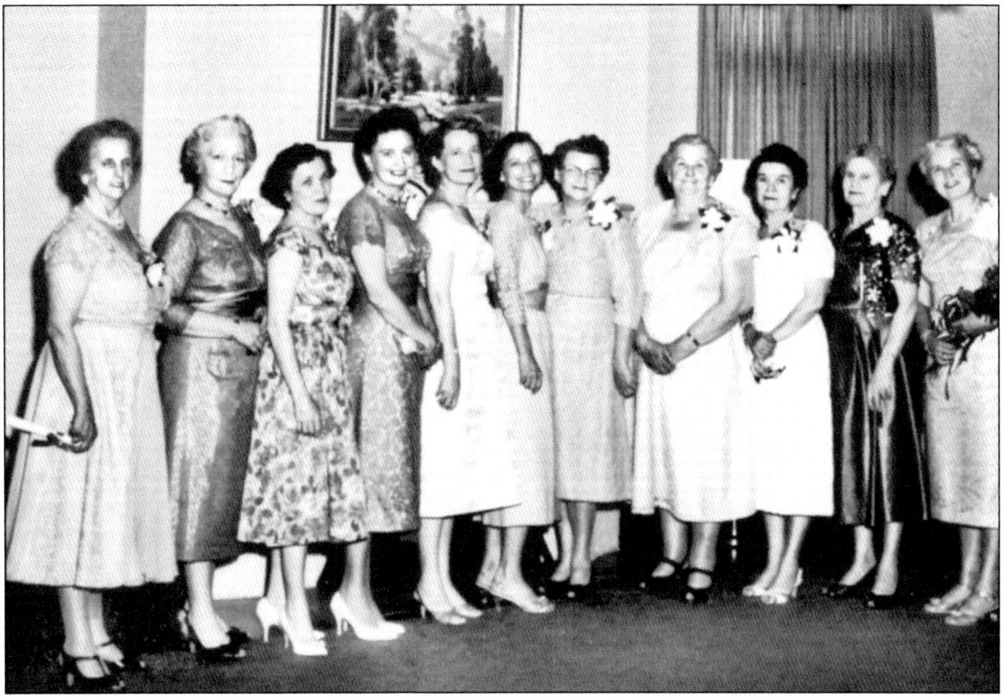

**ROCKRIDGE WOMEN'S CLUB, 1959.** Genevieve Larkins, second from right, was president of the Rockridge Women's Club in 1941. She stands next to Jeannette Righter, president of the club in 1959. Genevieve Larkins played an active role in the club as curator of the club's literature section for many years. From the 1930s through the 1950s, she gave book reviews and directed plays and skits. From left to right are Beatrice Booth, Bea Finch, Peggy Henchel, Margaret Fowler, Selma Weymouth, Connie Spilker, Mrs. Naomi, Mrs. Lane, Myrtle Fisher, Genevieve Larkins, and Jeannette Righter. (Courtesy William Larkins.)

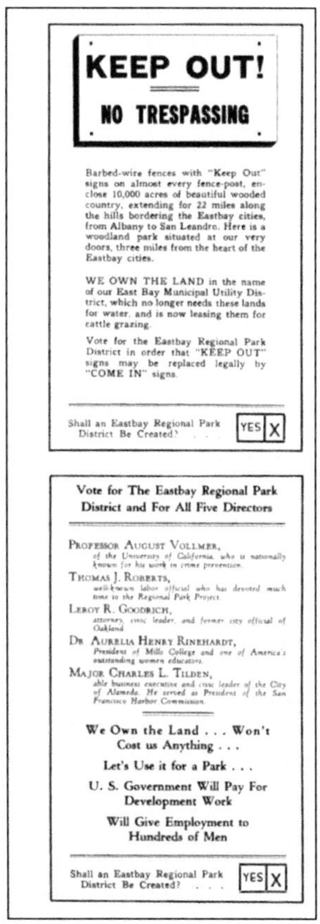

KEEP OUT!

NO TRESPASSING

Barbed-wire fences with "Keep Out" signs on almost every fence-post, enclose 10,000 acres of beautiful wooded country, extending for 22 miles along the hills bordering the Eastbay cities, from Albany to San Leandro. Here is a woodland park situated at our very doors, three miles from the heart of the Eastbay cities.

WE OWN THE LAND in the name of our East Bay Municipal Utility District, which no longer needs these lands for water, and is now leasing them for cattle grazing.

Vote for the Eastbay Regional Park District in order that "KEEP OUT" signs may be replaced legally by "COME IN" signs.

Shall an Eastbay Regional Park District Be Created? . . . YES X

Vote for The Eastbay Regional Park District and For All Five Directors

PROFESSOR AUGUST VOLLMER,
*of the University of California, who is nationally known for his work in crime prevention.*

THOMAS J. ROBERTS,
*well-known labor official who has devoted much time to the Regional Park Project.*

LEROY R. GOODRICH,
*attorney, civic leader, and former city official of Oakland.*

DR. AURELIA HENRY RINEHARDT,
*President of Mills College and one of America's outstanding women educators.*

MAJOR CHARLES L. TILDEN,
*able business executive and civic leader of the City of Alameda. He served as President of the San Francisco Harbor Commission.*

We Own the Land . . . Won't Cost us Anything . . .

Let's Use it for a Park . . .

U. S. Government Will Pay For Development Work

Will Give Employment to Hundreds of Men

Shall an Eastbay Regional Park District Be Created? . . . YES X

**ADVERTISEMENT URGING VOTE FOR PARKS.** After Lake Temescal no longer supplied water to Oakland, there was a movement in the 1930s to turn the property around Lake Temescal into a park by forming the East Bay Regional Park District. This advertisement from 1935 warns that if the East Bay Regional Park District ballot measure does not pass, there will be a "Keep Out" sign barring people from enjoying recreation around Lake Temescal. (Courtesy East Bay Regional Park District.)

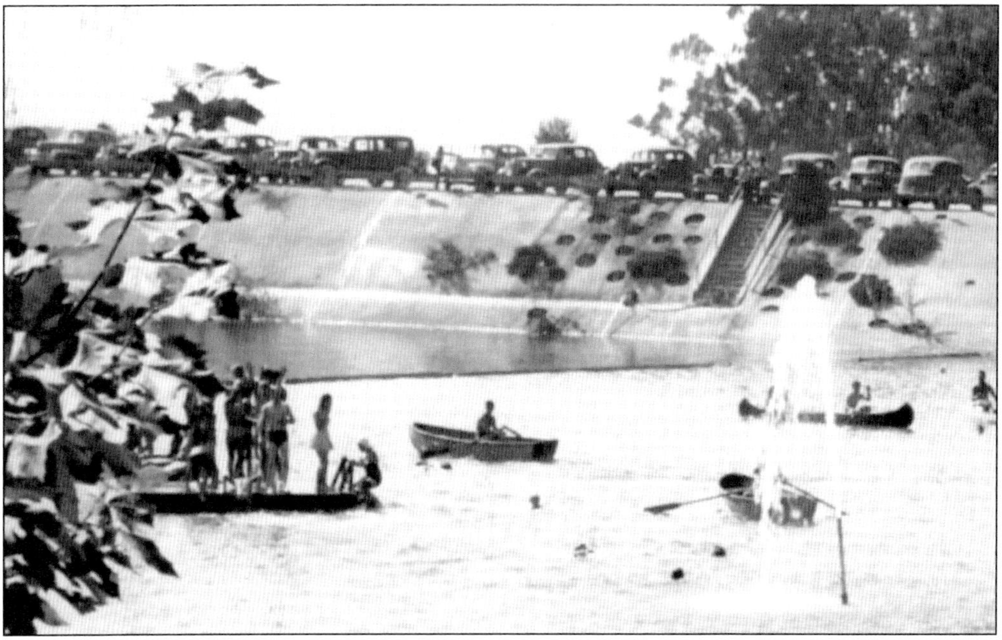

**LAKE TEMESCAL, LATE 1930S.** After the lake became part of the East Bay Regional Parks District, a parking lot was built above Lake Temescal for cars. By the 1930s, cars made access to the lake in the hills easy. Water for the early Rockridge housing developments came from Lake Temescal. Now with water for Oakland piped in from the Sierra, Lake Temescal became a recreation area. (Courtesy J. Kent.)

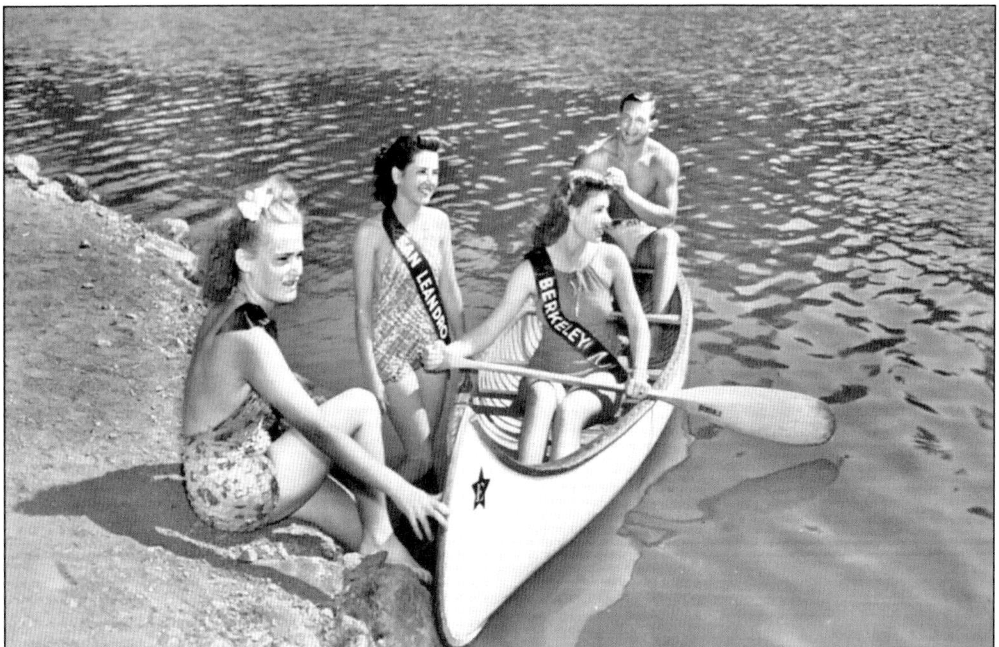


**BATHING BEAUTIES, 1958.** Winners of the titles Miss San Leandro, Miss Berkeley, and a title that cannot be seen are shown at Lake Temescal in a canoe. The beauty of Lake Temescal provided a popular backdrop for photographs. (Courtesy East Bay Regional Park District.)

# *Five*

# COMMERCE

College Avenue, the commercial street that has long anchored Rockridge, was a dirt road in the 1890s that strung together farm buildings, a dozen residential buildings, and a few saloons. (Two of the College Avenue houses built in the 1880s survive today, converted to commercial use.) By 1900, tradesmen were opening shops on the ground floor of their homes while living upstairs. Shops sold groceries, dry goods, tools, and lamp oil. These home shops, together with saloons and a roadhouse for overnight travelers, were the first commercial establishments on College Avenue. When automobiles began to appear, shops often diversified into selling gasoline by the can, along with cabbages and tomatoes. Farther down Broadway, the Rockridge Saloon and the Broadway Market both catered to quarry work crews, made up mostly of Italian immigrant men. Workers bought boots and coveralls from the family living upstairs over the market.

Along with the housing boom set off by the 1906 earthquake, College Avenue experienced a commercial boom, becoming a bona fide shoppers' Main Street for Rockridge. Growth leveled off around 1914, but by the 1920s, stores and shops had replaced the farms bordering College Avenue. The new commercial exuberance owed much to the service provided by the streetcar line. The Key System No. 6 streetcar ran from the intersection of College and Broadway and continued, with frequent stops, up College Avenue to the university. A major trolley stop was the Chimes Theater, located near the current BART station. The theater was a focal point of the College Avenue commercial scene, especially with the advent of talking pictures in 1929. Favorite confectionery shops sold candy, and in the 1940s, soda fountains became community gathering places. The Bulldog was a hangout for Oakland Tech students. In the 1930s, Dreyer's, the ice cream maker, moved onto College Avenue, first as Edy's and then as Dreyer's Grand Ice Cream. There Dreyer's operated both their manufacturing plant and a popular soda fountain.

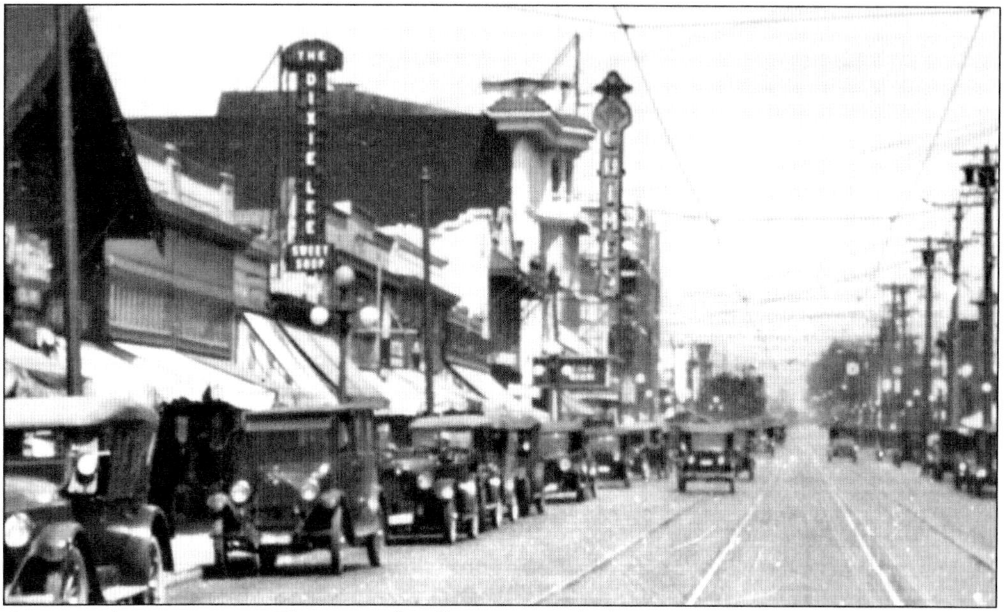


**COLLEGE AVENUE, 1924.** This view of College Avenue looks north from Lawton Avenue toward the Chimes Theater at Keith Avenue, by the current BART station. Rails run down the center of the street for the No. 6 Key System streetcar that ran between Rockridge and the University of California in Berkeley. The overhead electric wires powered the streetcars. Automobiles on the street had to drive over the rail lines to traverse College Avenue, making for a crowded street. (Courtesy John Bosko and Ray Raineri.)

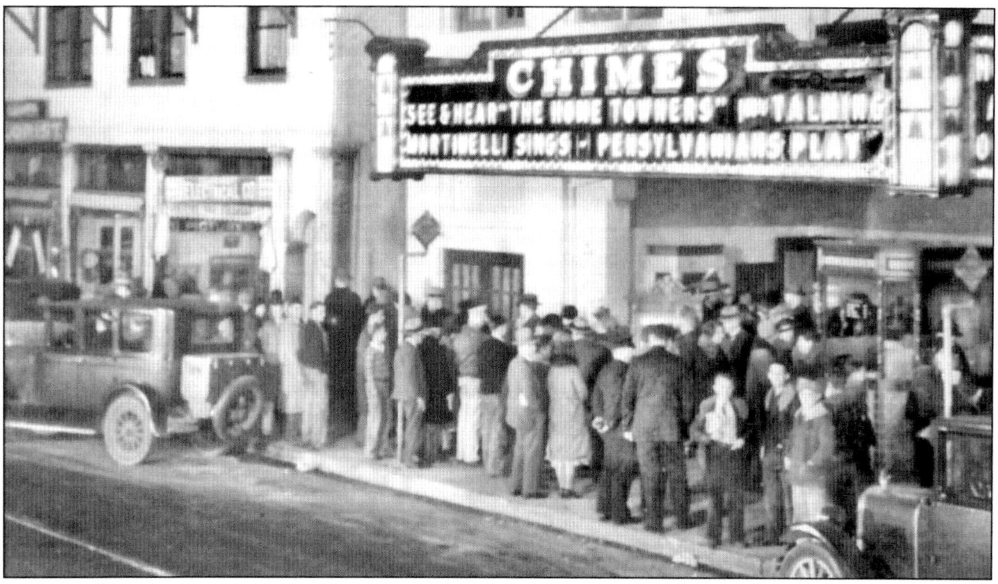


**CHIMES THEATER, 1929.** In the 1920s, the focal point of College Avenue was the Chimes Theater, which started out showing silent pictures. Here the theater is showing its first sound picture on Valentine's Day, 1929. The marquis reads: "See and Hear 'The Home Towners' 100% talking." The Chimes Theater was located at 5631 College Avenue near the current BART station and was known for ringing bell chimes to summon viewers before a film began. (Courtesy Jennifer Dowling.)

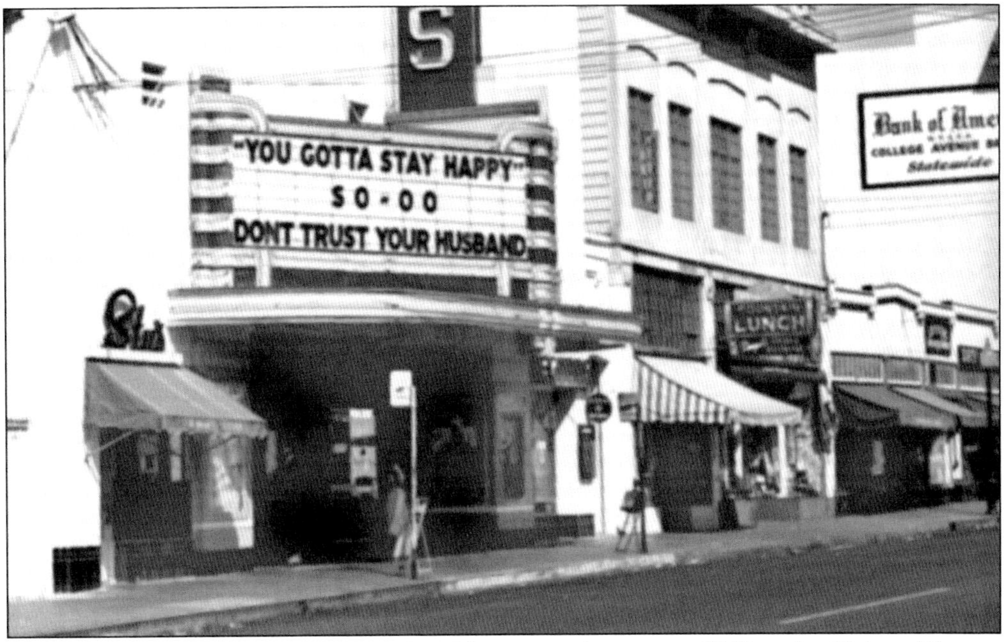


**CHIMES THEATER, 1948.** *You Gotta Stay Happy* was showing in 1948 at the Chimes Theater starring Joan Fontaine and James Stewart. Earlier, in 1910, a duck pond and barn were located where the Chimes Theater stood on College Avenue. The pond and barn had been part of a truck farm that stretched east from College Avenue to Forest Street, south of Shafter Avenue. (Courtesy William Larkins.)

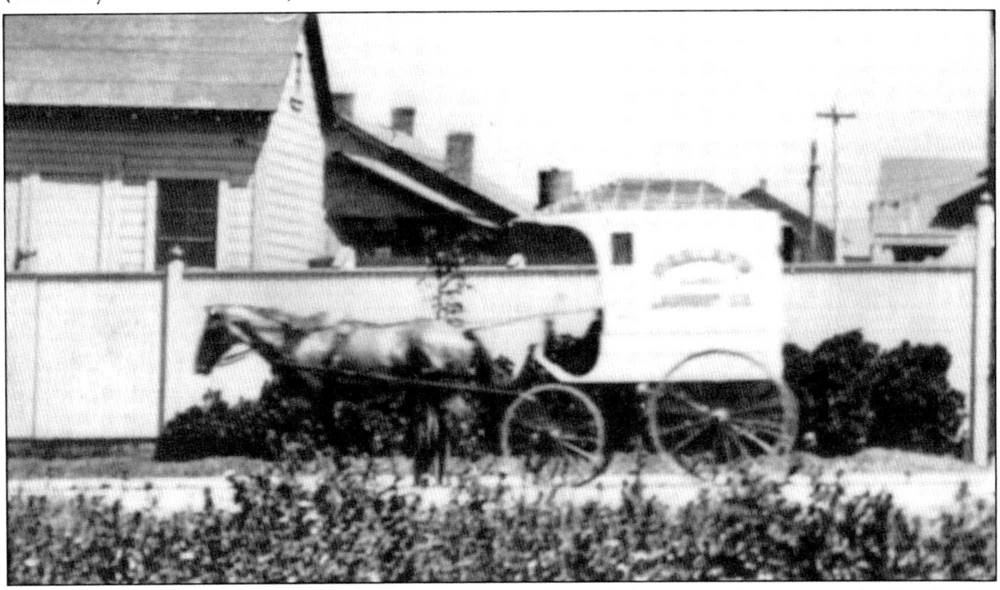

**DELIVERY WAGON, C. 1906.** A milk wagon is making deliveries to homes in the Rockridge neighborhood west of College Avenue. Many vendors came to Rockridge homes in the decades before 1930, including vegetable vendors and ice salesmen. As telephone ownership became common in the 1920s, it was typical for a housewife to place an order by phone at a College Avenue market and receive the groceries delivered to the home. Shoe repairmen would both pick up and deliver shoes. (Courtesy Kevin Flynn and Marion Citron.)

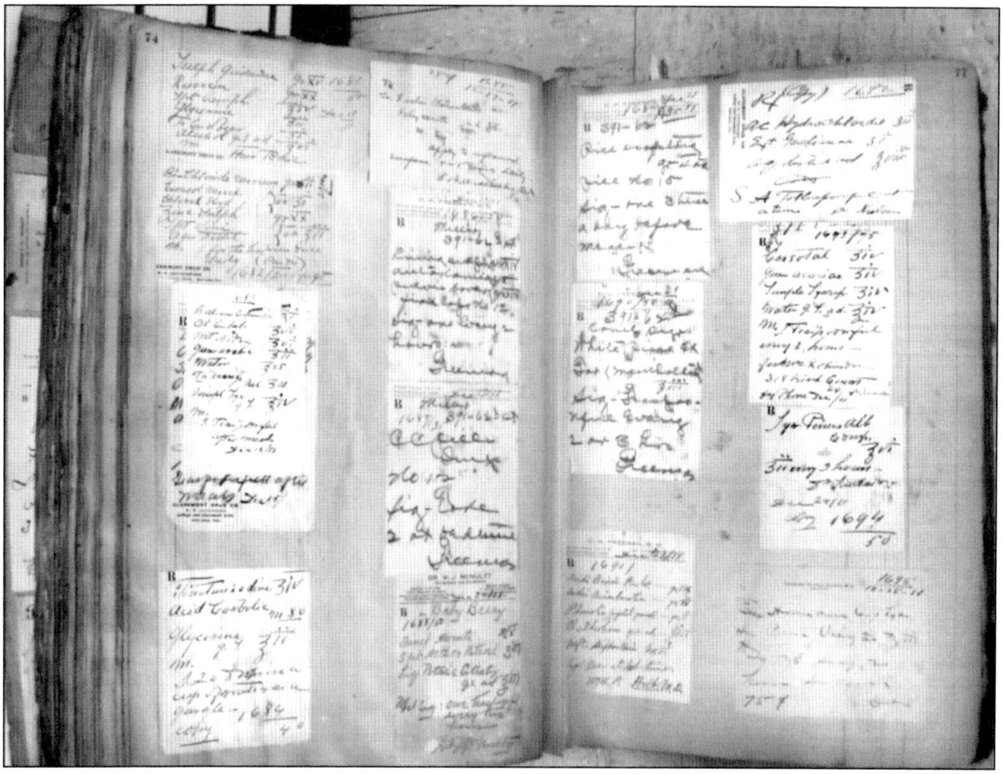

**PRESCRIPTION BOOK, 1911.** The pharmacist at Chimes Pharmacy on College Avenue pasted prescriptions into this book to keep track of them in 1911. Before the age of computers, the pharmacist would flip back through the book to find a prescription. (Courtesy John Gelinas.)

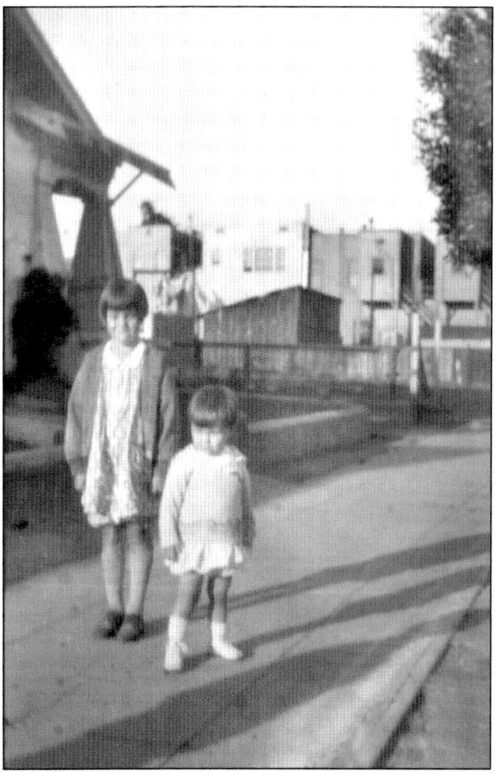

**THE BACK OF COLLEGE AVENUE, 1920S.** Marian Combs and a younger friend play on Sixty-second Street. This view looks east up Sixty-second Street toward College Avenue, showing the back side of College Avenue buildings. The neighborhood around College Avenue was changing from farms to housing. A barn can be seen at the end of the block, just before the back side of College Avenue stores that housed a milliner who blocked hats and a butcher who also sold vegetables in the 1920s. (Courtesy Marian Combs.)

**QUARRY WORKER'S HOUSE.** Thomas Madden, a mechanic at the Bilger Quarry, had this College Avenue house (photographed in the 1990s) built for his family in 1892. In 1908, Madden added a storefront to the ground floor of his house, quit his quarry job, and opened a grocery and notions store. He also sold coal from a bin in the yard next to the house. In the early 1900s, most College Avenue shopkeepers lived above or next to their businesses. (Courtesy Jennifer Dowling.)

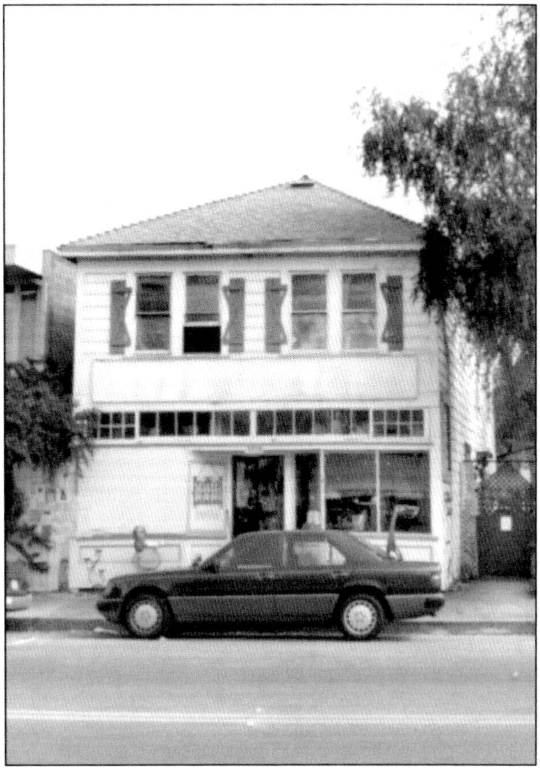

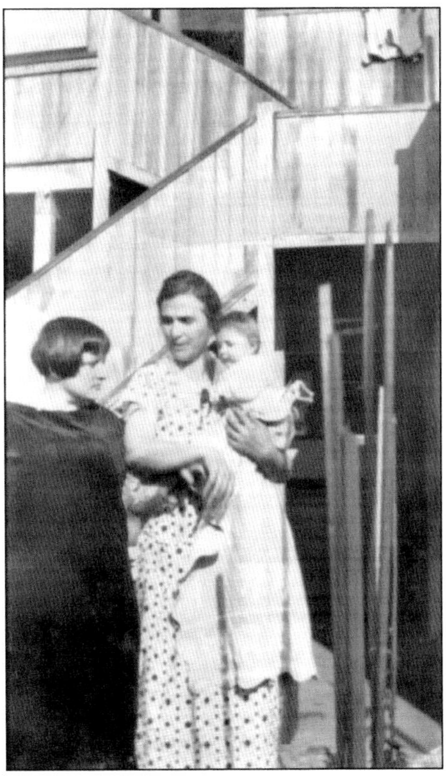

**BROADWAY MARKET LIVING QUARTERS, 1920S.** Eliza Ollino stands with her daughter, Camilla, and granddaughter, Evelyn, at the stairs that lead from the Broadway Market to their living quarters above the store. Eliza's husband, quarry worker Guiseppe Ollino, built the market across the street from the Bilger Quarry at the southwest corner of Broadway and Pleasant Valley Road. The market sold coveralls, boots, men's shirts, hats, and handkerchiefs to quarry workers. (Courtesy Evelyn Avidano Clevenger.)

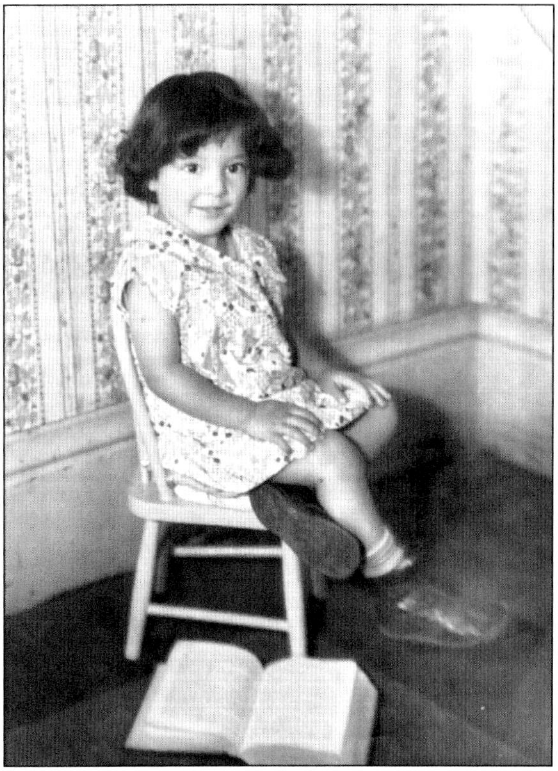

**BROADWAY MARKET HOME, 1920S.** Four-year-old Evelyn Avidano sits on a chair in her bedroom above the Broadway Market. At her feet is a leather-bound copy of *Grimm's Fairy Tales*. She lived above the market with her parents, grandparents, and aunt while growing up and while later attending Oakland Technical High School. (Courtesy Evelyn Avidano Clevenger.)

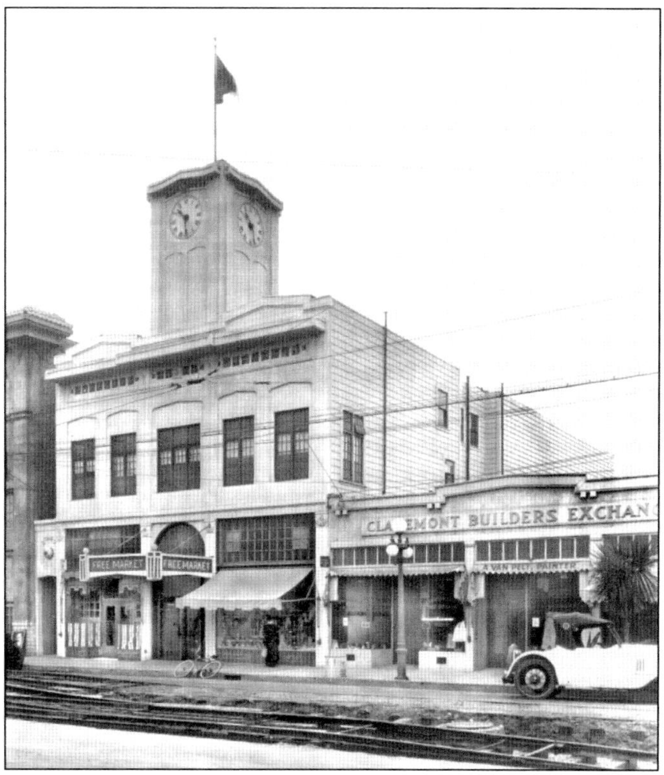


**THE FREE MARKET, C. 1920.** In 1918, the Free Market opened on College Avenue near Keith Avenue housing vendors of produce, meat, fish, baked goods, coffee, and ice cream under one roof. Next door was the Claremont Builders' Exchange where workers in "building mechanics," such as painters and carpenters, were available for work. The electrolier street lamp in front was one of 33 installed on College Avenue in 1914. (Courtesy Jennifer Dowling.)

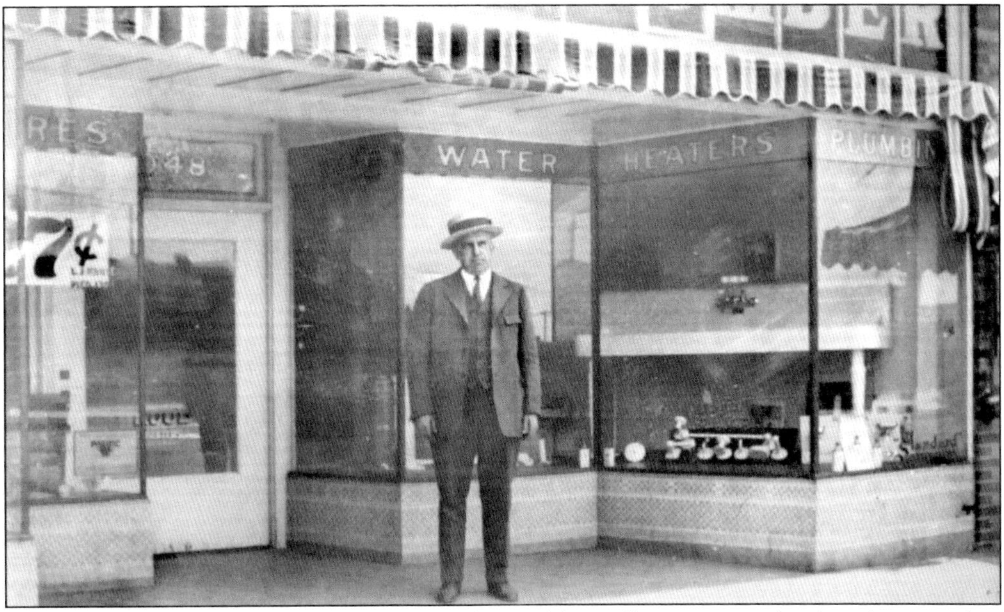


**L. J. KRUSE, 1920S.** Louis J. Kruse stands in front of the College Avenue plumbing business that he established in 1916 at age 27. Louis was the son a miner, Herman Kruse, who had a gold claim in Grass Valley. After a mining accident killed his father, Louis's mother moved the family to San Francisco. There Louis learned plumbing in the repair work that followed the 1906 earthquake. (Courtesy David Kruse.)

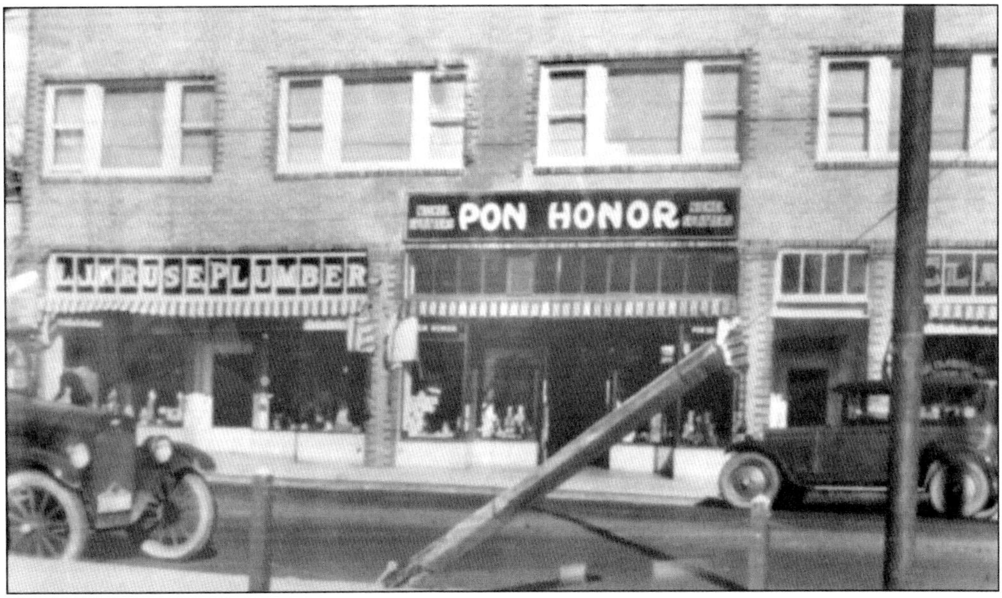


**PLUMBING BUSINESS, 1920S.** L. J. Kruse migrated from San Francisco to Rockridge around 1910 where he worked as a plumber in the housing boom that followed the influx of refugees after the 1906 earthquake. Six years later, he opened his own plumbing business on College Avenue and became president of the National Masters Plumbing Association in the early 1930s. L. J. Kruse Plumbing is now owned by his grandsons. (Courtesy David Kruse.)

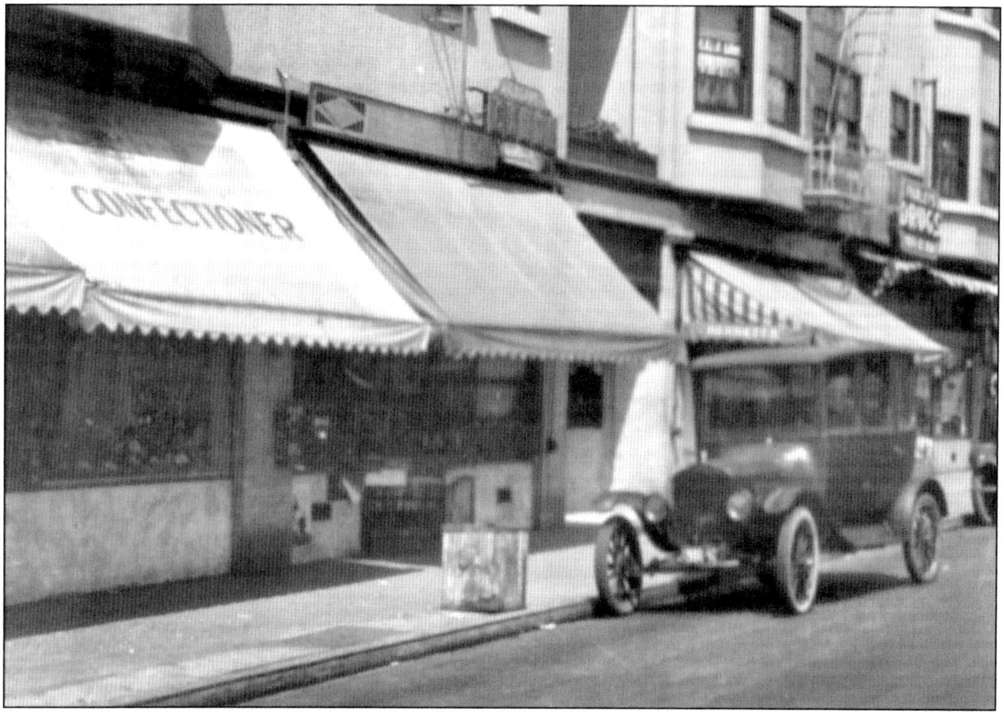


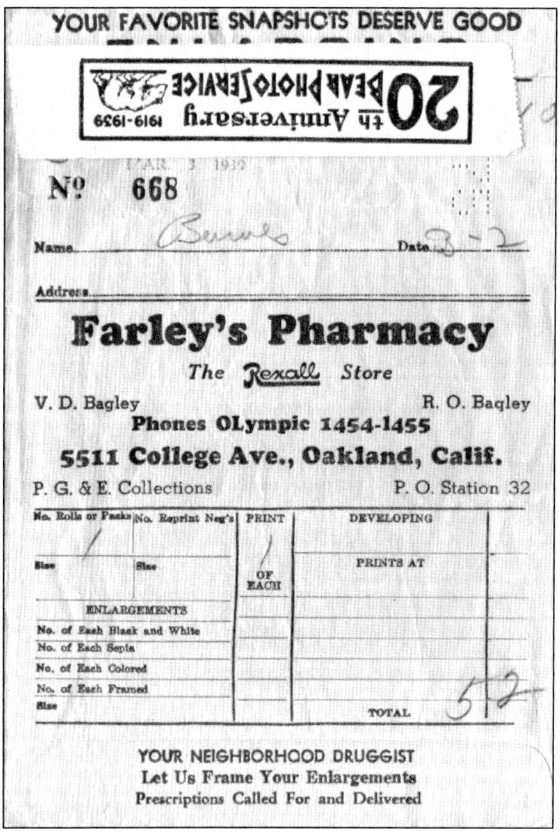
YOUR FAVORITE SNAPSHOTS DESERVE GOOD

20th Anniversary 1919-1939 BEAR PHOTO SERVICE

MAR 3 1939

No. 668

Name Burns Date 3-2

Address

**Farley's Pharmacy**

*The Rexall Store*

V. D. Bagley R. O. Bagley

Phones OLympic 1454-1455

5511 College Ave., Oakland, Calif.

P. G. & E. Collections P. O. Station 32

| No. Rolls or Packs | No. Reprint Neg's | PRINT | DEVELOPING |
|---|---|---|---|
| 1 | | 1 OF EACH | |
| Size | Size | | PRINTS AT |
| ENLARGEMENTS | | | |
| No. of Each Black and White | | | |
| No. of Each Sepia | | | |
| No. of Each Colored | | | |
| No. of Each Framed | | | |
| Size | | | TOTAL 52 |

YOUR NEIGHBORHOOD DRUGGIST
Let Us Frame Your Enlargements
Prescriptions Called For and Delivered

**CONFECTIONER, 1924.** In the 1920s, College Avenue had many sweets shops or confectioners that sold candies and pastries, which was perhaps a sign of the affluent times in Rockridge and elsewhere that preceded the Great Depression of the 1930s. This College Avenue confectioner near Lawton Avenue has marble trim under the plate-glass window. (Courtesy John Bosko.)

**FILM ENVELOPE, 1939.** This Farley's Pharmacy film envelope is stamped with a 1939 date. The phone number on the envelope is OLympic 1454, or OL-1454, from an era when phone numbers had four digits and a prefix. The envelope says, "prescriptions called for and delivered." Farley's would send a boy, usually a student who worked after school, to pick up a prescription and then deliver the medicine. (Courtesy Ray Raineri.)

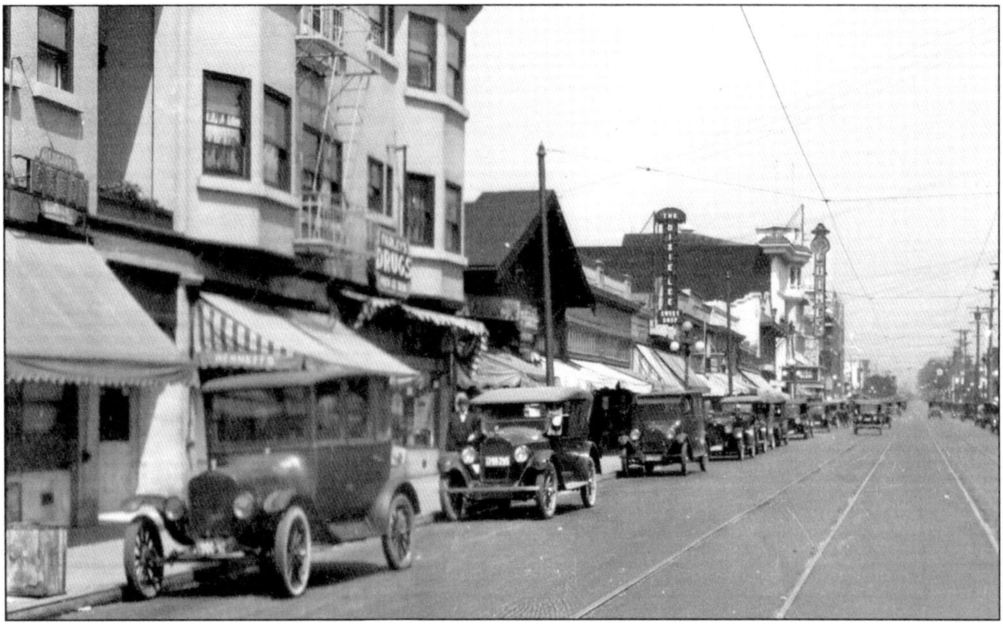


**FARLEY'S DRUGS, 1924.** In the foreground is Farley's Drugs on the left at 5511 College Avenue (later Farley's Pharmacy). In this view looking north on College Avenue, Farley's Pharmacy is underneath the third awning from the left. The Dixie Sweet Shop is farther north. Above Farley's Pharmacy are apartments. Street parking was free in the 1920s with no parking meters. Awnings were in fashion to protect customers from sun and rain. (Courtesy Ray Raineri and John Bosko.)

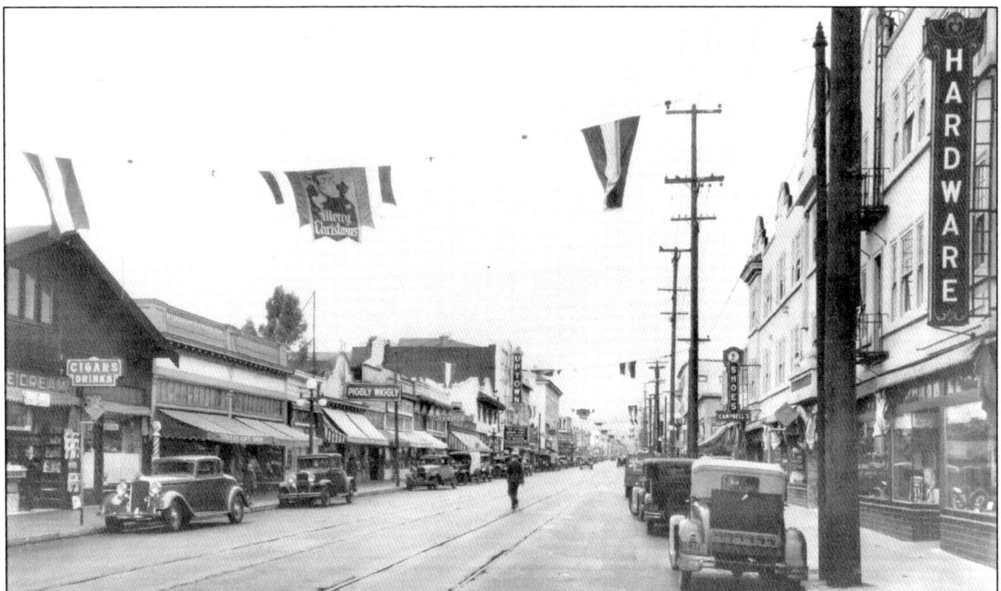


**COLLEGE AVENUE, 1930.** This photograph looks north on College Avenue from around Kales Avenue. The Uptown Theater can be seen in the distance on the left. The Chimes Theater closed in 1929 to install new sound equipment for the talking pictures. It then reopened as the Uptown Theater. On the left, in the middle of the block, is the Piggly Wiggly grocery store. (Courtesy Oakland History Room.)

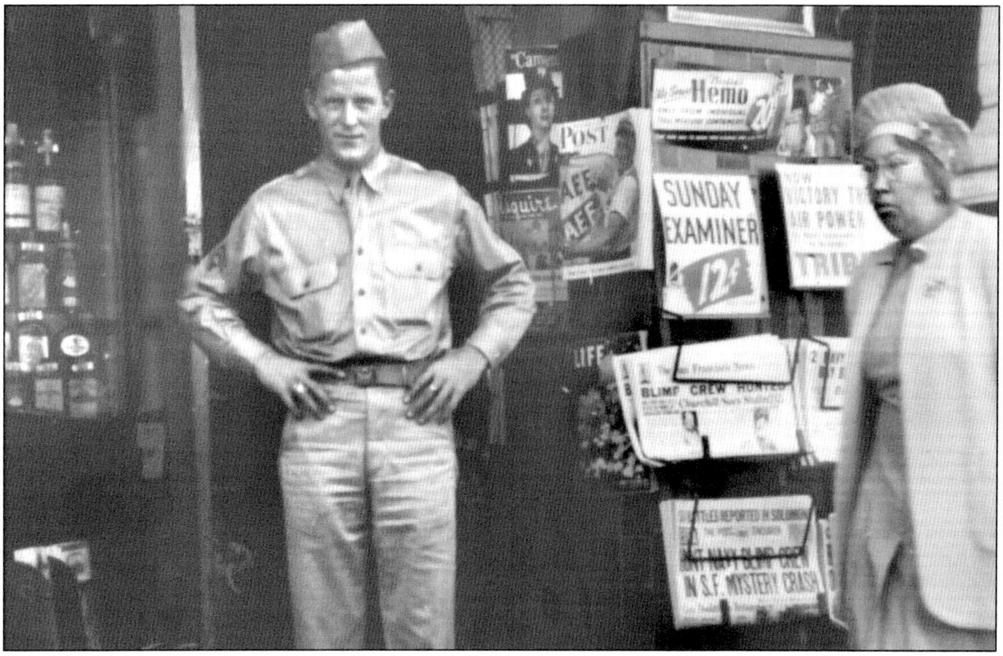


**CHIMES PHARMACY NEWSSTAND, 1942.** A World War II soldier stands by the front door of Chimes Pharmacy on College Avenue in 1942 where newspapers and the *Saturday Evening Post* were sold. The serviceman is Jack Peacock, nephew of the pharmacy owners, Clyde and Pearl Howes. (Courtesy John Gelinas.)

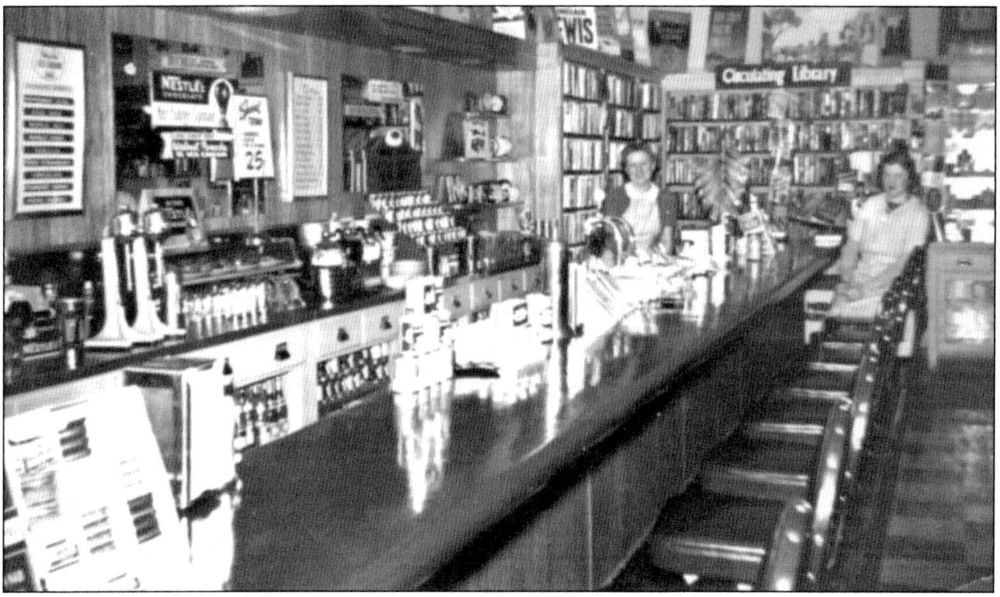


**CHIMES PHARMACY SODA FOUNTAIN, 1941.** Chimes Pharmacy had a new soda fountain installed in 1941 just before this photograph was taken. The stationary stools at the counter have backrests, which was considered luxurious. On the shelf behind the counter are two milk shake mixers and a large metal milk shake mixing cup. At the far end of the counter, the sign above the bookshelf says "Circulating Library." Chimes Pharmacy lent books to its customers. (Courtesy John Gelinas.)

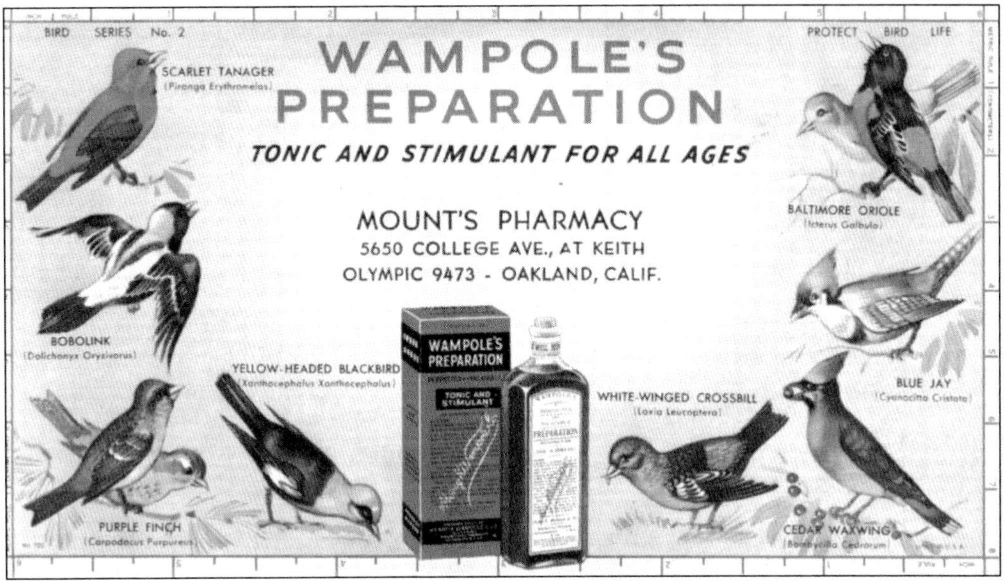


**INK BLOTTER, EARLY 1930S.** Mount's Pharmacy gave customers this ink blotter as a form of advertisement. Ink blotters were useful in an era when pens were filled from ink bottles and the written words needed to be blotted so that the ink did not smudge before drying. Mount's Pharmacy was located on College Avenue near Keith Avenue. (Courtesy Ray Raineri.)

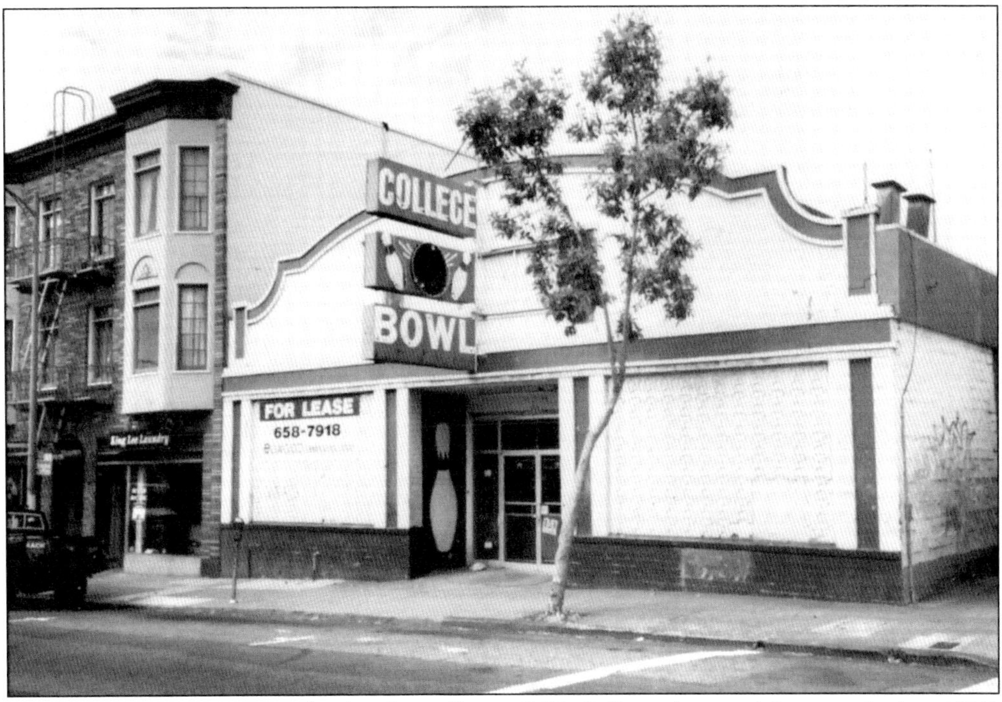


**COLLEGE AVENUE BOWL.** This bowling alley at 5433 College Avenue (photographed in 1990) was originally built as a one-story parking garage. The apartment buildings that were built along College Avenue in the 1920s did not include off-street parking. Auto owners often rented a space to securely park a car in a covered garage. The building was later converted into Diesel Bookstore. (Courtesy Jennifer Dowling.)

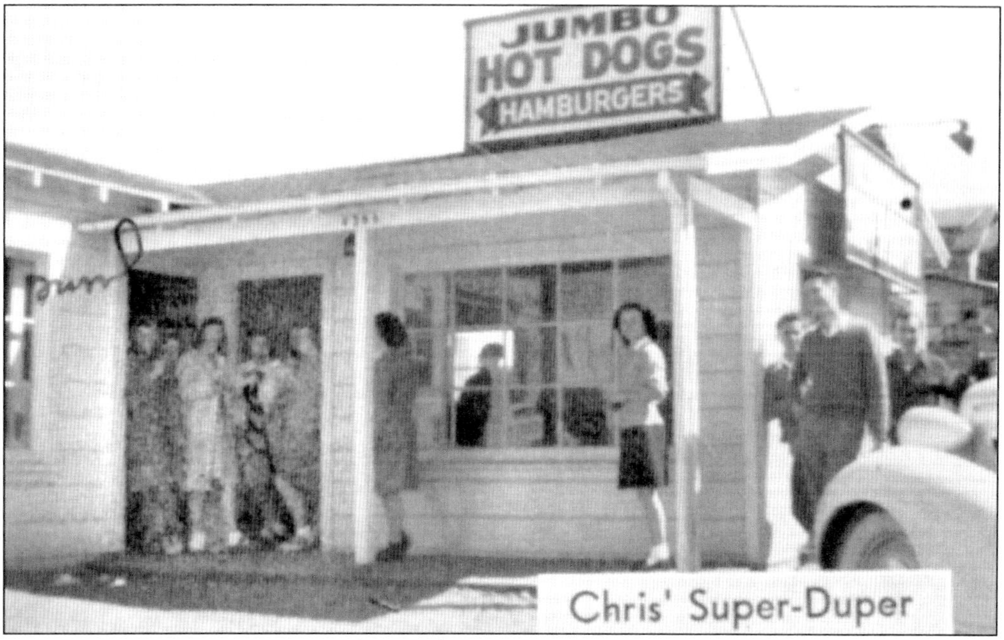


**CHRIS'S SUPER-DUPER, 1946.** A favorite hangout of Oakland Technical High School students in the 1940s was Chris's Super-Duper, across the street from the school. The sign advertises jumbo hot dogs and hamburgers. Here students could meet up with members of the opposite sex. (Courtesy Barbara Maltvy Follini.)

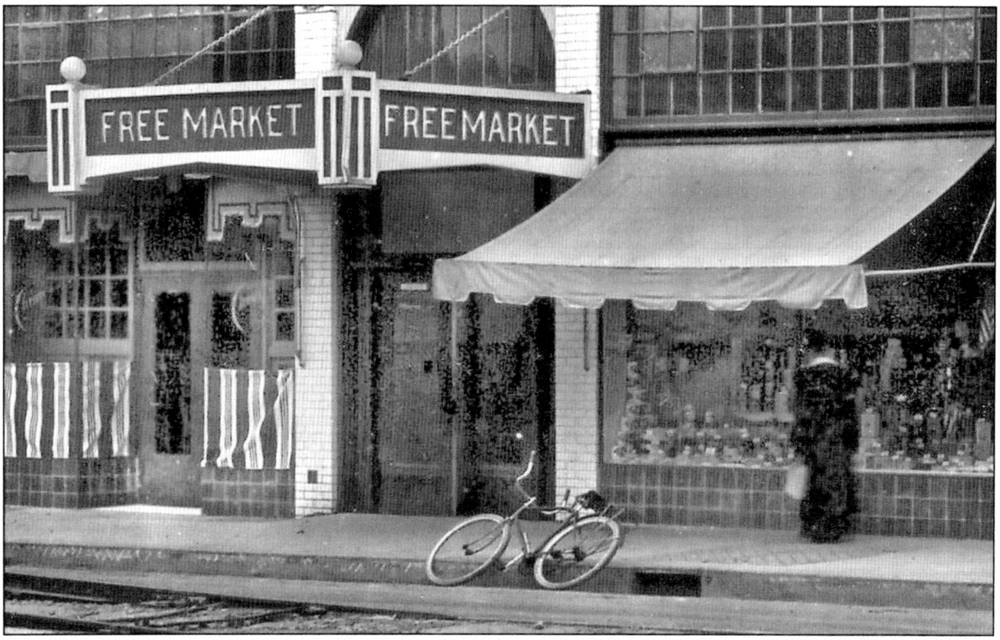


**ENTRY TO THE FREE MARKET.** The Free Market brought a bit of Old World markets to College Avenue in the 1920s when it housed a variety of food venders under one roof. The same concept inspired the building of Market Hall on the same block of College Avenue across from the Rockridge BART Station three generations later. The Free Market was unique in 1920 because it did not deliver groceries to the home and sought to thereby reduce prices. (Courtesy Jennifer Dowling.)

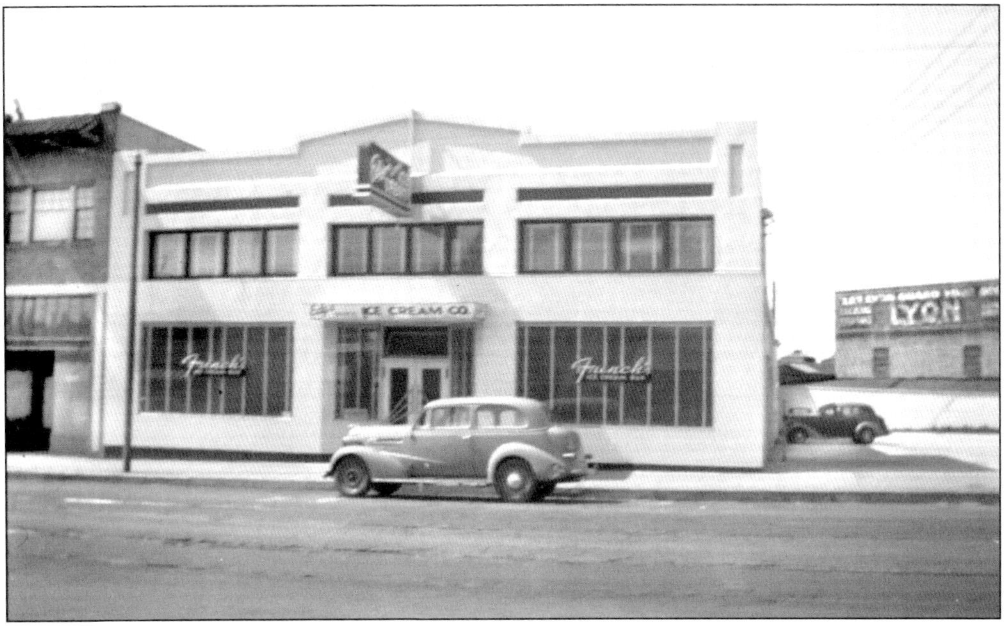


**EDY'S ICE CREAM, C. 1948.** The forerunner of Dreyer's Grand Ice Cream on College was Edy's, which opened this store in 1946. Bill Dreyer and Joe Edy were partners in Edy's, a chain of restaurants and candy stores. Bill Dreyer ran the ice cream operation that supplied Edy's coffee shops. In 1947, they split the partnership, with Bill Dreyer taking over the ice cream business. For several years, the ice cream store retained the name Edy's. (Courtesy Ed Archer.)

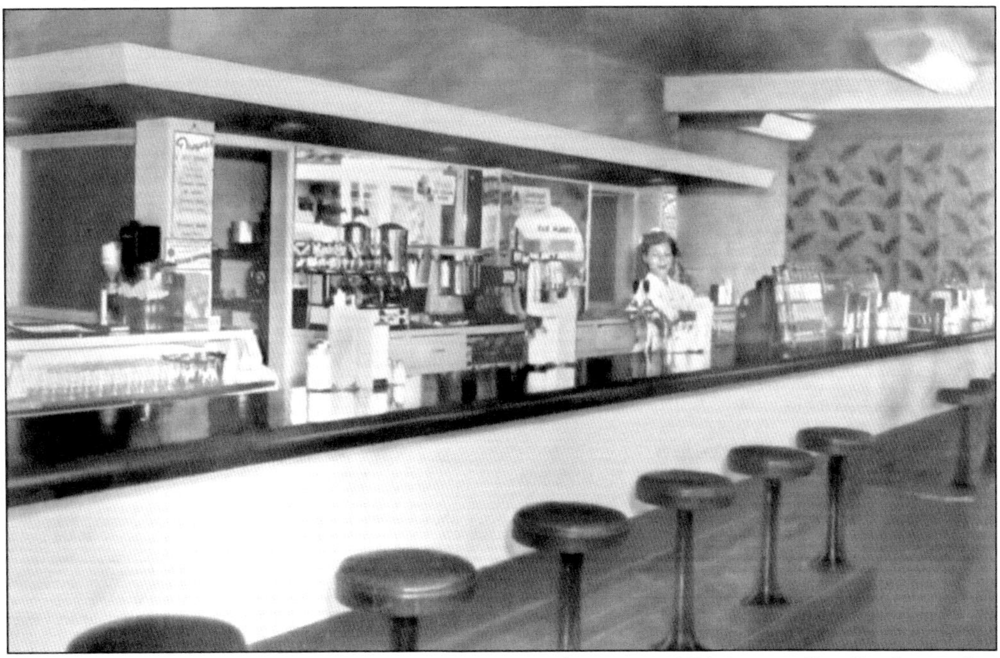

**DREYER'S SODA FOUNTAIN, EARLY 1950S.** In 1948, the name of Edy's was officially changed to Dreyer's Grand Ice Cream. This photograph shows the classic 1950s soda fountain at 5929 College Avenue. A long counter and stools attracted single individuals and pairs of friends. (Courtesy Dryer's Grand Ice Cream, Inc.)

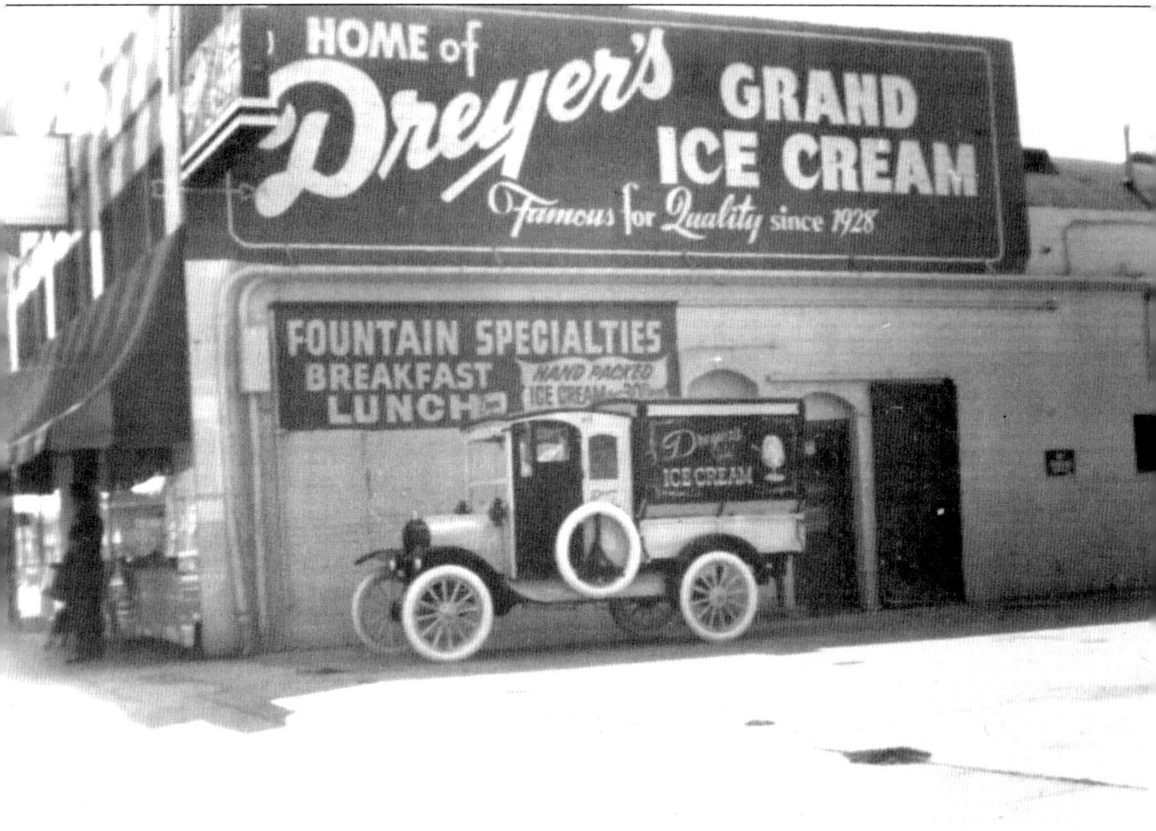


**DREYER'S TRUCK, C. 1949.** This 1920s delivery truck was purchased by Bill Dreyer in 1928 when he was in partnership with Joe Edy. The truck was used for deliveries from the Edy's location on Grand Avenue in Oakland. Bill Dreyer brought the truck to the new College Avenue location of Dreyer's Grand Ice Cream in the 1940s. The truck was eventually sold when it was out of date. In the early 1960s, the truck was purchased and restored by Ed Archer, a driver for the Dreyer's ice cream plant and lover of antique vehicles. (Courtesy Ed Archer.)

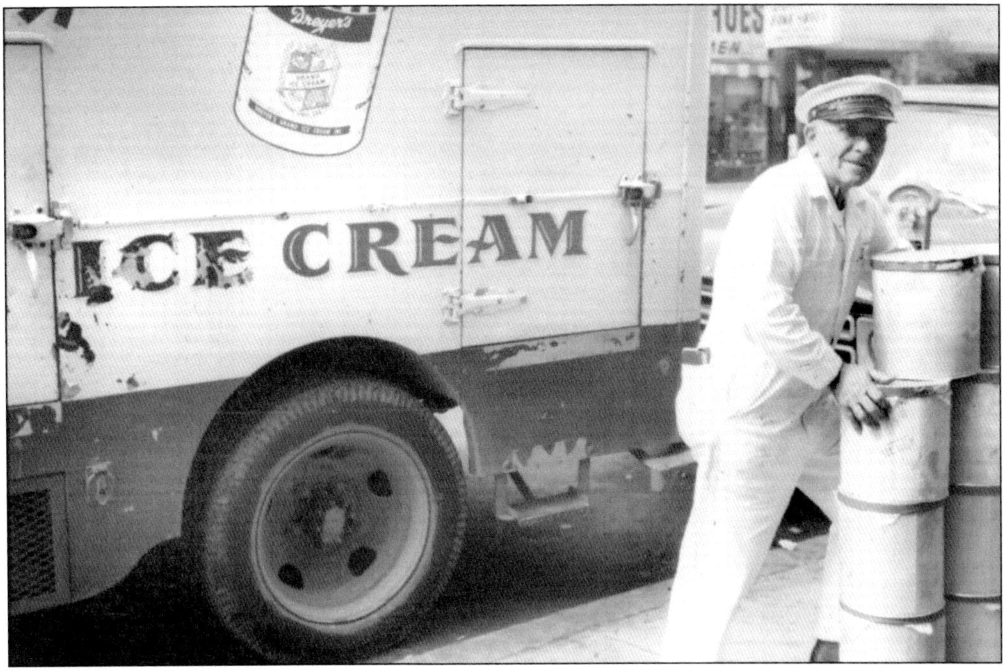


**LOADING A DREYER'S TRUCK, EARLY 1950S.** Behind Dreyer's soda fountain on College Avenue was a plant to manufacture ice cream and a yard where delivery trucks were loaded. The entrance to the truck yard was from Chabot Road. Ice cream was made on-site and then loaded onto trucks in the yard for delivery. (Courtesy Ed Archer.)

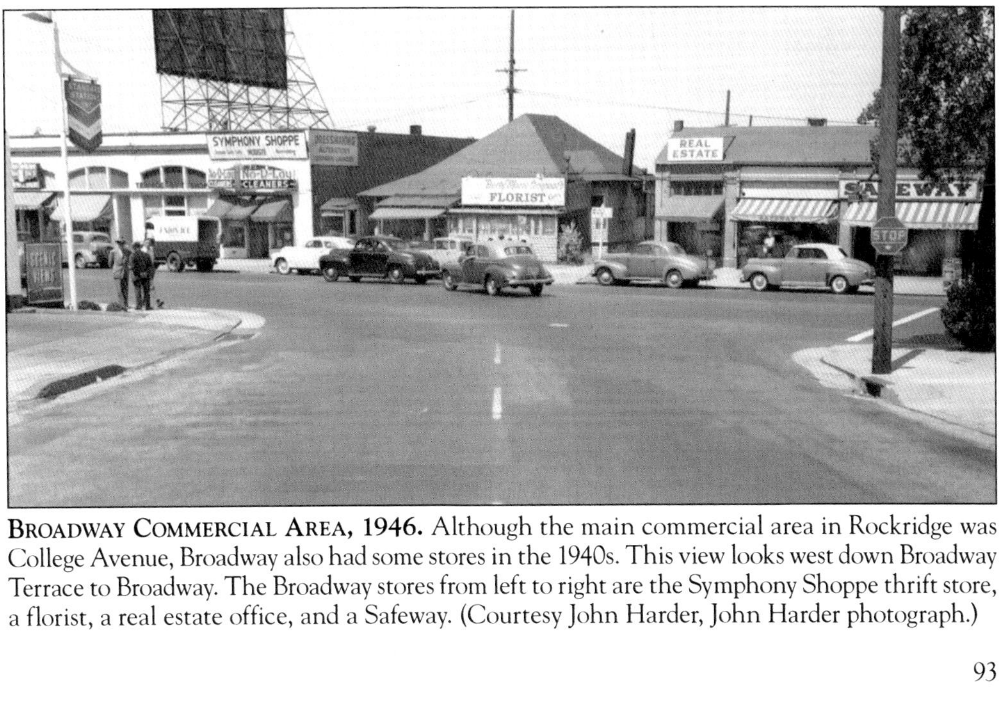


**BROADWAY COMMERCIAL AREA, 1946.** Although the main commercial area in Rockridge was College Avenue, Broadway also had some stores in the 1940s. This view looks west down Broadway Terrace to Broadway. The Broadway stores from left to right are the Symphony Shoppe thrift store, a florist, a real estate office, and a Safeway. (Courtesy John Harder, John Harder photograph.)

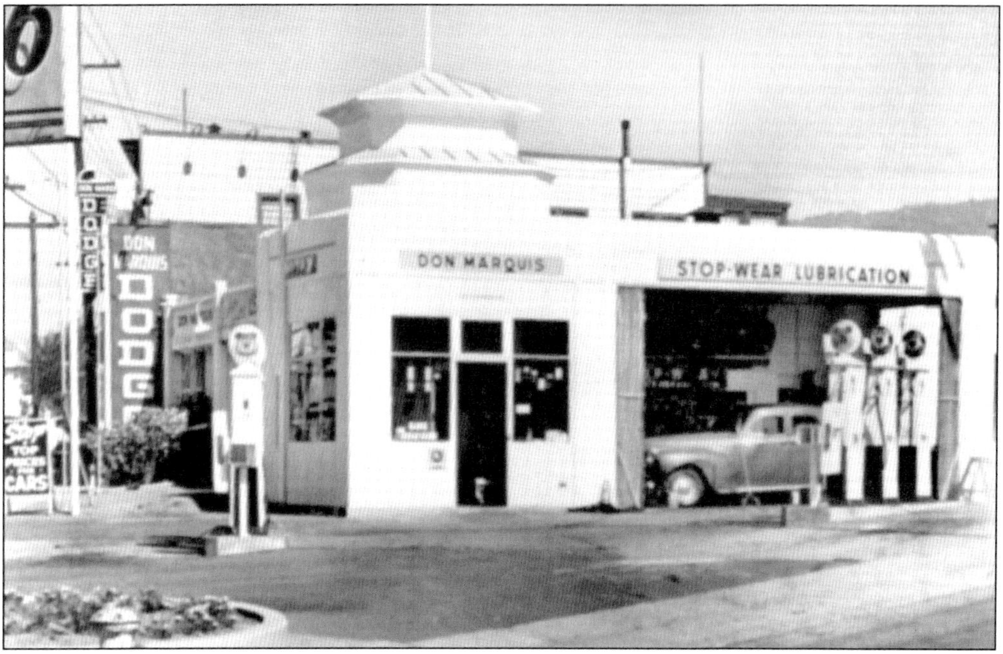


**A 1940s Gas Station.** The Don Marquis gas station was located at the intersection of College and Claremont Avenues. A sign above the auto repair shop reads, "Stop Wear Lubrication." A Dodge dealership is next door. The gas station was previously the location of George Ferrier, horseshoer and general blacksmith. (Courtesy Jennifer Dowling and John Coffin, Patrick Rippee photograph.)

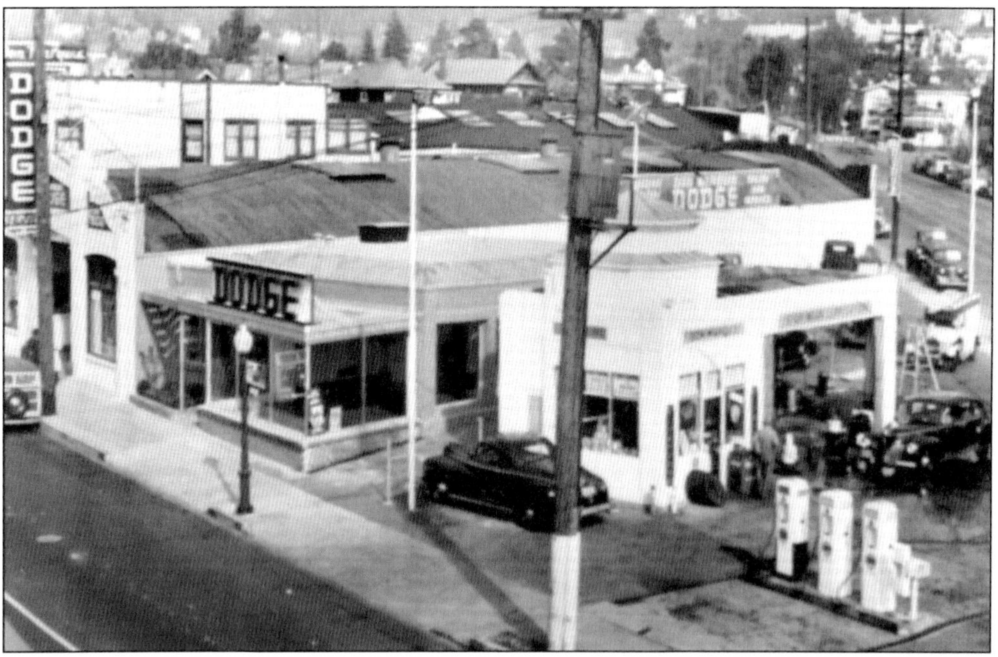


**Dodge Dealership, 1950s.** The Dodge dealership at Claremont and College Avenues is shown next to the Don Marquis gas station in the 1950s. Rockridge was changing from a streetcar suburb to a culture based on cars as auto ownership became widespread. (Courtesy Jennifer Dowling and John Coffin.)

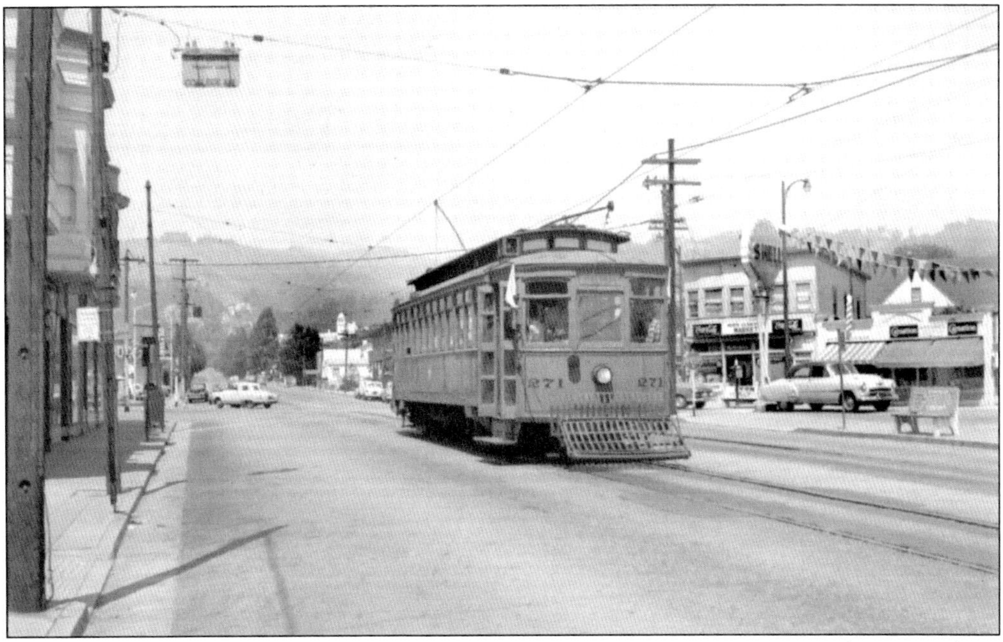

**KEY SYSTEM STREETCAR.** This Key System streetcar No. 271 is on a Bay Area Electric Railway Association excursion on May 22, 1955. It is traveling down Claremont Avenue and has stopped at the intersection of College and Claremont Avenues. The streetcar is using the E Line that originally ran between the Claremont Hotel and the Fortieth Street ferry to San Francisco. The Claremont Hotel is in the background. (Courtesy Ray Raineri.)

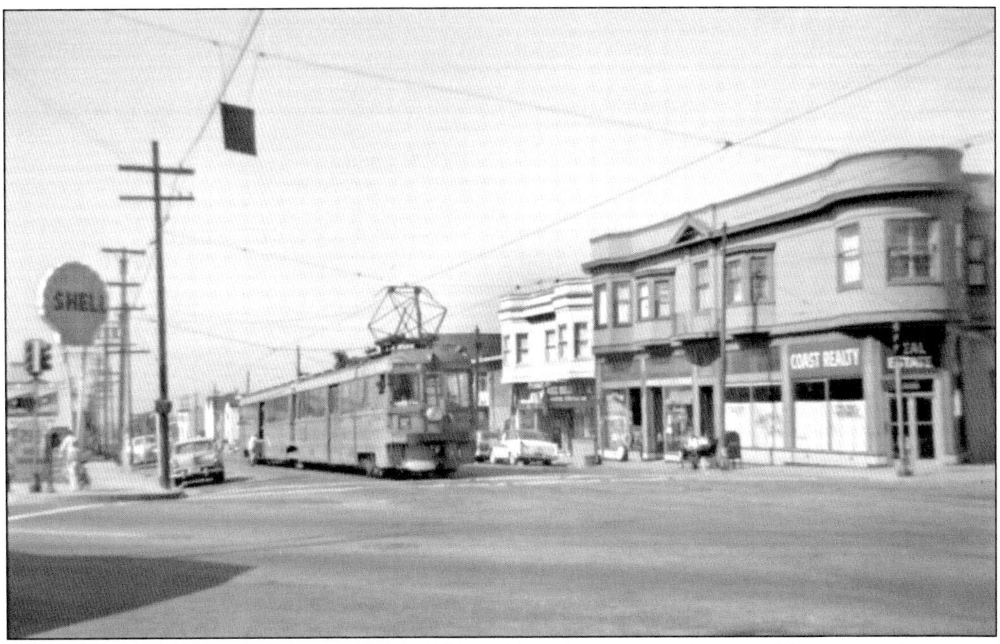


**INTERURBAN TRAIN.** Here Key System Unit 182 is shown traveling on Claremont Avenue at the intersection with College Avenues on the last day of service April 19, 1958. The Shell gas station is on the left and Coast Realty is on the right of the train. (Courtesy John Harder, John Harder photograph.)

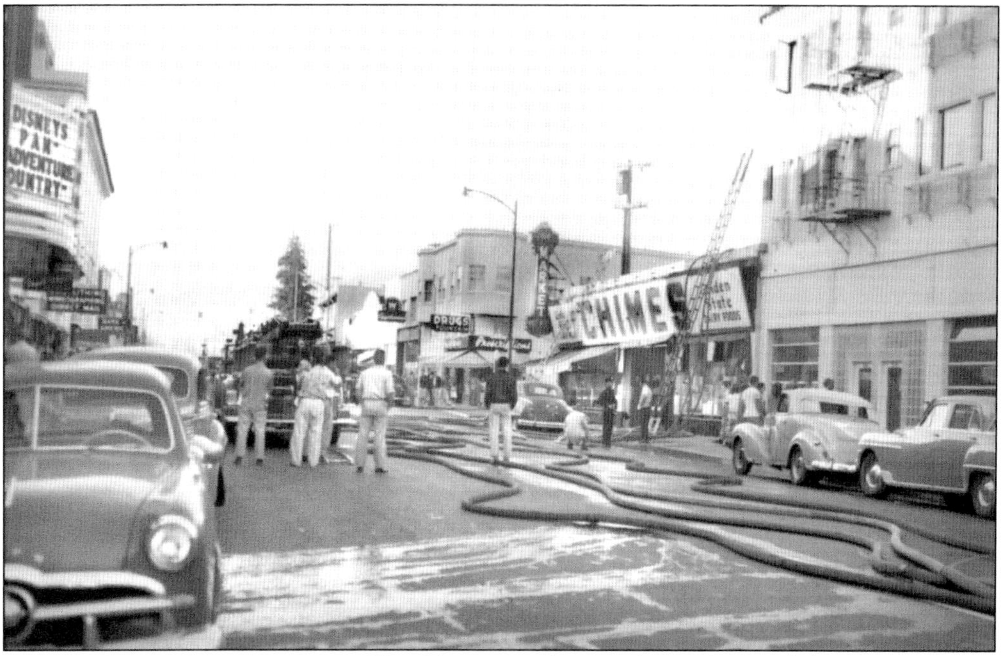


**FIRE AT CHIMES MARKET, 1953.** The Chimes Market was located several doors south of the Chimes Theater on College Avenue. The market burned in a major fire in 1953. (Courtesy Jennifer Dowling, Bob Arnold photograph.)

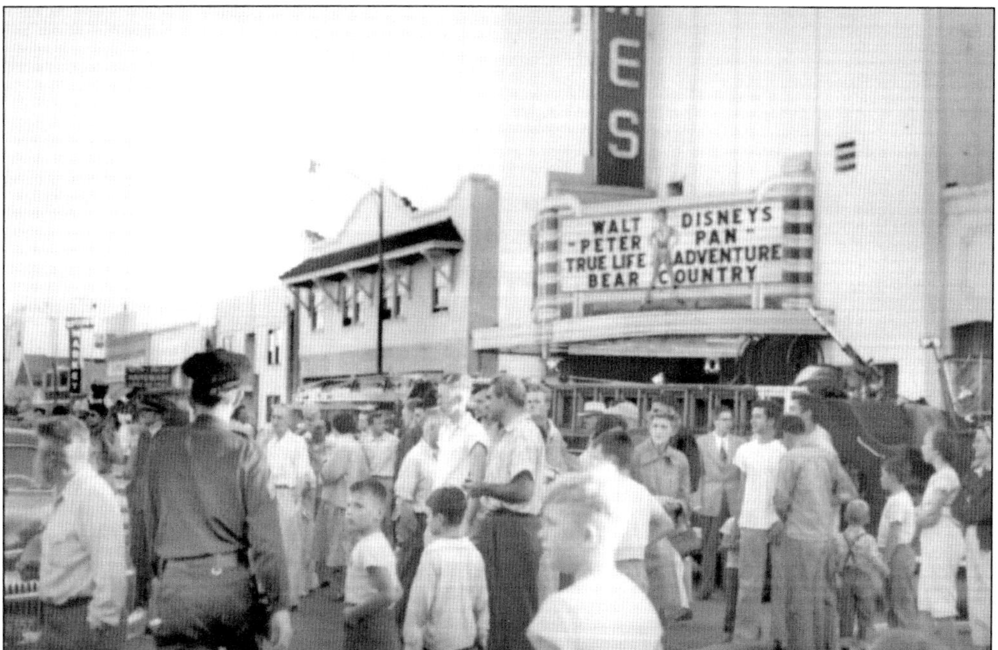


**CHIMES THEATER, 1953.** When word of the Chimes Market fire reached theater patrons, they poured into the street to watch the conflagration. The Chimes Theater was showing Disney's *Peter Pan* at the time. The Chimes Theater had reverted to its original name after being known as the Uptown Theater in the 1930s. (Courtesy Jennifer Dowling, Bob Arnold photograph.)

# *Six*

# ARTS AND CRAFTS

Rockridge has long had an attraction for artists. Probably most renowned was the group that became known as the Society of Six. Louis Siegriest, who lived on Miles Avenue and whose work is now collected by the Oakland Museum and whose personal papers and photographs are collected by the Smithsonian Institution, was a member of this group. Between 1910 and 1930, members met and painted in the hills of Rockridge. They felt blessed that the climate encouraged their specialty—outdoor painting.

Selden Gile was the leader of the group, and besides Siegriest, members included August Gay, Bernard von Eichman, William Clapp, and Maurice Logan. Most of them lived and painted in Rockridge. On weekends, they would gather to paint in the orchards near the Chabot Road home of Selden Gile. In the evening, Gile would cook dinner, and they might be joined by Jack London and Ambrose Bierce. After dinner, they would critique each others' paintings of the day. The Society of Six was a group of *plein air* painters who painted only outdoors and completed a painting in a single sitting without touching up back at the studio. They painted both landscapes and buildings with an eye to the way natural light played on the landscape.

In the early 1920s, the California College of Arts and Crafts (now the California College of the Arts) moved to Rockridge, taking over the estate of James Treadwell. The students and faculty formed work crews to refurbish the mansion and grounds, which were in a state of disrepair. Struggling Rockridge artists often found artistic nourishment and employment at the school. The mansion still stands and serves now as Macky Hall.

Peter Bosko, an alumnus of the California College of Arts and Crafts, returned home from World War II and used loan guarantees in the GI Bill to purchase a College Avenue business and turn it into Bosko's Picture Framing and Gallery. During the late 1940s and 1950s, Bosko's Gallery was the venue for a series of noted exhibits by major artists, including Rockridge's Louis Siegriest and Lundy Siegriest.

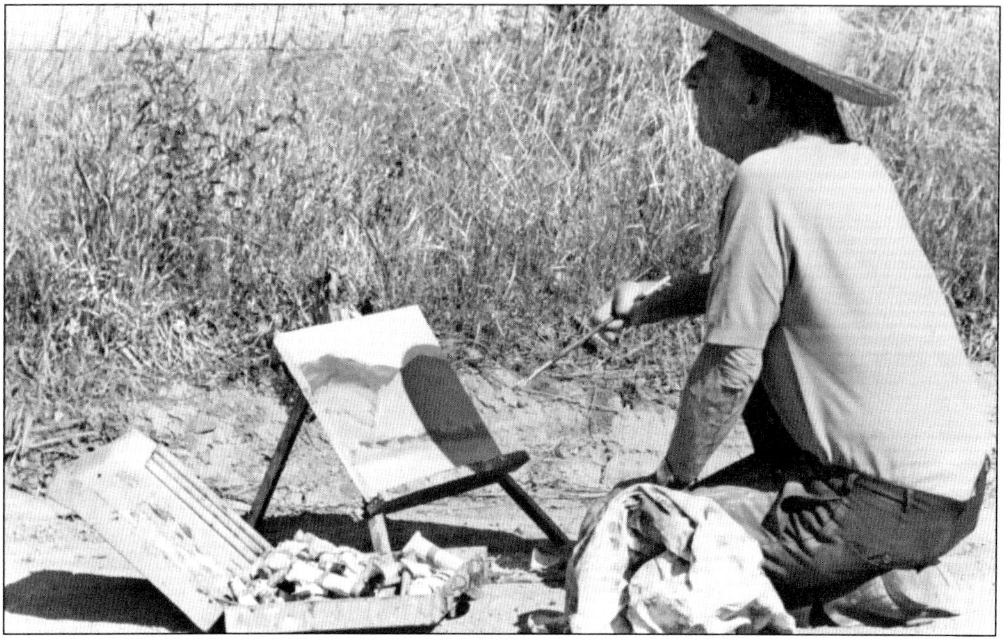

**LOUIS SIEGRIEST, 1978.** Louis Siegriest is a well-known artist who both lived and painted in Rockridge. His work is now collected by the Oakland Museum. Here Siegriest is shown kneeling and painting on a short easel in the countryside of Rockridge. In the second and third decades of the 20th century, Louis Siegriest painted with the Society of Six in the Rockridge hills, including Selden Gile, Bernard von Eichman, August Gay, William Clapp, Maurice Logan, and the youngest member, Louis Siegriest. (Courtesy Louis Siegriest estate, Peter Brown photograph.)

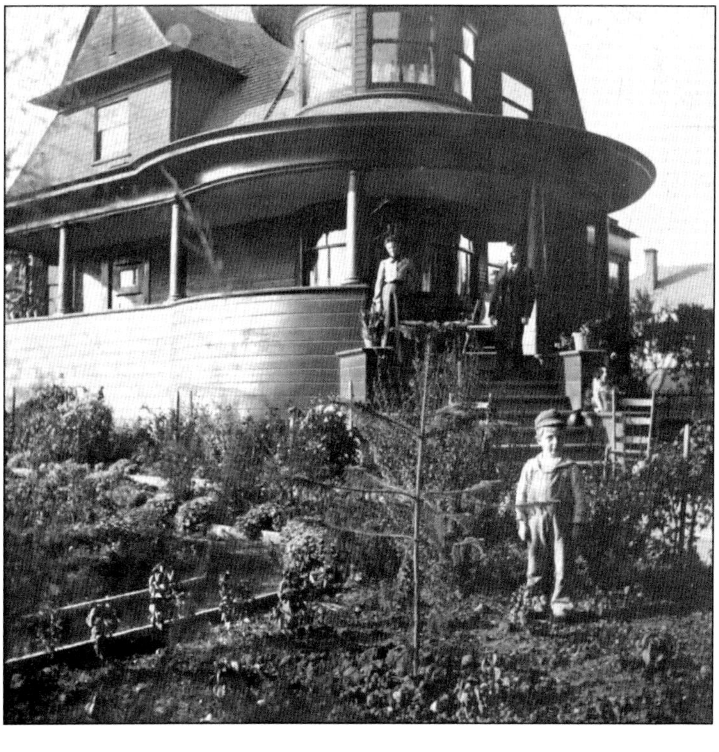

**LOUIS SIEGRIEST HOME, 1903.** Artist Louis Siegriest is shown here as a child with his father, Louis Napoleon Siegriest, and mother, Amelia, at their home on the corner of Miles Avenue and Cavour Street in the western part of Rockridge. Artist Louis Siegriest lived in this home until he died. When young Louis was a teenager, he was introduced to artist Selden Gile, the leader of the Society of Six artists, who had a studio around the corner on James Avenue. (Courtesy Louis Siegriest estate.)

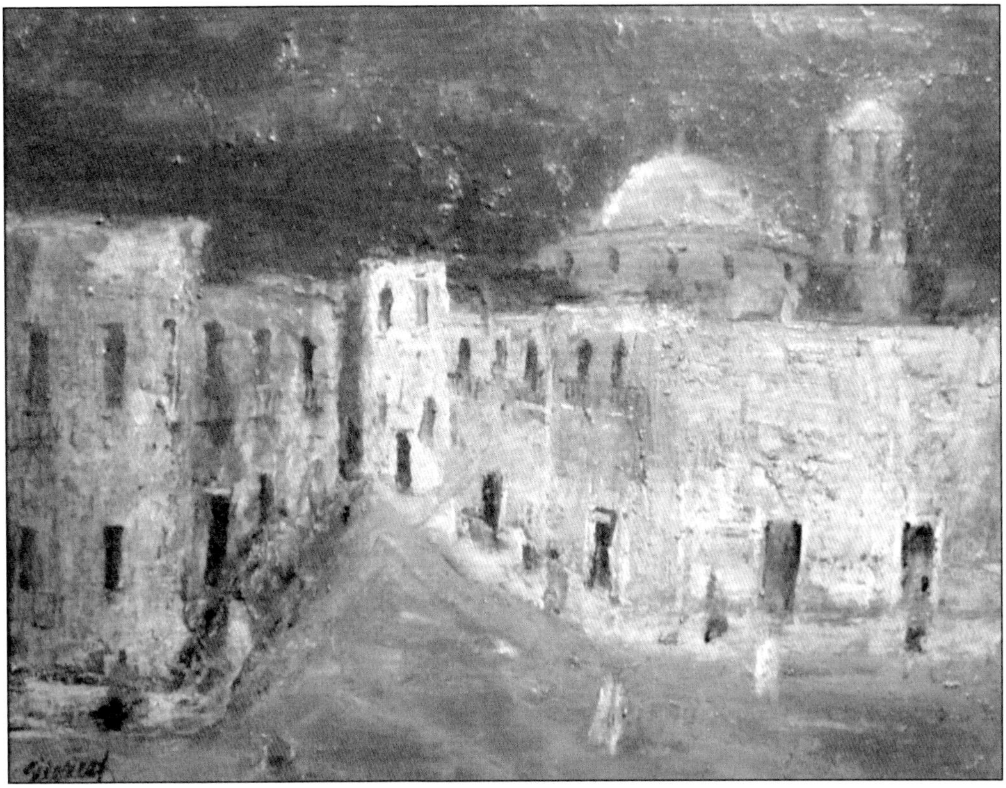

**GUANAJUTO, 1955.** In addition to painting scenes in Rockridge and other parts of Oakland, Louis Siegriest traveled internationally to find additional subjects for his painting. Siegriest and the Society of Six used a style of painting known as *plein air*, in which painting was always done outside, not in the studio. The subjects of *plain air* painters were outdoor structures, such as buildings or landscapes. (Courtesy Louis Siegriest estate.)

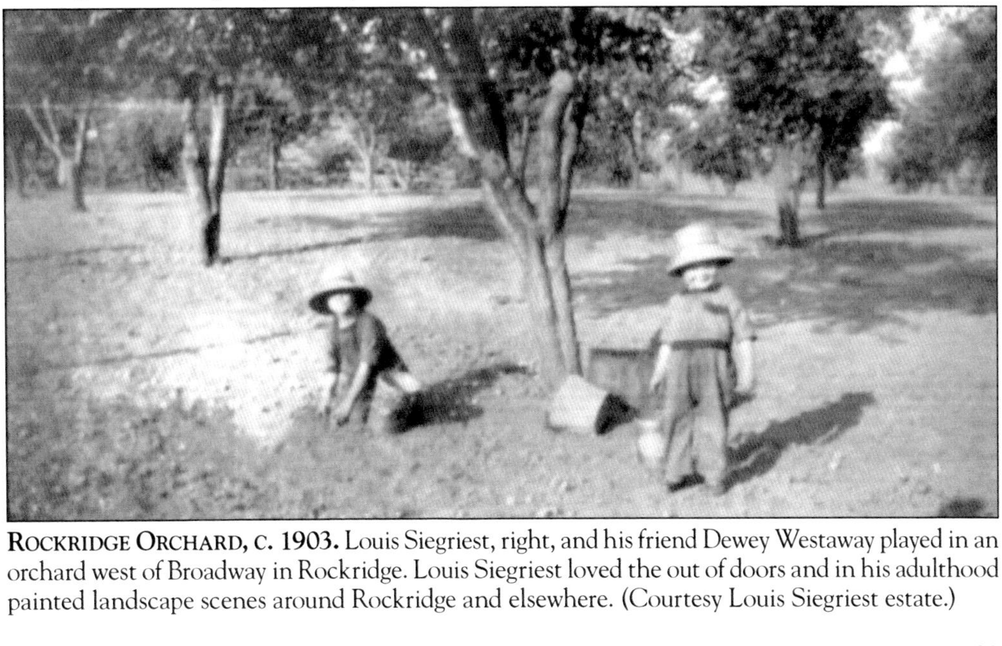

**ROCKRIDGE ORCHARD, C. 1903.** Louis Siegriest, right, and his friend Dewey Westaway played in an orchard west of Broadway in Rockridge. Louis Siegriest loved the out of doors and in his adulthood painted landscape scenes around Rockridge and elsewhere. (Courtesy Louis Siegriest estate.)

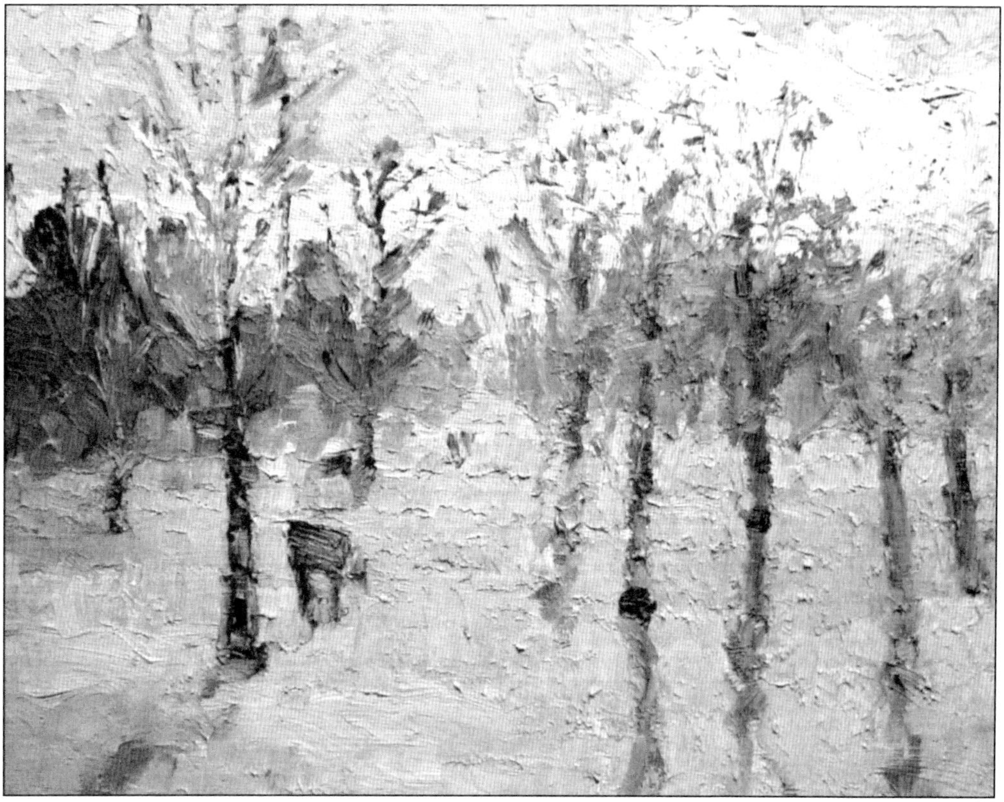

**NORTH OAKLAND ORCHARD, 1926.** Artist Selden Gile painted this scene of an orchard near his Chabot Road cabin. The orchards and fields around Chabot Road were a favorite location for the Society of Six to paint on weekends. The artists liked the way natural light in Rockridge illuminated the landscape. Rockridge weather was mild and provided many days of outdoor painting. (Courtesy Louis Siegriest estate.)

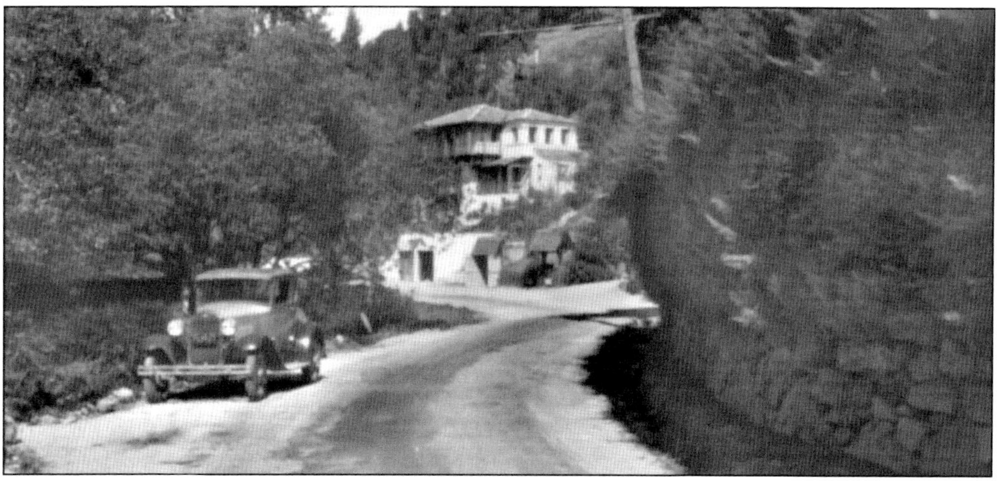

**CHABOT ROAD, 1931.** This is the road on which Selden Gile, leader of the Society of Six, lived in a cabin, not shown. When this photograph was taken in 1931, Chabot Road was still a dirt lane in the countryside. At Gile's cabin, the Society of Six gathered on weekends to have dinner, sometimes with Jack London and Ambrose Bierce. (Courtesy Louis Siegriest estate.)

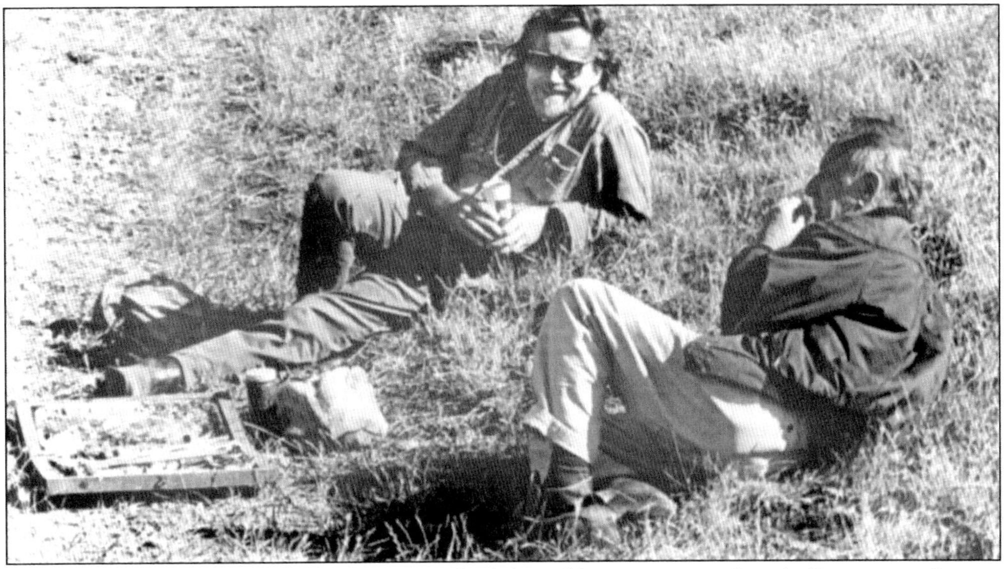

**Taking a Break, 1970.** Louis Siegriest (right) and his son, artist Lundy Siegriest, relax on the grass, taking a break from painting out of doors. A canvas is seen at their feet. They were comfortable in their outdoor painting environment. (Courtesy Louis Siegriest estate, Peter W. Brown photograph.)

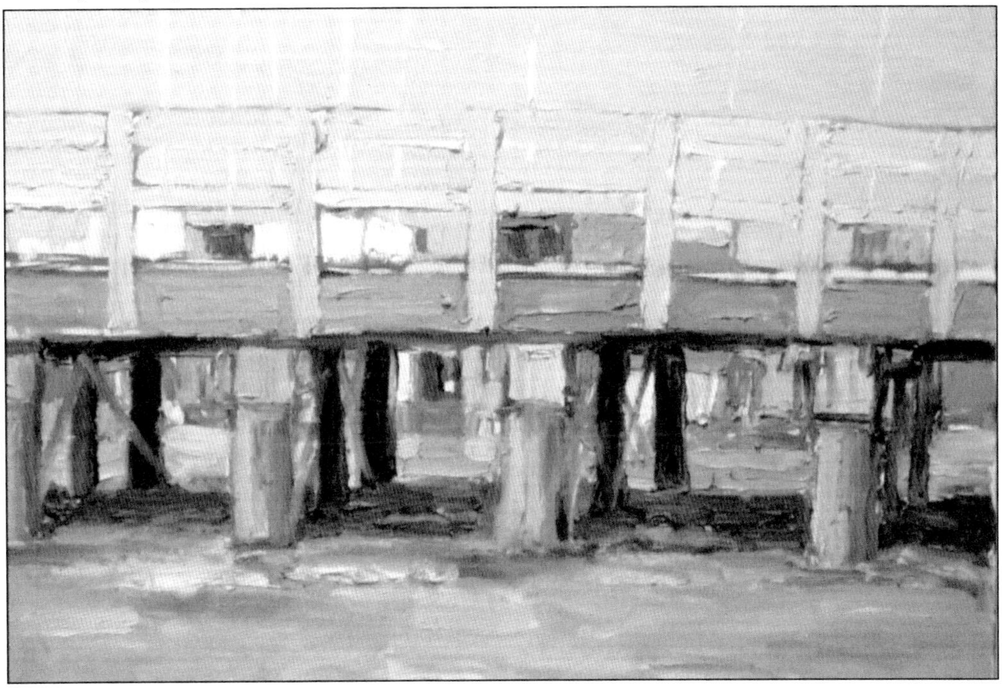

**Untitled Landscape, 1978.** This painting by artist Lundy Siegriest was done at the Fifth Avenue Marina in Oakland. The marina has long been a gathering place for Oakland artists. Like his father, Louis Siegriest, Lundy painted in the *plein air* style. This approach was a reaction to the stylized landscapes popular at the time that often used shades of brown. In contrast, plain-air painting used bold color to capture what William Clapp called the "joy of vision." (Courtesy Louis Siegriest estate.)

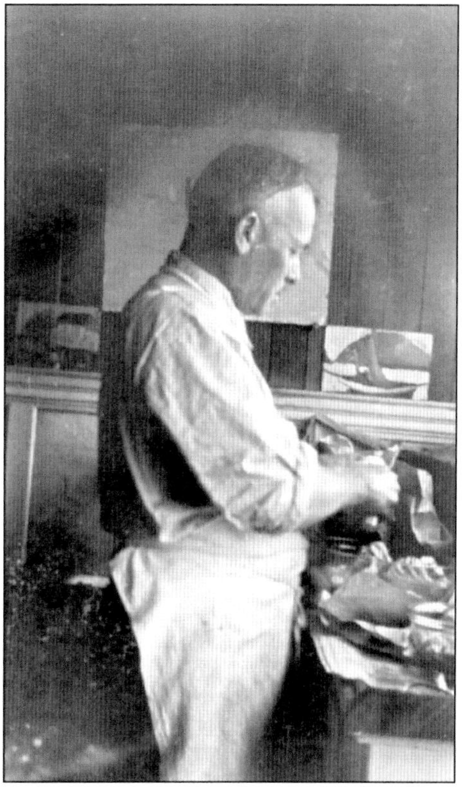

**SELDON GILE COOKING, C. 1920.** Selden Gile is cooking a weekend dinner for the Society of Six at his Chabot Road cabin. He moved to Chabot Road in 1916 from his earlier Rockridge home and studio on James Avenue. Dinner included red wine and was followed by critiques of paintings completed that day in the countryside around Chabot Road. *Plein air* paintings were typically completed in one sitting in a single day and not brought into the studio for retouching. (Courtesy Louis Siegriest estate.)

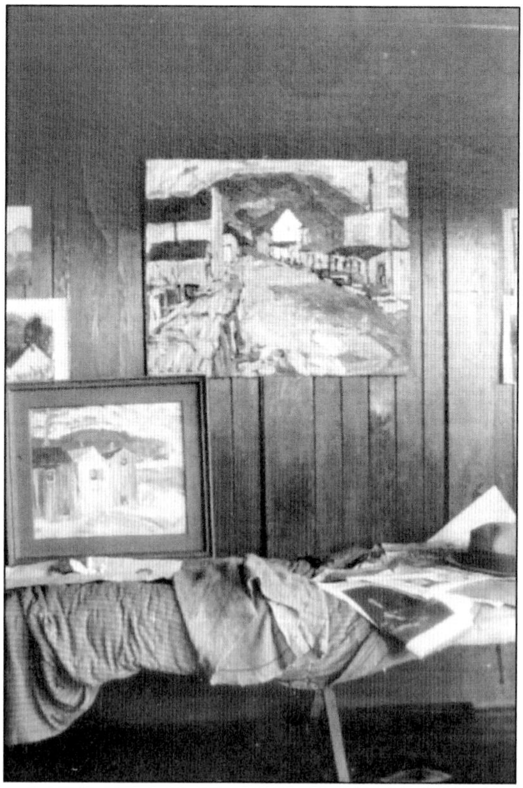

**SELDEN GILE'S BUNK, 1920S.** The cabin where the Society of Six met was more primitive than the comfortable homes now on Chabot Road. Selden Gile spent a decade hosting the Society of Six at his country cabin before moving to Marin County. *Plein air* painters from California represented what was untamed in the West. In the early part of the 20th century, Rockridge was still largely sparsely settled countryside. (Courtesy Louis Siegriest estate.)

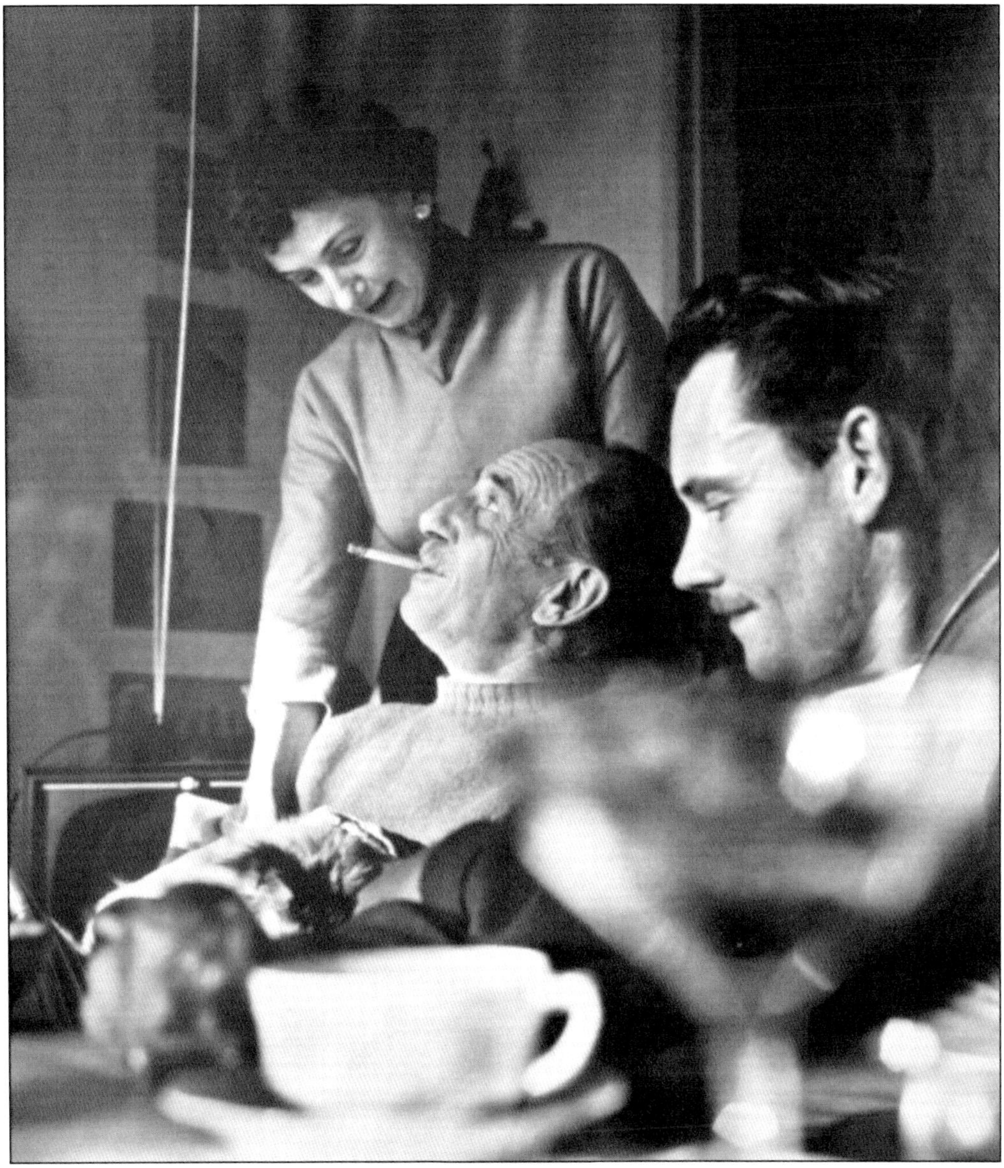

**SIEGRIEST AT KITCHEN TABLE.** Artist Louis Siegriest, center, sits with his wife, artist Edna Stoddart, and son, artist Lundy Siegriest, at the kitchen table of their Miles Avenue home. Louis Siegriest worked professionally as a graphic artist, even painting camouflage designs for military use in World War II. As a young man, his paintings were a weekend endeavor. (Courtesy Louis Siegriest estate.)

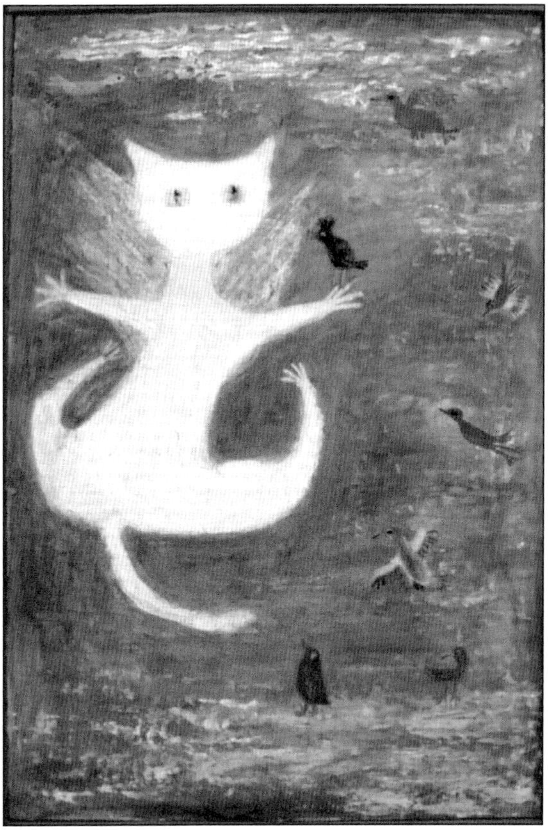

**Pussy Cat Angel, c. 1960.** Edna Stoddart, wife of Louis Siegriest, was a known artist. Here she captured a cat in a whimsical scene. Louis and Edna often welcomed students from California College of the Arts (then California College of Arts and Crafts) into their home on Miles Avenue. (Courtesy Louis Siegriest estate.)

**Treadwell Mansion, 1928.** In 1922, California College of Arts and Crafts purchased the four-acre estate of mining tycoon James Treadwell in order to move the college from downtown Berkeley to Rockridge. Enrollments increased at the earlier campus after veterans returned home from World War I and a larger facility was needed. James Treadwell had the stone fence and stair entrance built, which can still be seen on Broadway. (Courtesy the archives of California College of the Arts, Meyer Library; copyright © California College of the Arts.)

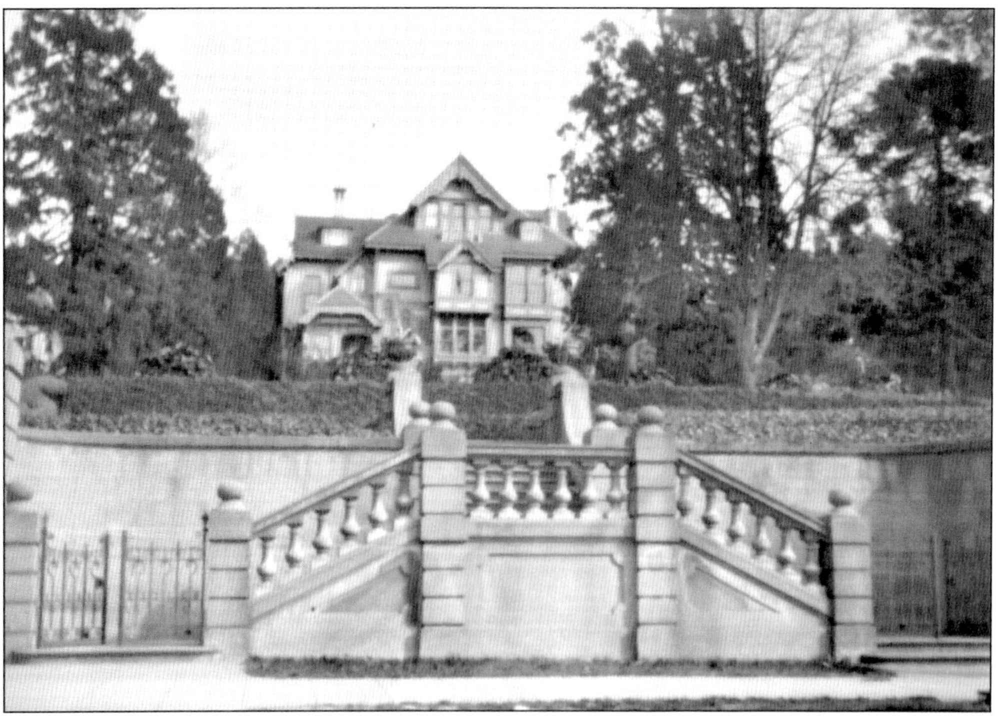

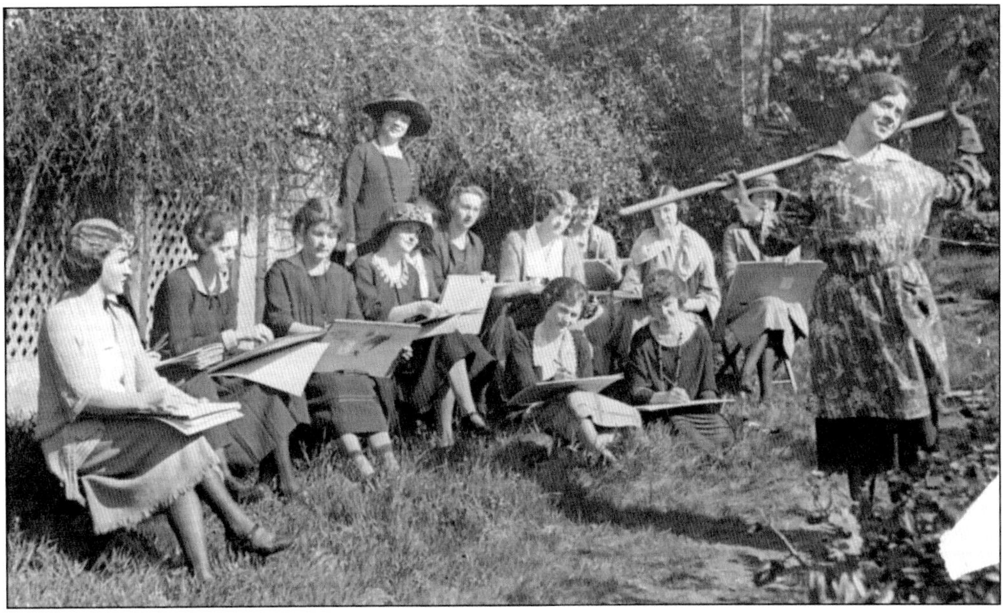

**SKETCHING CLASS, 1923.** Students at California College of Arts and Crafts (now California College of the Arts) attend a sketching class beside the Treadwell mansion, now Macky Hall. The model stands in the foreground of the photograph holding a pole. (Courtesy the archives of California College of the Arts, Meyer Library; copyright © California College of the Arts.)

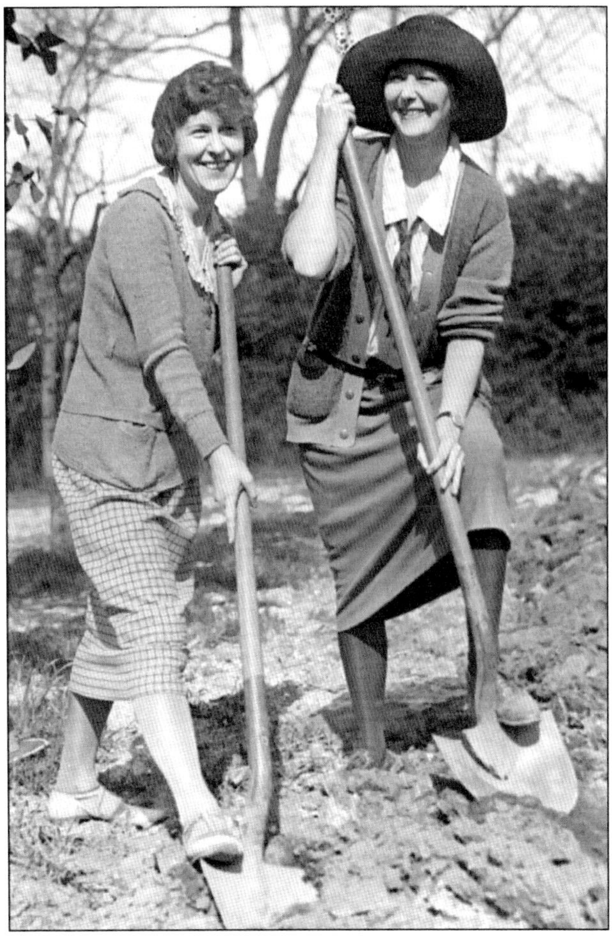

**CREATING A CAMPUS, 1923.** The Treadwell mansion and grounds were run-down when the California College of Arts and Crafts purchased it. During the next four years, work crews made up of students, teachers, and alumni labored to turn the estate into an attractive campus. College founder Frederick Meyer and his family also pitched in to work. Here two young women, Letitia Archambault (right) and Minerva Hogadone, take up shovels on Labor Day to work on the grounds. (Courtesy the archives of California College of the Arts, Meyer Library; copyright © California College of the Arts.)

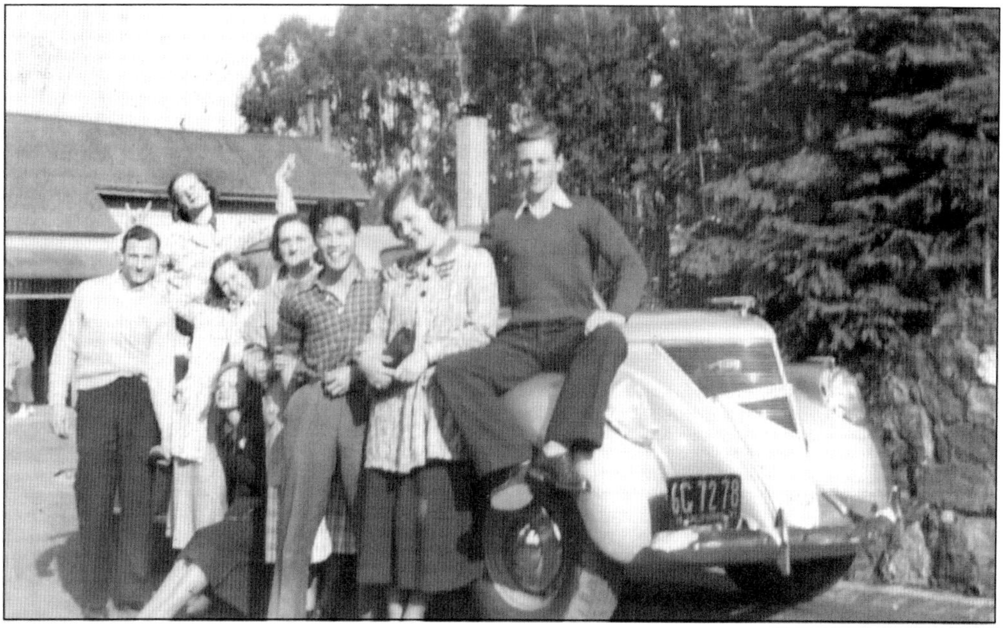


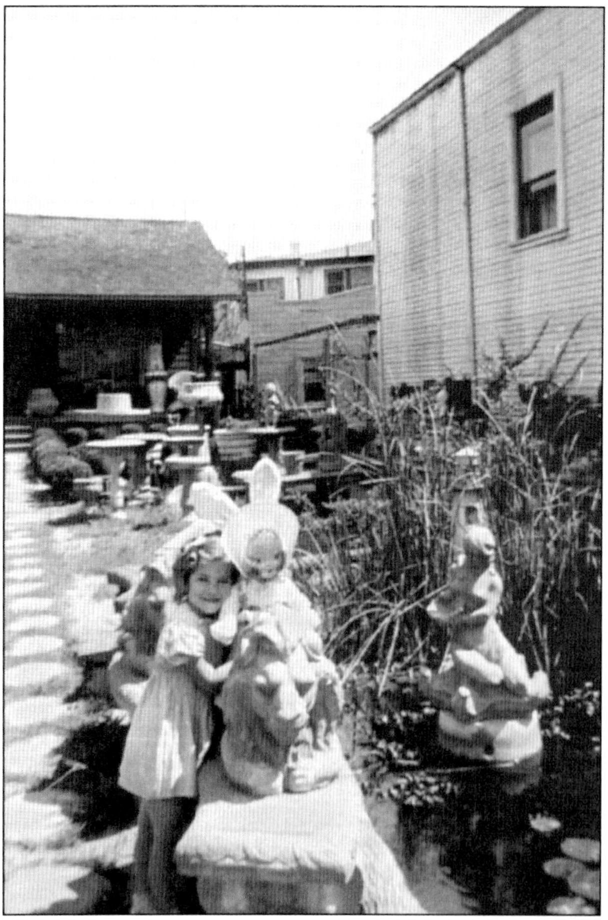

**ART STUDENTS, 1937.** Peter Bosko (far left) relaxes with fellow students on the campus of California College of Arts and Crafts. Peter Bosko later owned Bosko's Picture Framing and Art Gallery on College Avenue. (Courtesy John Bosko.)

**LONGO ART STONE AND POTTERY WORKS.** This chapter looks at Rockridge craftsmen artists in addition to painters. Raffaele Longo and family emigrated from Italy, bringing with them the techniques that they had used in their village to create statues and sculptures out of cement. Art Stone statues can be seen in the foreground, and in the background are birdbaths. (Courtesy the estate of Louis Follini Jr. and Barbara Maltvy Follini.)

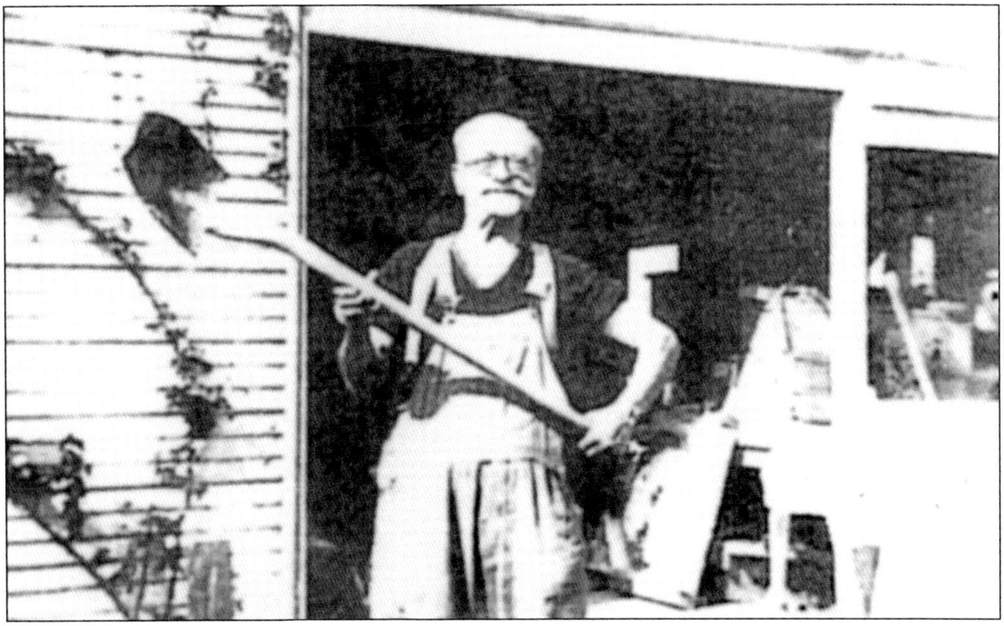

**RAFFAELE LONGO.** Raffaele "Pa" Longo gets ready to mix cement in front of the pottery shed on the Art Stone property. He and the family members who worked for him used both molds and a potter's wheel to shape cement into sculptures. (Courtesy the estate of Louis Follini Jr. and Barbara Maltvy Follini.)

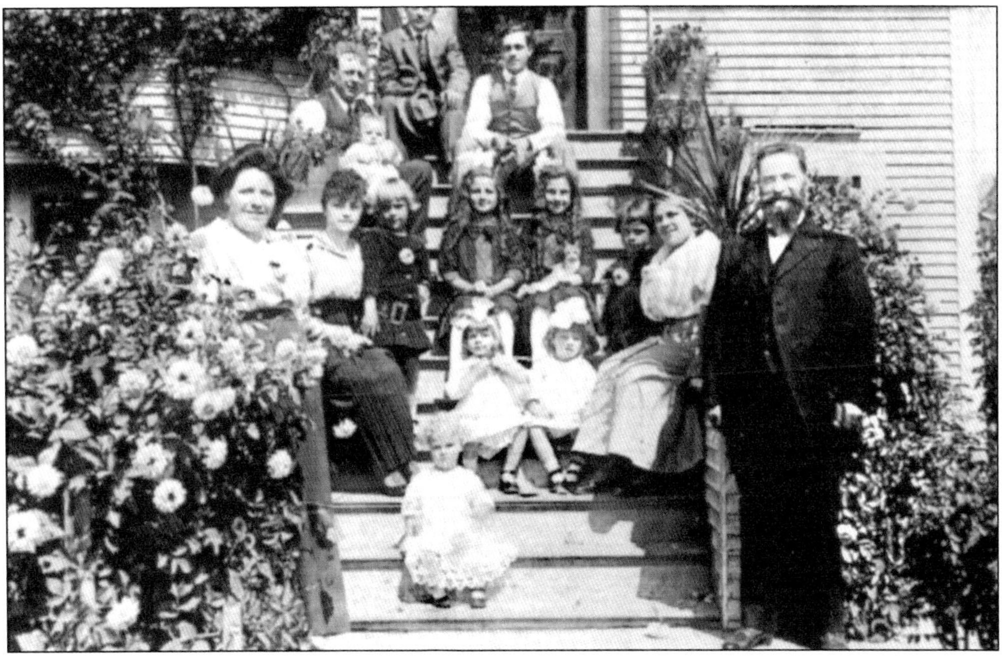

**LONGO FAMILY.** The Longo family stands on the front porch of their College Avenue house. It was typical in the early 20th century for families to live and work on the same property, either living above a store or, in this case, having a house next to the barn where the art stone sculptures were created. The Longo family lived in a house next door to their art stone business on College Avenue. (Courtesy the estate of Louis Follini Jr. and Barbara Maltvy Follini.)

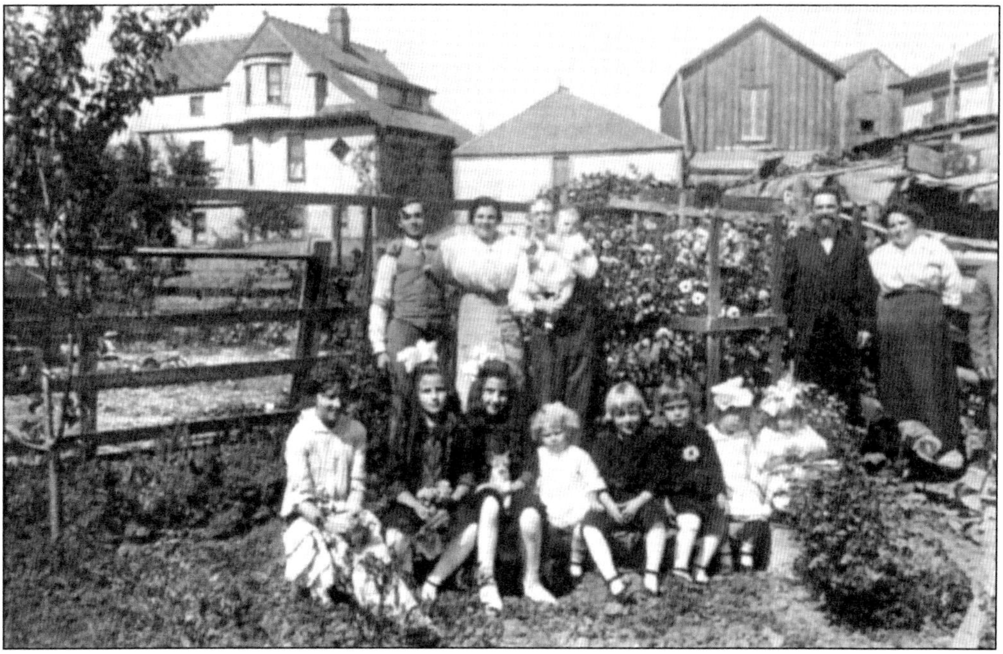

**BACKYARD OF ART STONE.** Longo family is shown in the backyard of the pottery works. The view looks east toward Broadway. A barn can be seen in the background. The family name Luongo in Italy was shorted to Longo when Raffaele immigrated to the United States. They had 11 children, and each one was taught to play a musical instrument. Raffaele organized the children into a band that played for family gatherings. (Courtesy the estate of Louis Follini Jr. and Barbara Maltvy Follini.)

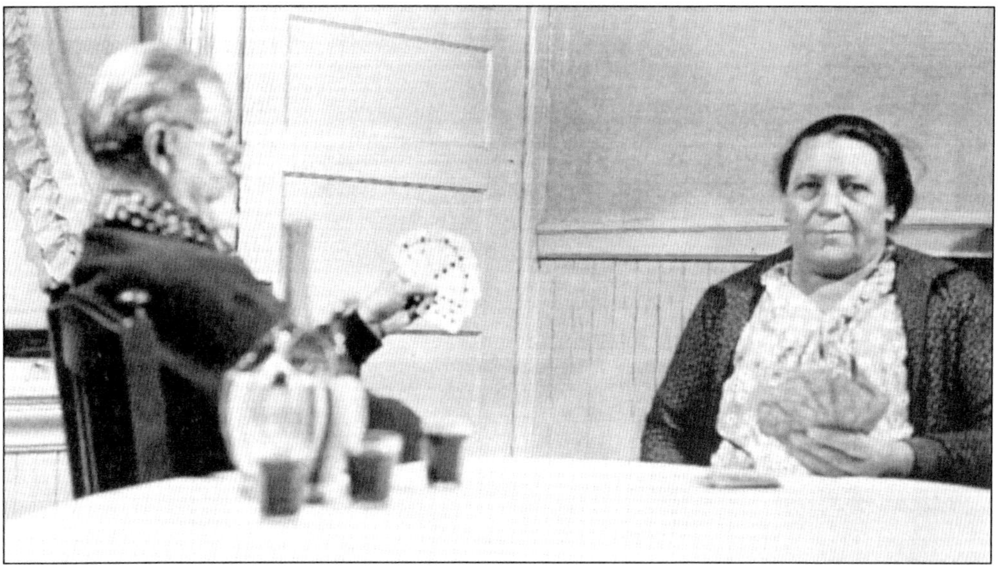

**PLAYING SCOPA.** Raffaele and his wife, Giuglia (Julia), are sitting in their kitchen in their house on the art stone property at College Avenue and Manila Avenue. They are playing an Italian card game, scopa. Raffaele had large vats of fermenting wine in the cellar of their home. Visitors drank wine out of cheese jar glasses (jars that cheese was sold in). (Courtesy the estate of Louis Follini Jr. and Barbara Maltvy Follini.)

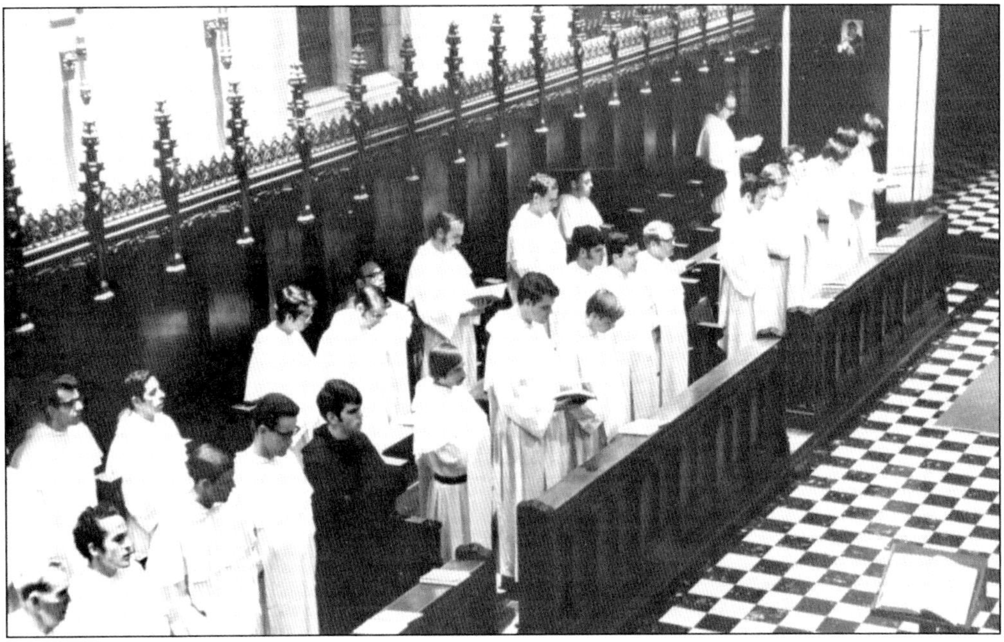

**St. Albert's Priory Chapel, 1950s.** The Dominican brothers are accomplished vocalists. Here they are shown in the chapel at St. Albert's Priory on College Avenue. The choir stalls were carved by German craftsmen. (Courtesy and © Western Dominican Province.)

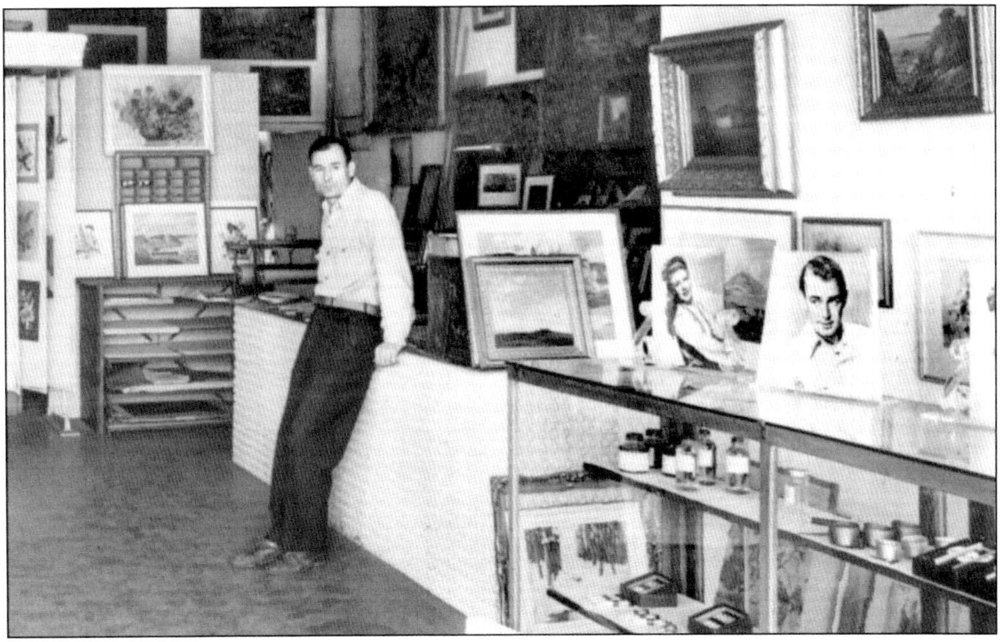

**Peter Bosko, Late 1940s.** Peter Bosko stands in Bosko's Picture Framing and Art Gallery on College Avenue. Bosko served in World War II in the early 1940s, then bought this gallery when the war ended, using a government-guaranteed loan provided through the GI Bill. A decade earlier in the 1930s, College Avenue business had been in a slump during the Great Depression. Business on College Avenue picked up after returning veterans bought businesses and infused new energy into College Avenue. (Courtesy John Bosko.)

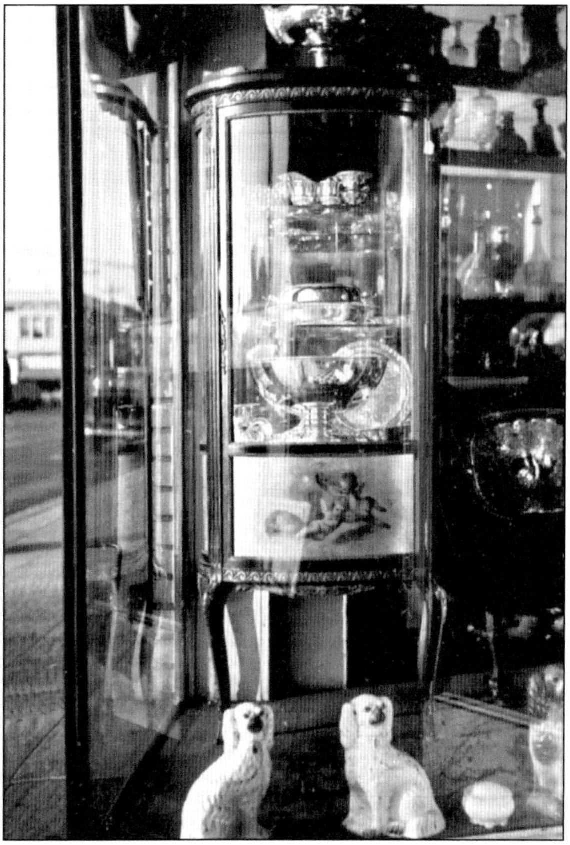

**EL CAPITAN ANTIQUE STORE, 1930.** A decade before Peter Bosko opened Bosko's Picture Framing Gallery on College Avenue, this antique store occupied the same space that Bosko would later use. College Avenue has a long history of attracting antique and collectible dealers, most of whom are now gone because of higher rents. (Courtesy Lynne Bosko.)

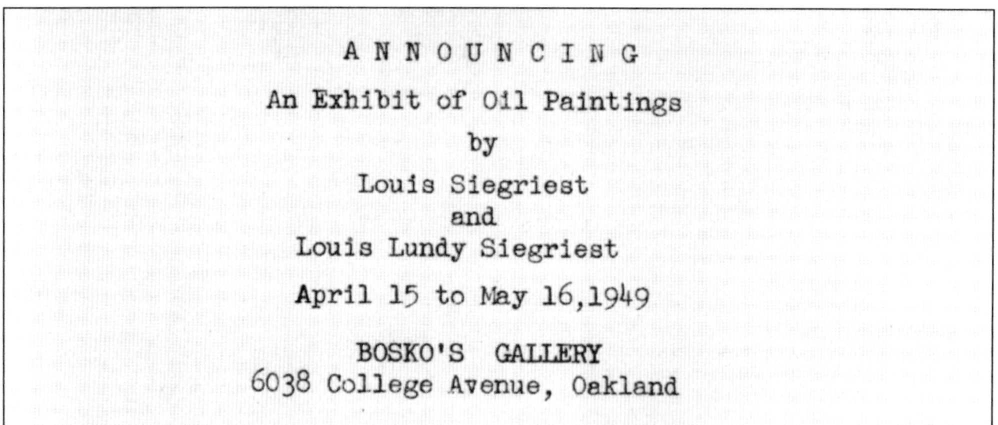

A N N O U N C I N G

An Exhibit of Oil Paintings

by

Louis Siegriest

and

Louis Lundy Siegriest

April 15 to May 16,1949

BOSKO'S GALLERY

6038 College Avenue, Oakland

Reception

Friday, April 15

From 7:30 to 10:30

**BOSKO ART SHOW ANNOUNCEMENT.** This hand-typed announcement from Bosko's Gallery on College Avenue says, "Announcing an Exhibit of Oil Paintings by Louis Siegriest and Louis Lundy Siegriest" in April 1949. Numerous artists showed their work at Bosko's Gallery. (Courtesy John Bosko.)

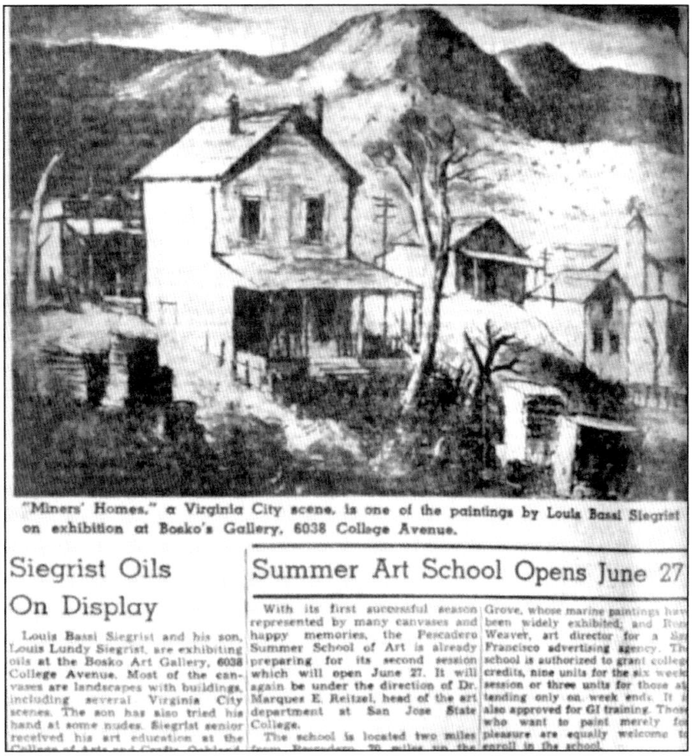

"Miners' Homes," a Virginia City scene, is one of the paintings by Louis Bassi Siegrist on exhibition at Bosko's Gallery, 6038 College Avenue.

## Siegrist Oils On Display

Louis Bassi Siegrist and his son, Louis Lundy Siegrist, are exhibiting oils at the Bosko Art Gallery, 6038 College Avenue. Most of the canvases are landscapes with buildings, including several Virginia City scenes. The son has also tried his hand at some nudes. Siegrist senior received his art education at the

## Summer Art School Opens June 27

With its first successful season represented by many canvases and happy memories, the Pescadero Summer School of Art is already preparing for its second session which will open June 27. It will again be under the direction of Dr. Marques E. Reitzel, head of the art department at San Jose State College.

The school is located two miles

Grove, whose marine paintings have been widely exhibited; and Weaver, art director for a Francisco advertising agency. The school is authorized to grant college credits, nine units for the six week session or three units for those attending only on week ends. It is also approved for GI training. Those who want to paint merely for pleasure are equally welcome to enroll in the school.

**NEWSPAPER ARTICLE ON ART SHOW.** Bosko's Gallery had numerous art exhibits with extensive newspaper coverage in the late 1940s and 1950s. Here an article describes a 1949 show of oil paintings by Louis Siegriest and his son, Lundy Siegriest. (Courtesy John Bosko.)

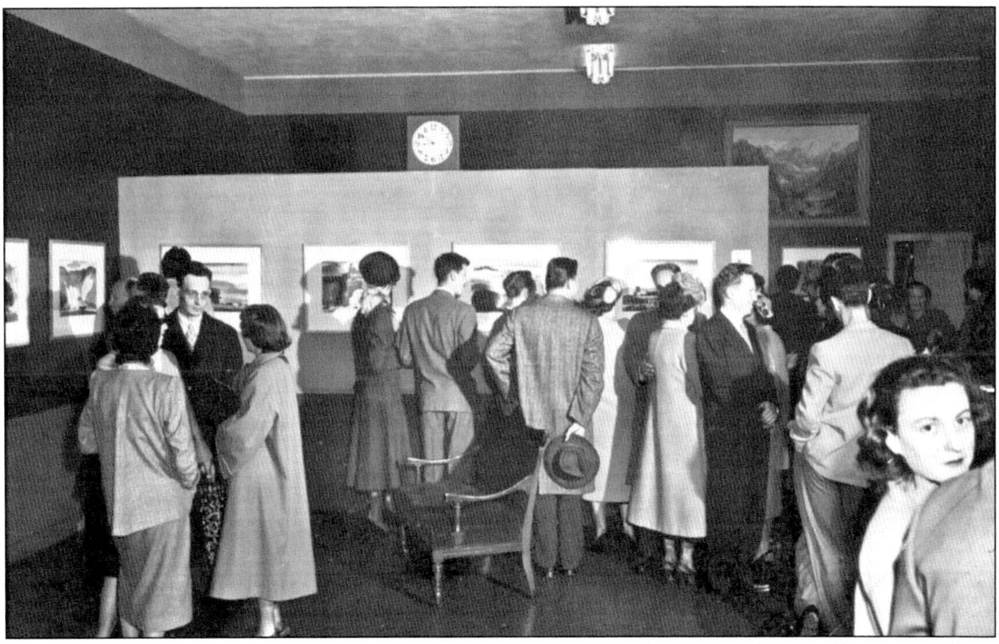

**SHOW AT BOSKO'S GALLERY, EARLY 1950S.** Here a crowd gathers at Bosko's Gallery on College Avenue to view the work of artist William Wintle. Rockridge has attracted artists since the early 1900s. College Avenue was a hub for art exhibitions in the late 1940s and 1950s. The presence of California College of the Arts has anchored Rockridge as a place to appreciate the arts. (Courtesy John Bosko.)

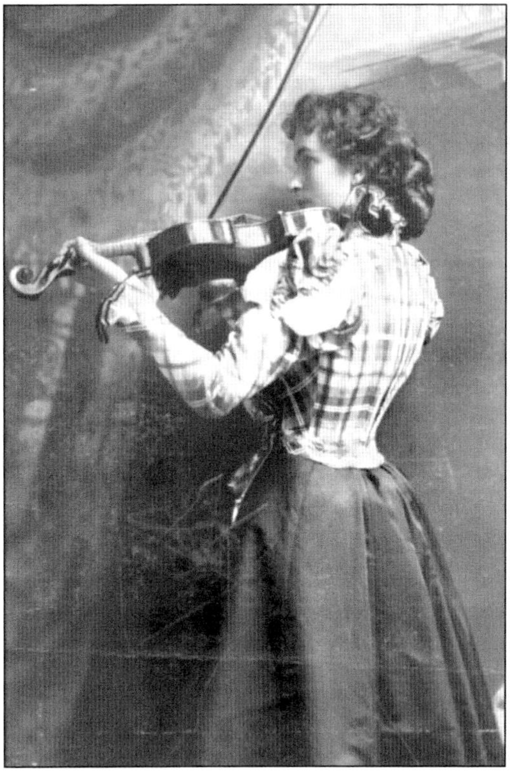

**WINIFRED PERRY, C. 1911.** Winifred Perry was the wife of Raymond Perry, who built a Rockridge mansion in 1910 nearby the Roselawn estate on Chabot Road. Here she is playing a violin in her home. Winifred was an artist who was known in the Rockridge area. (Courtesy Patricia Browne Arthur.)

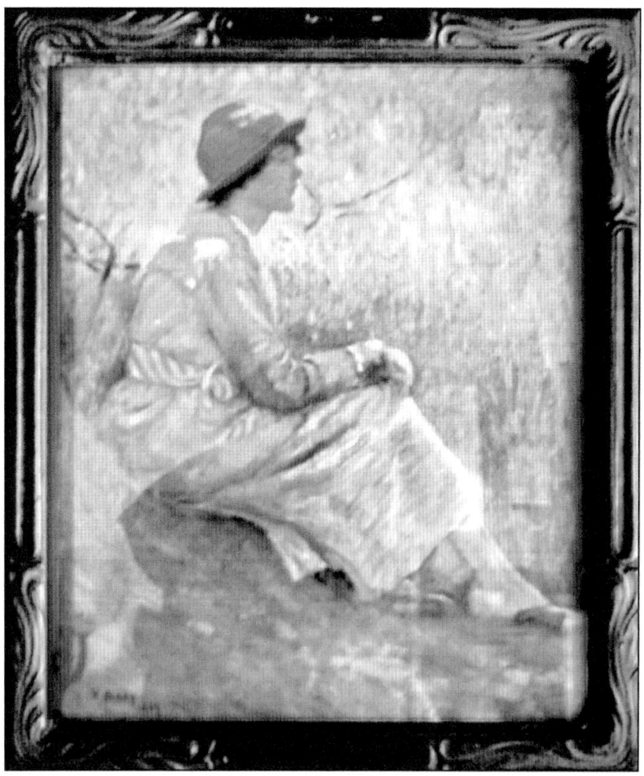

***SELF-PORTRAIT*, C. 1915.** This self-portrait of Winifred Perry was painted on her Chabot Road estate. Her work was frequently shown in local galleries. (Courtesy Patricia Browne Arthur.)

## *Seven*

# CHALLENGES

Rockridge has faced challenges over its history. In the Depression, the federal Works Progress Administration put unemployed people to work building the bathhouse at Lake Temescal. Because many of the houses in Rockridge were purchased in the 1920s by a cohort of young families, when America entered World War II, there were many families with sons of draftable age. Roger Heller, a Thomas Avenue resident and draftee who had recently graduated from Oakland Tech, today recalls knowing eight draftees from his neighborhood.

Differing visions of land use have repeatedly stirred debate on College Avenue. In the 1940s, controversy arose over the effort to get rid of the trains. The Vernon Rockridge Improvement Club, which in 1911 had campaigned to bring in the Sacramento Northern (then the Oakland, Antioch, and Eastern Railroad), a generation later lobbied to have it shut down. The 1950s saw the demolition of the Fortieth Street and Shafter train depot. The elevated tracks of BART were later built on the Sacramento Northern right-of-way down Shafter Avenue (now Miles Avenue).

Following World War II, College Avenue brightened with a wave of new shops opened by returning veterans using the GI Bill. The big public works project of the 1960s, construction of BART and the Grove Shafter Freeway, forced the demolition of many houses and brought a slump to College Avenue. This was compounded by the out-migration of residents to the Contra Costa County suburbs.

Prosperity returned, but numerous land use issues followed upon the opening of the BART station. The convenience of BART to San Francisco heightened Rockridge's appeal to young professionals who appreciated the charm of the bungalows that lined Rockridge streets. Their influx helped change College Avenue from a street of barbershops, laundries, shoe repairs, a bowling alley, and other service shops into a popular urban stroll of rated restaurants, independent bookstores, cafés, and boutiques. Advocates squared off on the merits of urban density and preservation. Home prices soared, and earlier generations who gave a working-class European ethnic cast to the neighborhood were less evident.

The 1991 Oakland firestorm destroyed more than 3,000 homes, most of them in Rockridge. Homes have been rebuilt and neighborhoods have recovered, but the photograph of the posted notes outside the Chimes Market on College Avenue, where people sought to meet up with relatives and friends, is a poignant reminder of that difficult period and the spirit of recovery.

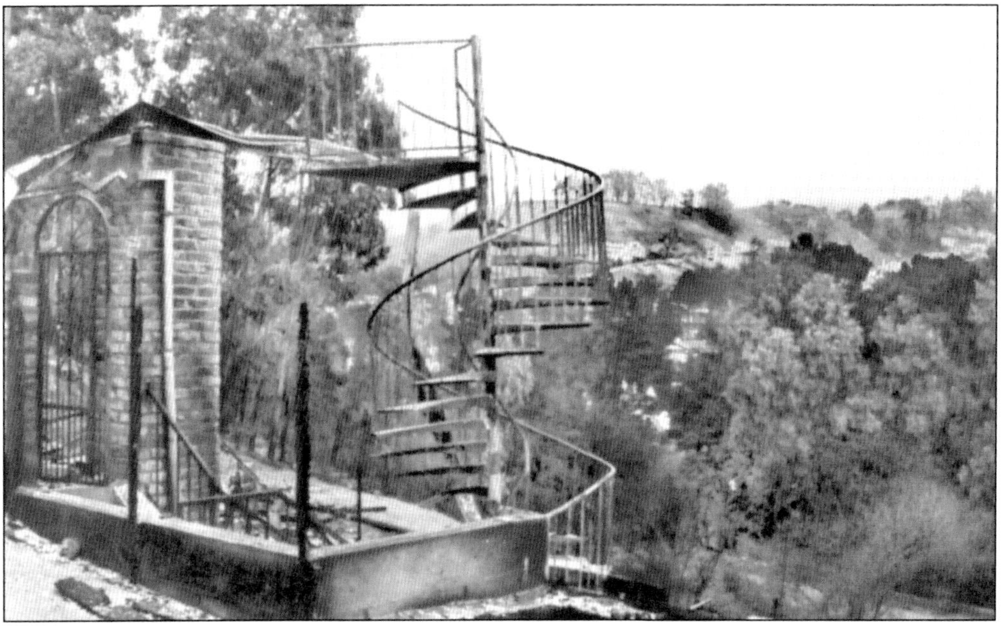

**OAKLAND FIRE.** The 1991 Oakland firestorm burned over 3,000 dwellings, most of them in Rockridge. Here a Rockridge house was burned, and only the metal stairwell still stands. The fire was one of a number of challenges faced by Rockridge over its history, and this chapter explores some of those challenges. (Courtesy Don Kinkead, Don Kinkead photograph.)

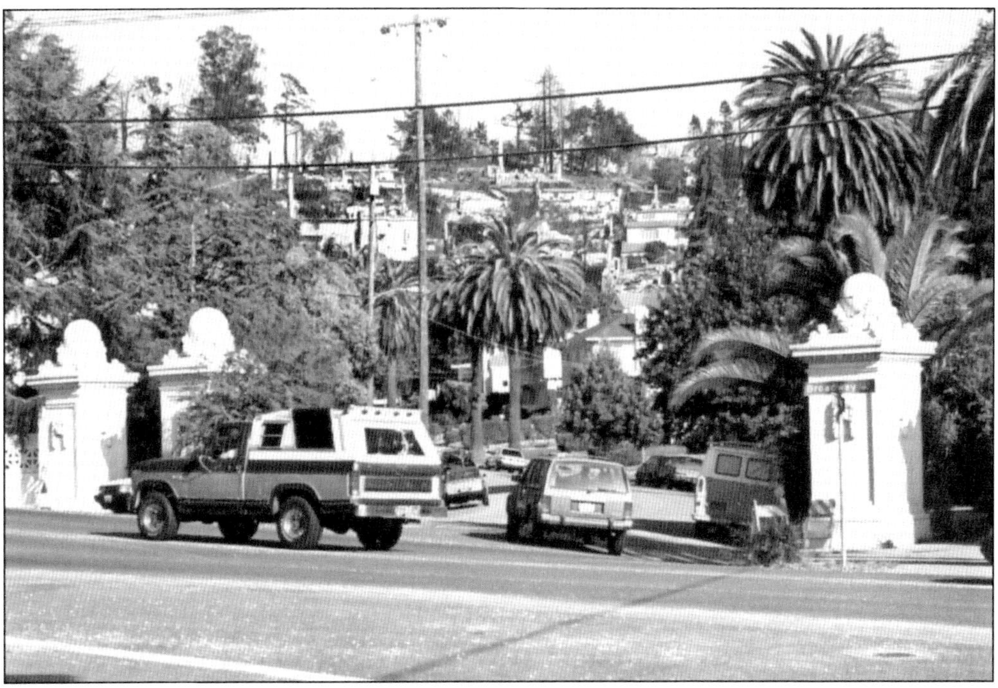

**BURNED HOMES, 1991.** This view is from Broadway looking east past the Renaissance Gates, up Rockridge Boulevard. The palm trees still stand near Broadway, but farther up the hill, houses have been burned to the ground. Only chimneys are still standing. (Courtesy Don Kinkead, Don Kinkead photograph.)

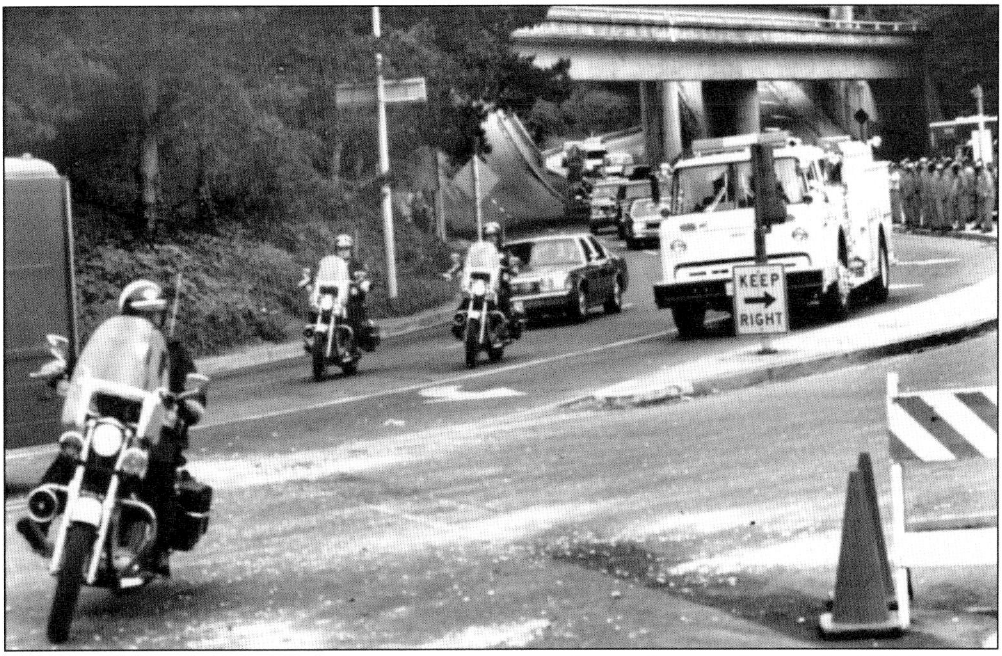


**POLICE RESPOND.** Motorcycle policemen accompany a fire truck responding to the 1991 firestorm in Rockridge. They are passing under Highway 24 on their way to the fire. (Courtesy Don Kinkead, Don Kinkead photograph.)

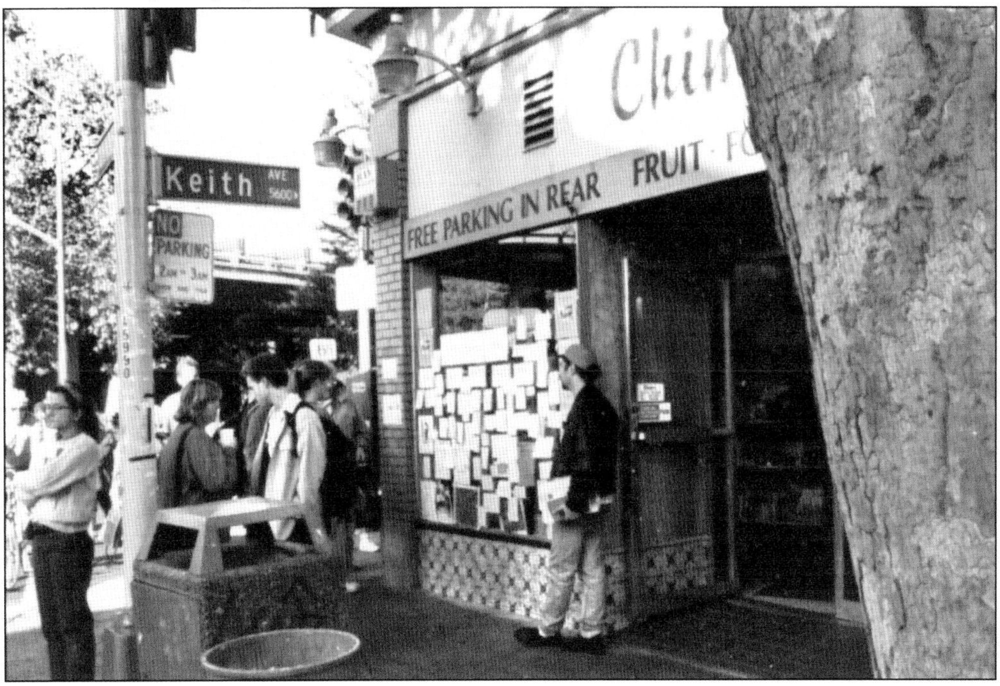


**FIRE BULLETIN BOARD.** After the 1991 fire, Chimes Market became a clearinghouse where Rockridge residents who were looking for friends or family members could leave a note. The community pulled together during the confusion that followed the fire. (Courtesy Don Kinkead, Don Kinkead photograph.)

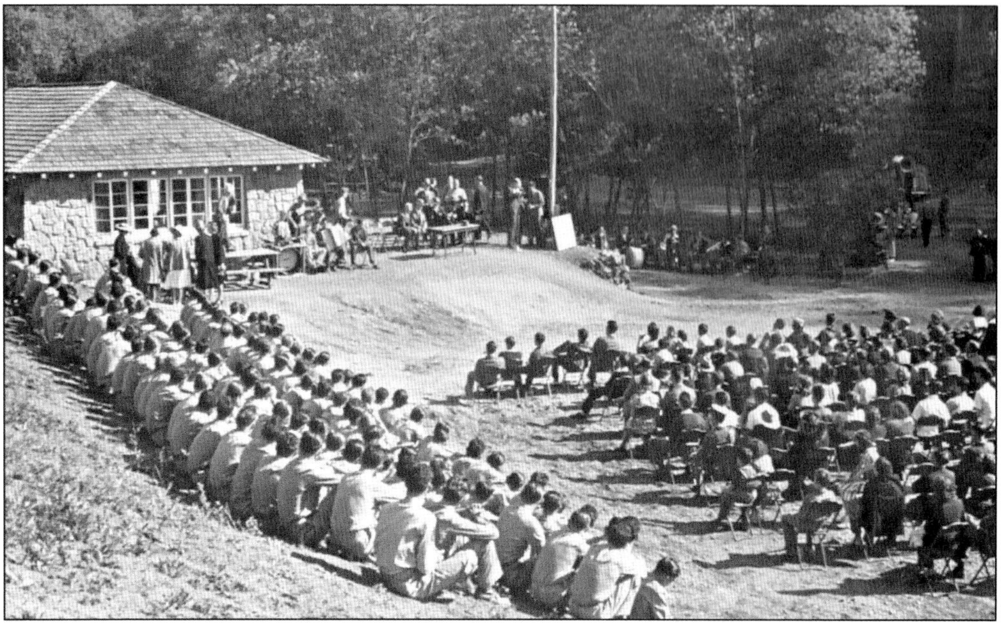

**STOCKING FISH, 1941.** During the Great Depression of the 1930s until the early 1940s, the federal government sponsored a Civilian Conservation Corps to put people back to work. Here the corps has gathered to stock fish in Lake Temescal. (Courtesy East Bay Regional Park District.)

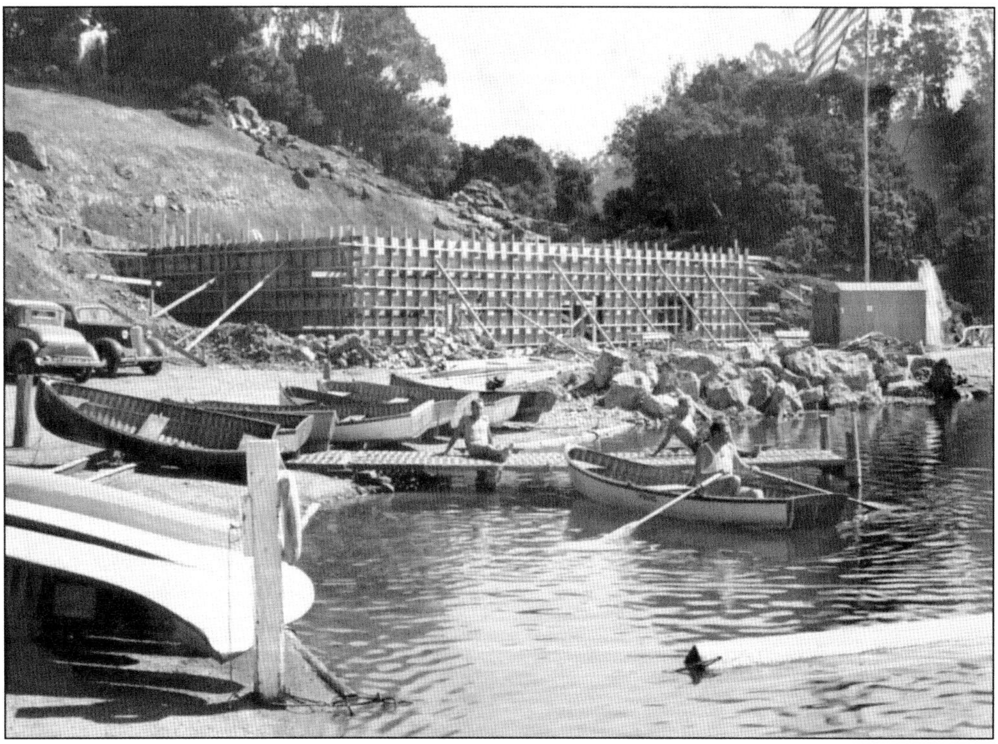

**BUILDING A BATHHOUSE, 1938.** Construction of the bathhouse at the northern end of Lake Temescal was another Depression-era project that provided jobs for out-of-work people. The bathhouse was a project of the Works Progress Administration (WPA). (Courtesy J. Kent.)

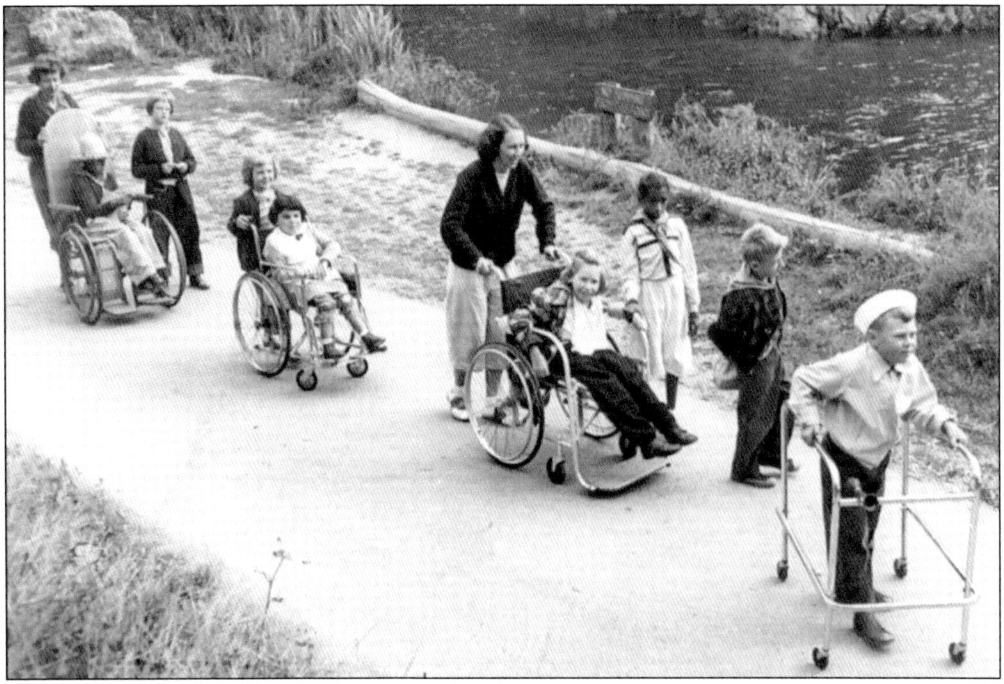

**TEMESCAL RECREATION.** Children with wheelchairs and walkers go on an outing at Lake Temescal. The photograph is from the 1950s when there was a polio epidemic, and these children may have been affected by polio. (Courtesy East Bay Regional Park District.)

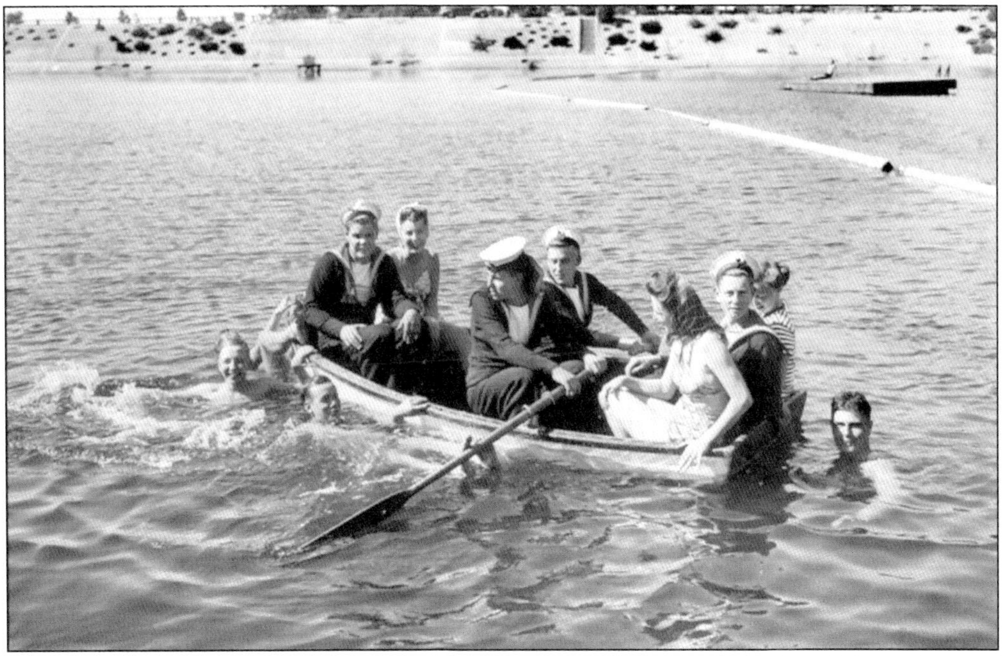

**SAILORS AT THE LAKE.** When the United States entered World War II in 1941, Oakland became a major port where soldiers and sailors shipped out for the war in the Pacific. Lake Temescal provided recreation for military personnel about to leave for war. (Courtesy East Bay Regional Park District.)

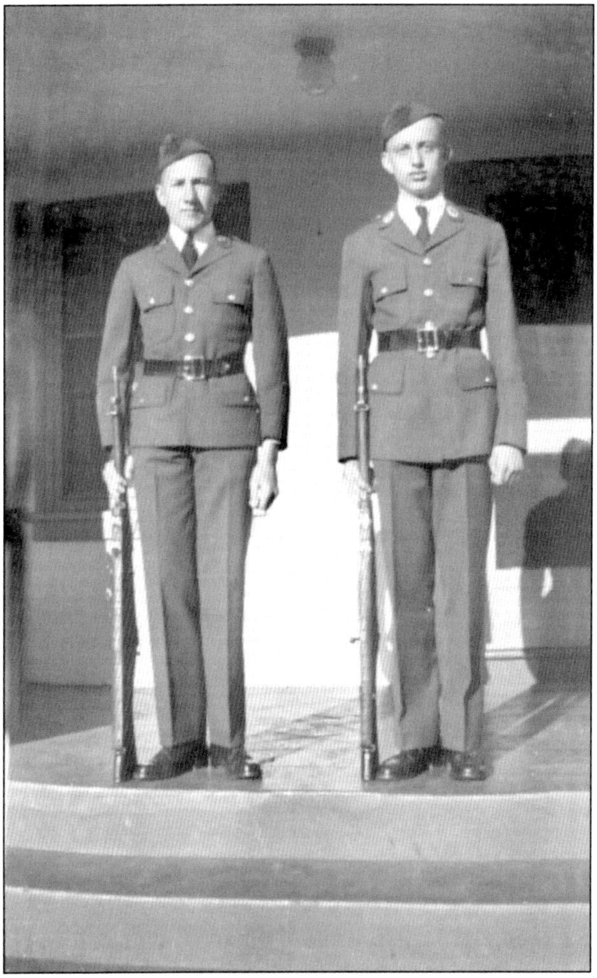

**ROTC AT TECH.** Roger Heller (right), a resident of Thomas Avenue, and a classmate took ROTC at Oakland Technical High School. They were drafted into World War II after graduation. Many of the houses around Thomas Avenue were built around 1920. By the time World War II arrived in the early 1940s, many families had sons old enough for military service. (Courtesy Roger Heller.)

**HALL PASS.** This hand-typed hall pass from Oakland Technical High School and dated 1940 allowed student Roger Heller to walk in the hallways at restricted times, which was a privilege. (Courtesy Roger Heller.)

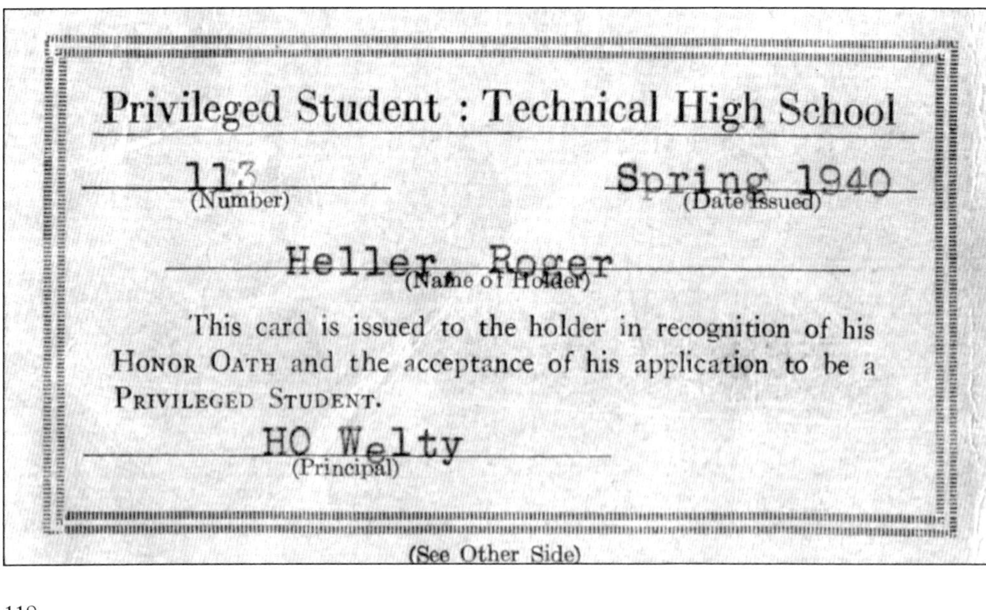

Privileged Student : Technical High School

113 (Number)

Spring 1940 (Date Issued)

Heller, Roger (Name of Holder)

This card is issued to the holder in recognition of his HONOR OATH and the acceptance of his application to be a PRIVILEGED STUDENT.

HO Welty (Principal)

(See Other Side)

OAKLAND TECH YEARBOOK. Paper was scarce during World War II. This Oakland Technical High School yearbook, produced in 1946 just after the war ended, dealt with the continuing paper shortage by limiting the book to 14 pages, meaning seven two-sided pages. (Courtesy Barbara Maltvy Follini.)

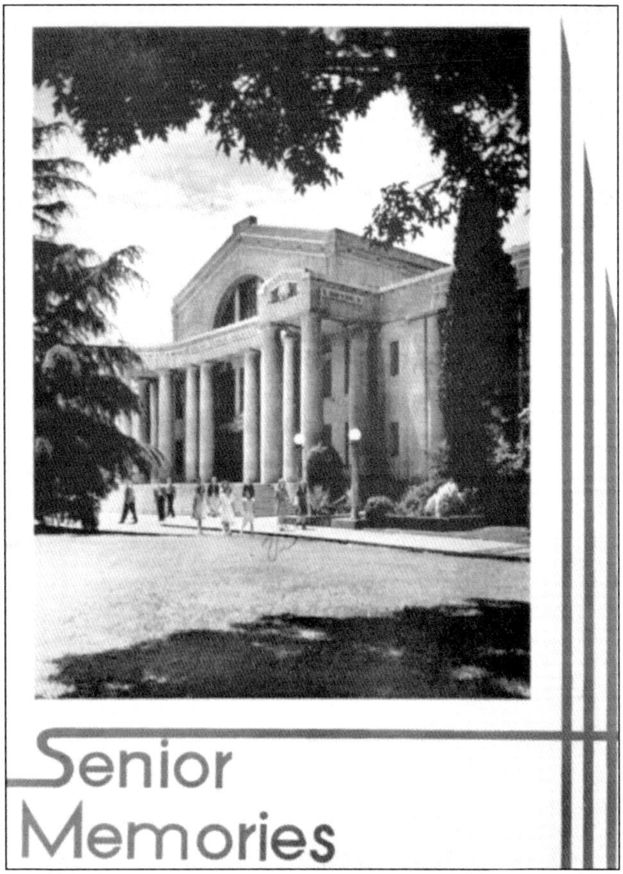


RELAXING AT HOME. William Larkins was home from World War II, sitting in his living room on Ocean View Drive. The Craftsman interior has natural-wood and leaded-glass doors on the bookcases. (Courtesy William Larkins.)

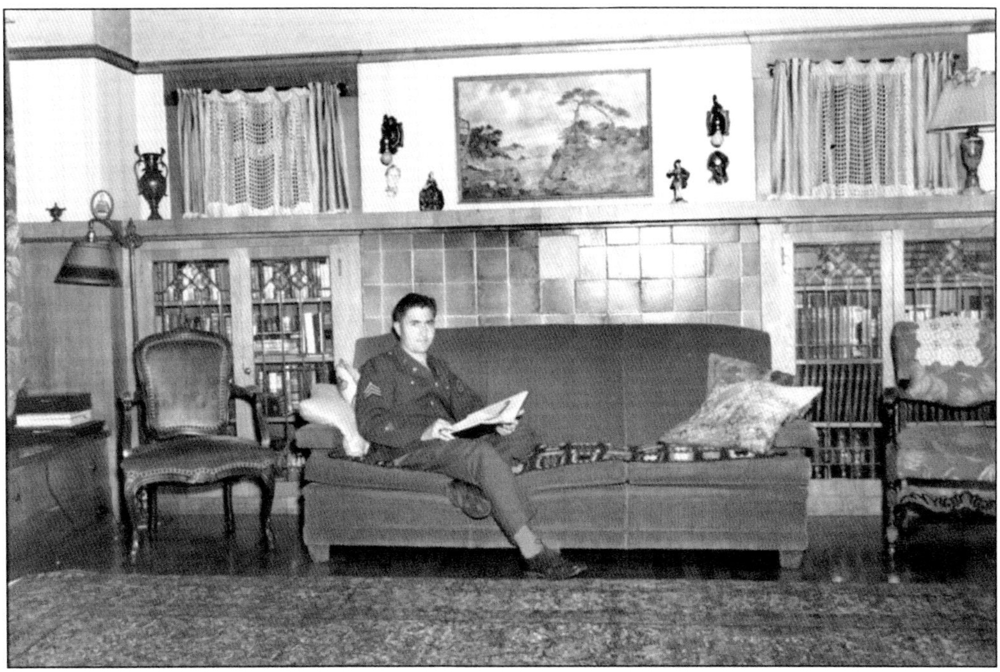

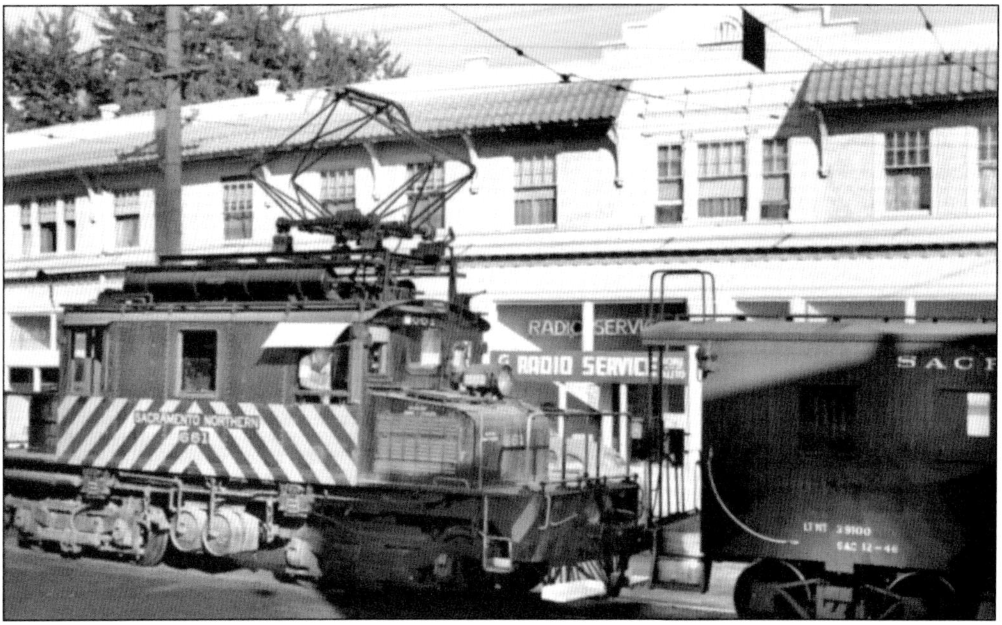


**SACRAMENTO NORTHERN FREIGHT TRAIN.** This freight engine is at the intersection of Shafter and College Avenues. After passenger service ended in 1941, freight service continued until 1957. The Sacramento Northern line connected with the Oakland Army Base and transported supplies for World War II from the Concord Naval Weapons Station. They were shipped to the action in the Pacific. (Courtesy William Larkins.)

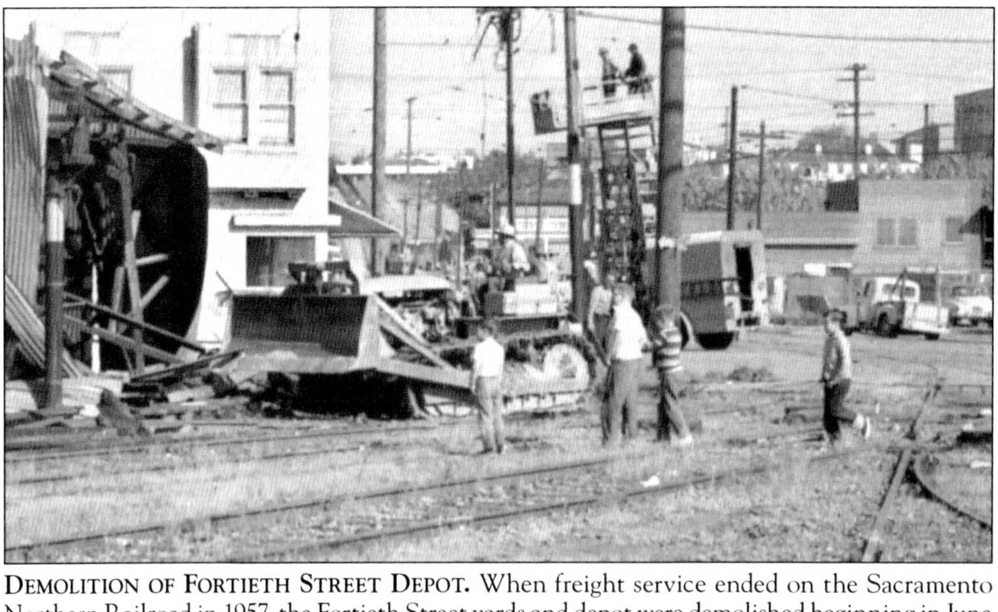

**DEMOLITION OF FORTIETH STREET DEPOT.** When freight service ended on the Sacramento Northern Railroad in 1957, the Fortieth Street yards and depot were demolished beginning in June of that year. Trains on Rockridge Streets had drawn complaints from neighbors as streets became crowded. Freight trains used two engines for added braking power. (Courtesy John Harder.)

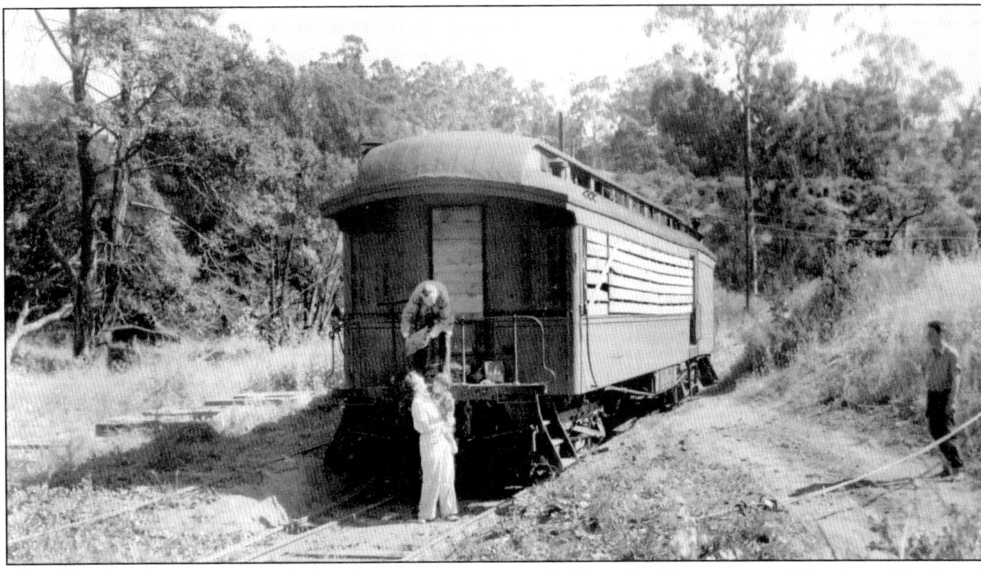

**RAILROAD CLUBHOUSE.** When passenger service ended on the Sacramento Northern Railroad, there were plans to convert this railroad car into a clubhouse for train enthusiasts. It is sitting on the rail spur behind Chabot School. This 1941 photograph shows Ralph Demoro, center, standing on the tracks and William Larkins standing to the right. Demoro's car, which is out of camera range, was used to position the railroad car on the track by towing it with a rope. To the disappointment of many, the railroad car was burned by vandals. (Courtesy William Larkins, Ralph Demoro photograph.)

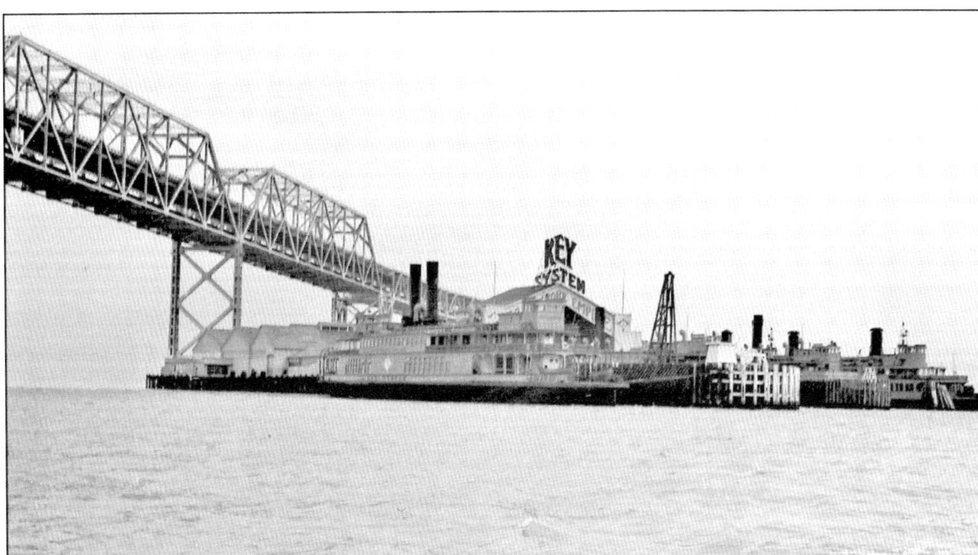


**KEY SYSTEM FERRY, 1938.** The Key System ferry is leaving the Key pier bound for San Francisco. The newly constructed Bay Bridge is overhead. Soon after this, Key trains began running on the lower deck of the Bay Bridge in January 1939 and ferry service from the pier was discontinued except to take passengers to the Golden Gate International Exposition in 1939 and 1940. (Courtesy John Harder, Ralph Demoro photograph.)

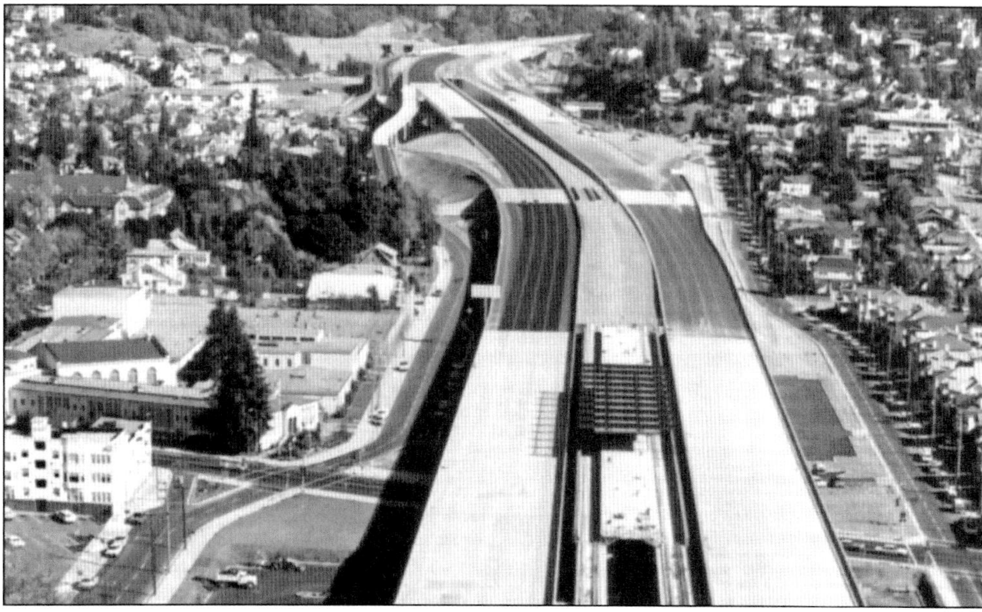

**Freeway and BART.** In the 1960s, the construction of the Grove Shafter Freeway and BART began. BART followed the right-of-way of the Sacramento Northern Railroad, but the much-wider freeway led to the demolition of a swath of houses between Shafter Avenue (now Miles Avenue) and Keith Avenue. (Courtesy John Harder.)

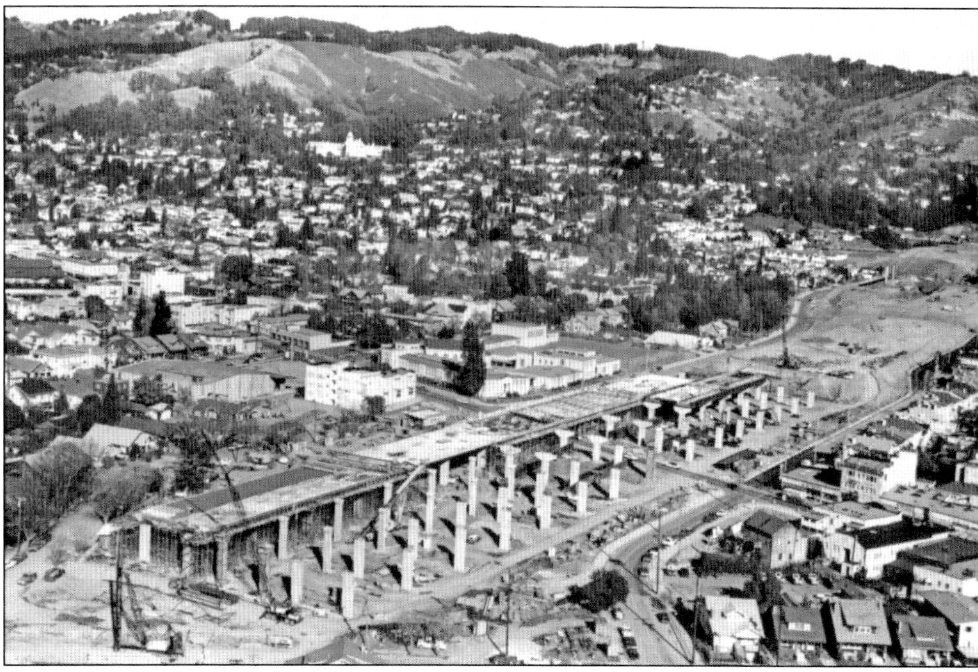

**BART Construction.** The building of the Grove Shafter Freeway and BART caused a disruption of merchant businesses on College Avenue. This coincided with an economic slump that occurred when many Rockridge residents moved to the Contra Costa suburbs in the 1960s and 1970s. Eventually BART and freeway access attracted commuters who made their homes in Rockridge. (Courtesy of John Harder.)

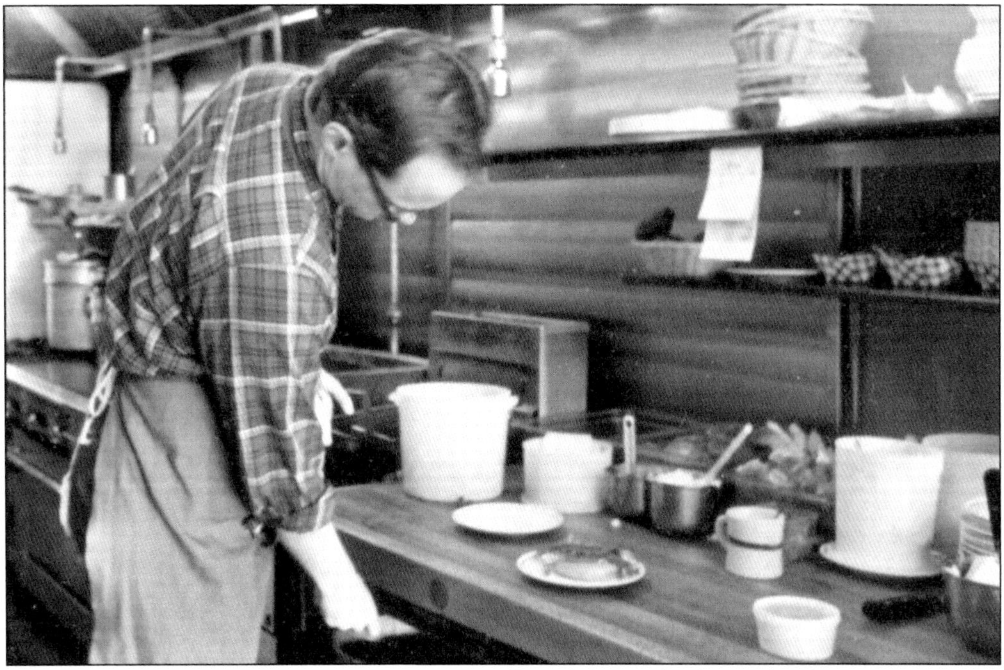

**ROCKRIDGE CAFÉ, 1973.** BART construction affected the Rockridge Café. The new owner, Bill Chung, reported that for the first few years after he and his wife bought the cafe in the 1970s, he could not afford to hire workers, although relatives helped out. He turned the lunch counter (which is now 70 years old) around so that he could cook and serve customers at the counter without having to leave the kitchen. By the end of the 1970s, business on College Avenue was improving, and now the popular Rockridge Cafe is doing well. (Courtesy Bill Chung.)

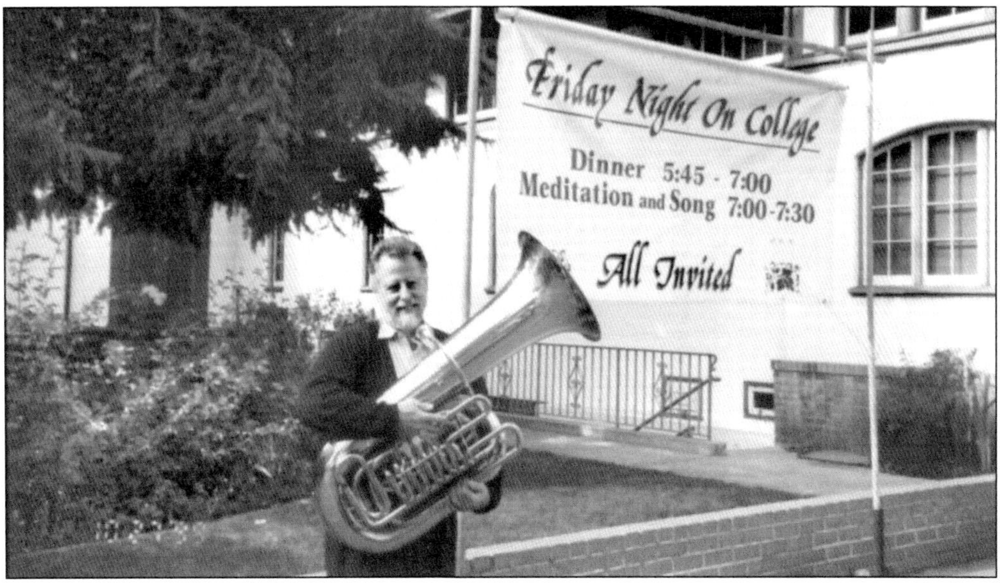


**COLLEGE AVENUE PRESBYTERIAN CHURCH, LATE 1990S.** Pastor Bill Beatty stands in front of the College Avenue Presbyterian Church. During World War II in the early 1940s, the church housed and fed over 7,000 soldiers who came to Oakland to ship out to the war in the Pacific. (Courtesy Don Kinkead, Don Kinkead photograph.)

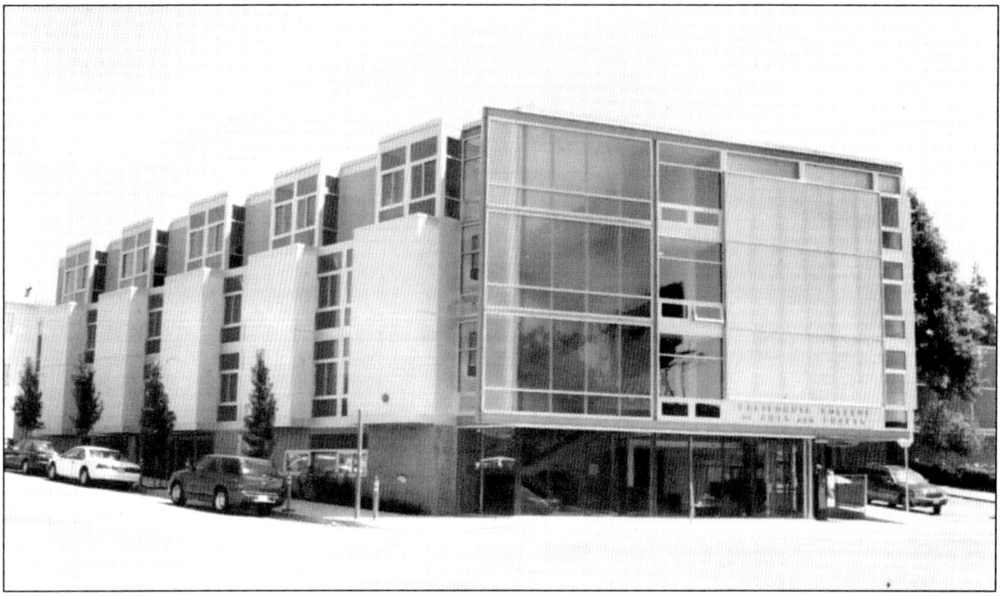

**New Dormitory.** California College of the Arts built this striking new freshman dormitory at the corner of Broadway Terrace and Broadway in the 1990s. The controversy over parking in the neighborhood led RCPC, the Rockridge Community Planning Council, to negotiate an agreement with the college to prevent a flood of parked cars into the neighborhood. (Courtesy Don Kinkead, Don Kinkead photograph.)

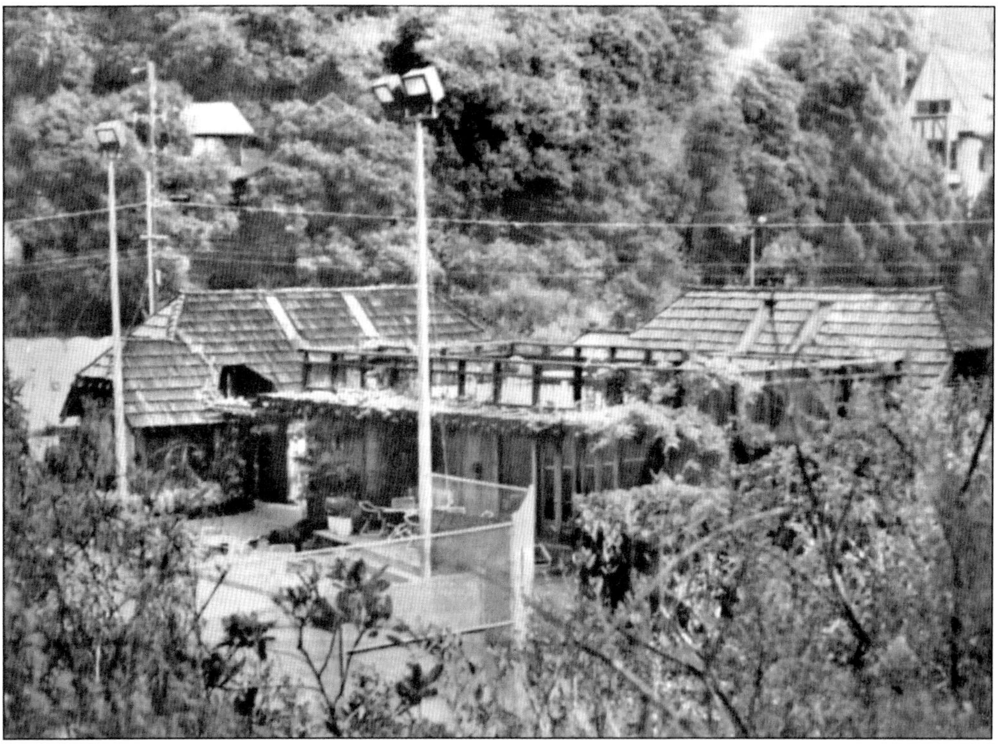

**Chabot Racquet Club.** The Chabot Racquet Club was established in the 1970s, then burned and was rebuilt after the 1991 firestorm. (Courtesy Pat Bracewell.)

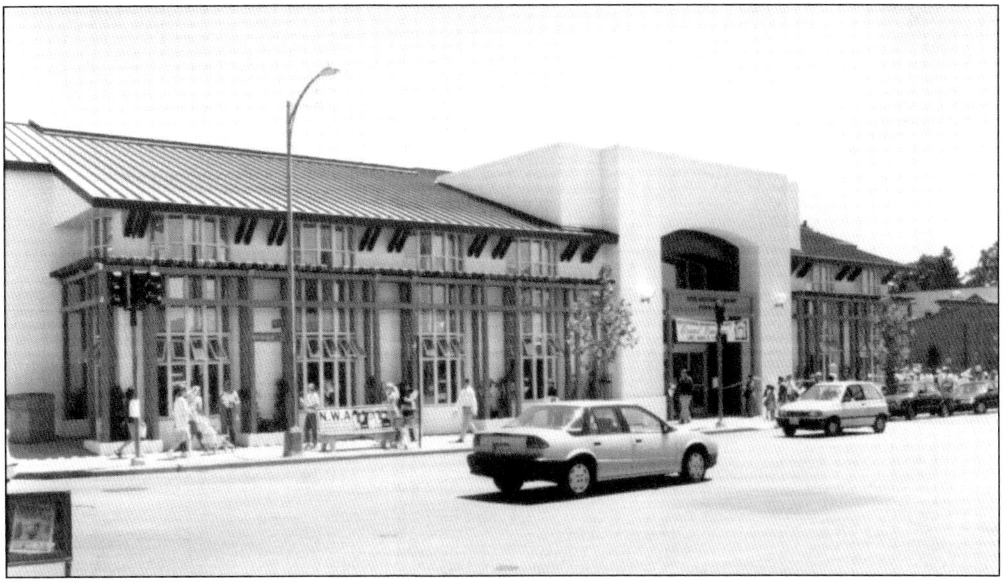

**Rockridge Library.** The Rockridge Community Planning Council took on the task of bringing a new branch library building to College Avenue in Rockridge, which opened in 1996. The previous branch lost its lease and was then temporarily housed at Claremont Middle School. The Rockridge community voted to add a temporary surcharge to their property taxes to help pay for the new library. (Courtesy Don Kinkead, Don Kinkead photograph.)

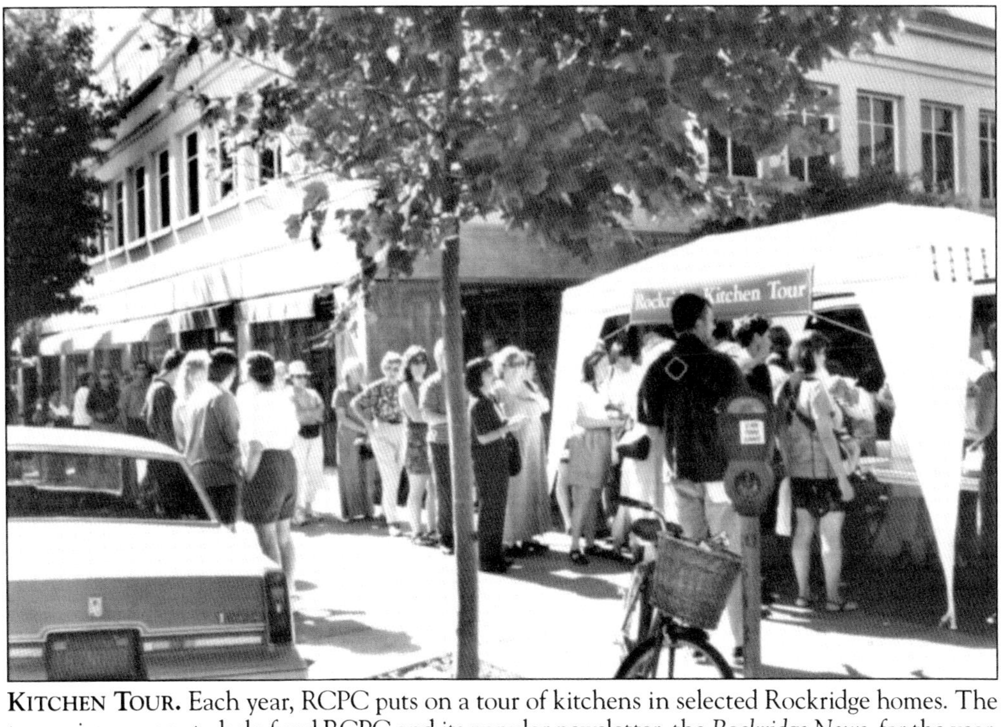


**Kitchen Tour.** Each year, RCPC puts on a tour of kitchens in selected Rockridge homes. The tour raises money to help fund RCPC and its popular newsletter, the *Rockridge News*, for the year. (Courtesy Don Kinkead, Don Kinkead photograph.)

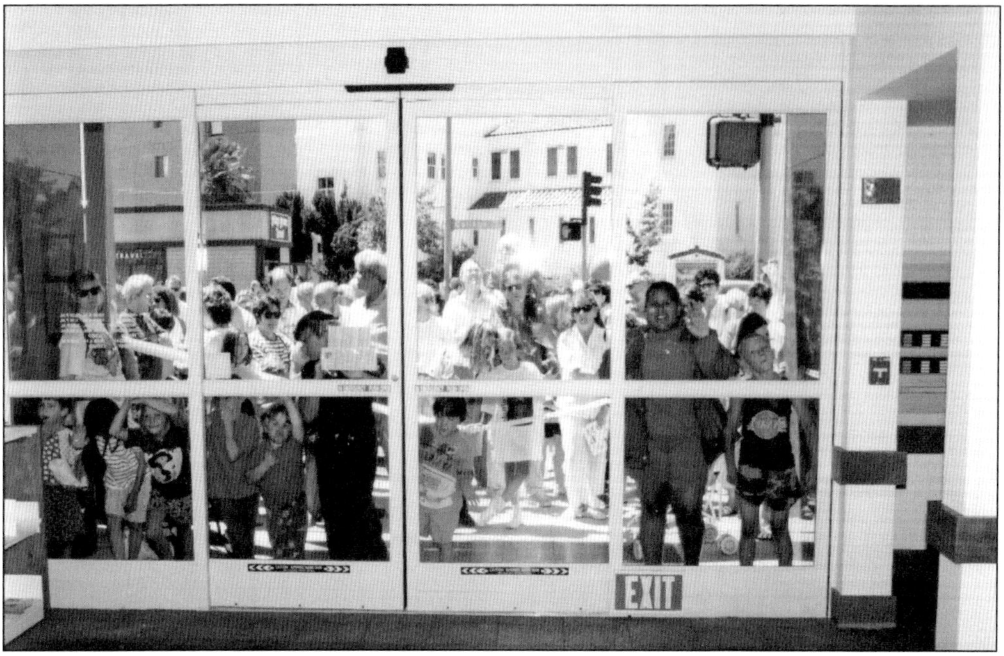


**LIBRARY DOORS.** When the doors of the new Rockridge branch of the Oakland Public Library opened in 1996, future library patrons stood outside the new glass doors waiting to enter. A good deal of community effort had gone into securing the library for Rockridge, led by the Rockridge Community Planning Council, RCPC. (Courtesy Don Kinkead, Don Kinkead photograph.)

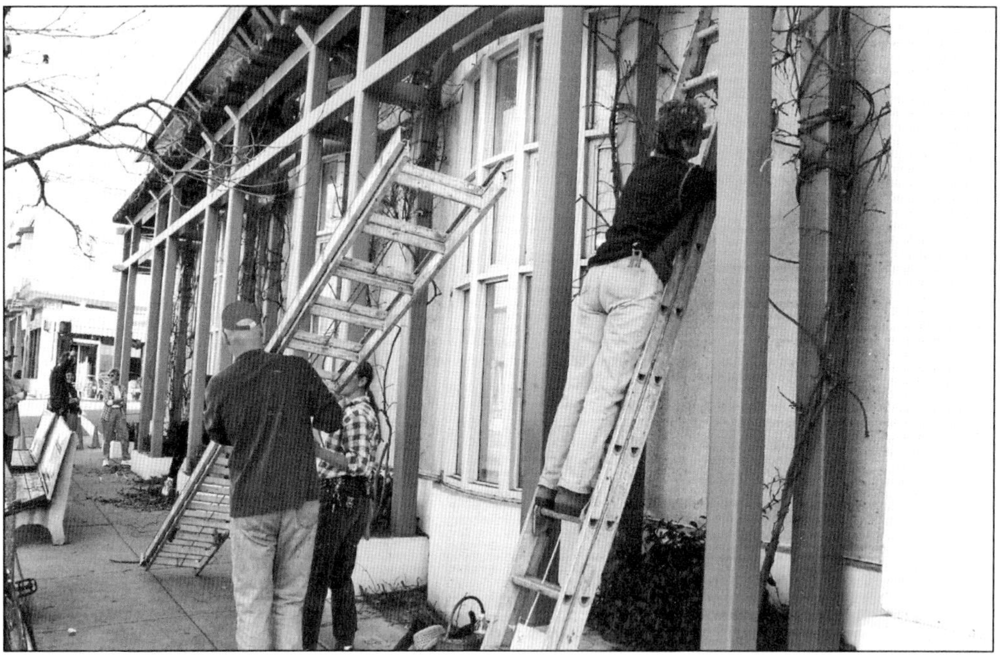

**LIBRARY EXTERIOR.** Students from Merritt College have gathered to help prune the vines that decorate the Rockridge Library in 2002. Rockridge has a good deal of community spirit which is exhibited in the effort to keep the new Rockridge Library beautiful. (Courtesy Susan Montauk, Susan Montauk photograph.)

# INDEX

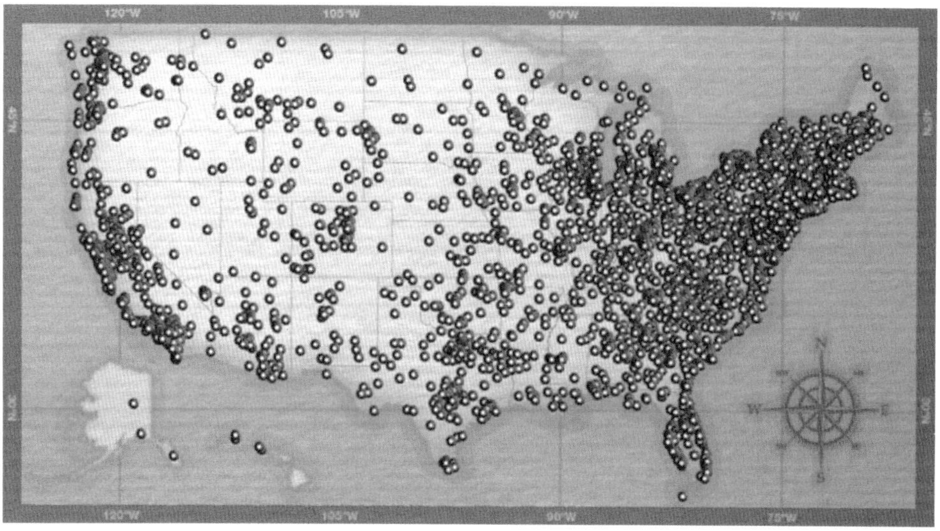